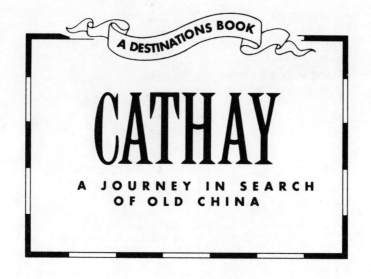

A DESTINATIONS BOOK

CATHAY

A JOURNEY IN SEARCH OF OLD CHINA

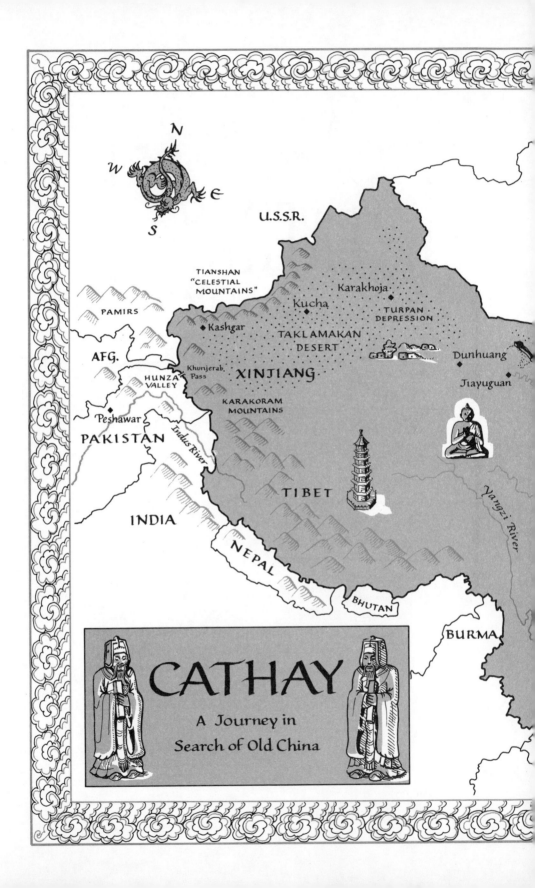

N

W   E

S

U.S.S.R.

TIANSHAN "CELESTIAL MOUNTAINS"

PAMIRS

Karakhoja

Kucha

TURPAN DEPRESSION

Kashgar

TAKLAMAKAN DESERT

Dunhuang

AFG.

Khunjerab Pass

XINJIANG

Jiayuguan

HUNZA VALLEY

KARAKORAM MOUNTAINS

Peshawar

PAKISTAN

Indus River

TIBET

Yangzi River

INDIA

NEPAL

BHUTAN

BURMA

CATHAY

A Journey in
Search of Old China

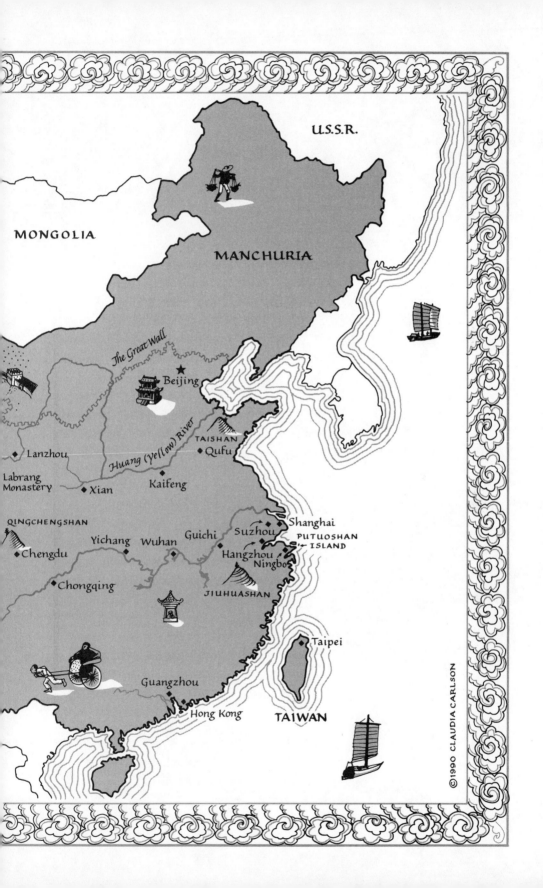

U.S.S.R.

MONGOLIA

MANCHURIA

The Great Wall

Beijing

TAISHAN

Lanzhou

Huang (Yellow) River

Qufu

Labrang
Monastery

Xian

Kaifeng

QINGCHENGSHAN

Yichang

Wuhan

Guichi

Suzhou

Shanghai

PUTUOSHAN
ISLAND

Chengdu

Hangzhou

Ningbo

Chongqing

JIUHUASHAN

Taipei

Guangzhou

Hong Kong

TAIWAN

©1990 CLAUDIA CARLSON

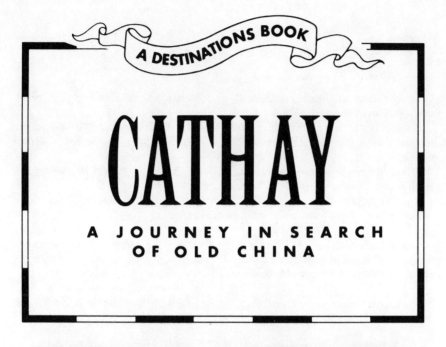

A DESTINATIONS BOOK

CATHAY

A JOURNEY IN SEARCH OF OLD CHINA

FERGUS M. BORDEWICH

INTRODUCTION BY JAN MORRIS

PRENTICE
HALL
PRESS

NEW YORK   LONDON   TORONTO   SYDNEY   TOKYO   SINGAPORE

Grateful acknowledgment is made to the following for permission to reprint previously published material:

Penguin Books Ltd.: "From the South Sea" by Tu Fu, from *Li Po and Tu Fu*, translated by Arthur Cooper (Penguin Classics, 1973). Copyright © 1973 by Arthur Cooper.

Islands magazine: "Putuo Shan: Isle of the Goddess" by Fergus M. Bordewich, published in different form in the March/April 1990 issue.

Reader's Digest: Portions of "The Outer Gate" and "The Desert Road" have appeared in different form in the international editions.

Grateful acknowledgment is made to the following for permission to print previously unpublished material: *Condé Nast Traveler*: "Qufu, China, and the Rediscovery of Confucius" by Fergus M. Bordewich.

The translations of Chinese poems appearing in this book are not by the author and can be found in the books listed in the "Suggestions for Further Reading."

Prentice Hall Press
15 Columbus Circle
New York, NY 10023

Originally published in U.S.A. by Prentice Hall Press

PRENTICE HALL PRESS and colophons are registered trademarks of Simon & Schuster, Inc.

Library of Congress Cataloging-in-Publication Data
Bordewich, Fergus M.
    Cathay : a journey in search of old China / Fergus M. Bordewich.
      p. cm.
    ISBN 0-13-202136-6
    1. China—Description and travel—1976–   I. Title.
DS712.B66   1991
915.104'5—dc20   90-7709
                                        CIP

Designed by Robert Bull Design
Manufactured in the United States of America
10 9 8 7 6 5 4 3 2 1
First Edition

For Jean, with love

CONTENTS

INTRODUCTION

by Jan Morris

OR CENTURIES the Chinese thought of their country as the unquestioned center of all things: the Middle Kingdom, the home of civilization, the fount of wisdom, and the source of power. They considered themselves self-sufficient materially and spiritually, and they treated the rest of the world with unconcealed contempt or condescension.

The rest of the world responded to this arrogance with nervous ambivalence. By the mid-nineteenth century Westerners, in particular, knowing themselves to be technologically infinitely more advanced than the Chinese, mocked the pretensions of the Middle Kingdom and exerted their own supposed superiority by bluster, by guile, and by force. It seems to me, however, reading between their often grandiloquent lines, that they never quite convinced themselves. Perhaps China *was* the ultimate place. Perhaps they really were, as the Chinese had always maintained, no more than Outer Barbarians.

Since the days of Marco Polo, after all, the Western peoples had been fed a diet of marvels out of Cathay, and the self-imposed isolation of China had helped to invest it with suggestions of mysterious omnipotence. The Chinese had indeed invented, long before, many of the appurtenances of civilized society (gunpowder, for instance), and the *objets d'art* that continued to emerge from the Middle Kingdom were of exquisite artistry and craftsmanship.

Besides, there was always the reputation of Confucian wisdom, which beguiled so many Westerners. Chinese wisdom became proverbial, and people tended to think that it was a special category of wisdom, different in kind from the more facile cleverness of the West—loftier of impulse perhaps, grander of style. Westerners who went to live in China, where Confucianism was embodied in splendid architecture too, often became neo-Chinese themselves, such was the osmotic power of the culture.

One such convert to "Chineseness" provides the opening of this book. He is an elderly American, confined in the late 1980s to a New England nursing home, looking back to the manners of the China he had known and loved long before. Forty years of Communist rule have greatly changed the Chinese reputation. In general, the ideologies of Mao Zedong, Zhou Enlai, and their successors have not seemed to possess any celestial distinction, being no more than crudely bucolic interpretations of Marxist-Leninist thought. The apparently insuperable problems of the Chinese economy; the pitiable hardships of the Chinese people; and the cruelty, intolerance, and fustian provincialism of official attitudes, all have adequately convinced most of us that the wisdom of contemporary China is less than absolute.

Always there remains in the back of the western mind, though, that old half-baffled, half-suspicious respect. We are still easily persuaded, not least by the Chinese, that the Chinese are wiser than we are. We still suppose that behind the melancholy facade of modern China—by now doubtful itself of Communism's merits—that an older, more profound China must still exist. This wistful conviction gives an extra meaning to Fergus M. Bordewich's book. Already familiar with Mao's China (he had worked for the Chinese news agency in Beijing), he set out for Cathay, and now he reports his findings.

It is like the revelation of a long-lost relative, hidden away as undesirable, old-fashioned, and perhaps embarrassing by an ambitious new generation. There have been hundreds of books about Communist China, making us familiar not merely with the drab look of the country but with the feel and the effect of its ideology. Mr. Bordewich, though, seeks out that other, hidden China: The China of tradition, religious speculation, and artistic fulfillment, which the Communists had dismissed as irrelevant and debilitating. Wherever it lingers he pursues it, through the remains of the discredited communes, beyond the supervision of the ever less dogmatic party cadres.

For such a quest is by no means a mere exercise in nostalgia. No one pretends that pre-Communist China, which was in many ways an appalling society, can ever be revived—as that venerable sinophile said from his nursing-home bed, "The China I knew is no longer there." Yet it becomes more apparent each year that the extinction of the old transcendence has deprived modern China of something powerful and, indeed, essential. The experience of Communism everywhere has demonstrated that an element of grace is necessary for the well-being of the most forceful and functional state; the condition of China today seems to cry out for an injection of beauty, serenity, and balance.

The Chinese of old may not have been as supremely all-knowing as they thought they were, or as the emissaries of the West perhaps half-consciously assumed, but their view of life, like their art and their architecture, was at least grand and spacious. There are signs that the modern Chinese leadership itself recognizes the national need for nobler philosophies, and it may well be that some aspects of the old China, so long hidden away in shame and contumely, will yet be brought out of the closet to revivify the new.

Perhaps some revival of classical standards may help to ease the Chinese people at last into the international comradeship so long denied them; perhaps Mr. Bordewich, by searching so assiduously, so affectionately, and so understandingly for legacies of the Chinese past, may paradoxically be giving us some foretastes of a China yet to be.

AUTHOR'S NOTE

The journey recounted in these pages took place before the violent suppression of the democratic movement in China, in June 1989. I have changed some names, and occasionally an identifying detail, in order to protect people who, in the current climate, might be made to suffer for the frankness and warmth with which they spoke to me.

I have generally followed the pinyin system of romanization that is now standard in the People's Republic of China. For the sake of clarity, however, I have retained older forms in the case of a few very familiar Chinese terms, thus "Tao Te Ching" instead of "Daodejing," "Confucius" instead of "Kong Fuzi," "tai chi" rather than "taiqi," and so on.

Several letters used in pinyin are sometimes disconcerting to the Western eye. They should be pronounced as follows:

x like the *sh* in "ship"
c like the *ts* in "that's"
z like the *ds* in "reads"
q like the *ch* in "cheer"
zh like the *g* in "large"

PROLOGUE

Middletown

HAD THE disconcerting sense that the lighter-than-air voice on the other end of the wire was speaking to me from beyond the grave. I said something, clumsily, about how excited I was to have found him.

"I don't hold with extravagance of expression, Mr. Bordewich," the voice replied. "Nevertheless, perhaps we may become friends."

THE NURSING home emanated an antiseptic suburban neutrality. A receptionist in a mint-colored uniform directed me down a bright corridor that smelled of disinfectant and boiled vegetables, past spotless rooms where elderly men and women were watching the soap operas. At the nurses' station, I was confronted by a fragile woman I had never seen before. A smile spread over her face as she flung her arms around me and planted a moist kiss first on one cheek and then the other. "I'm so happy to see you again! Thank you so much for coming!" Her expression turned to one of hurt and disappointment as a nurse pried her loose and led her away.

The door now swung open on a beige room identical to the others I had passed. The portly man I found inside was confined to a wheelchair. He wore khaki trousers, an oxford shirt, and a navy blue tie decorated with tiny carrots, everything a little askew, as if someone else had dressed him. What must once have been a rather austere face had collapsed into waves of loose flesh. Nevertheless, his heavy-lidded gaze was acute and intelligent. His grace of manner was recognizably more Asian than Western and immediately made me think of his description of the literary Chinese upon whom he had modeled himself, whose personalities had been "rubbed" to remove the "rasping edges of speech and manners."

A photocopied map of China was taped to the wall. Tacked to a large bulletin board was what he called his "mosaic": postcards of some of the great houses in Newport that he had known as a young man in the teens of the century, of Alpine scenery, of pavilions of the imperial Summer Palace in Beijing. "These are my memories," he said.

He knew that years had passed since he left Beijing, but the memory of everything that had happened to him since had melted away. I found myself talking, in effect, to a man who had just arrived from the China of 1940.

"It is as though the years between never existed," he said quite matter-of-factly.

THERE HAD been years spent in Scotland and Austria, living in hotels, working patiently on the biography of an obscure Austrian queen, a dignified life eked out on stocks and bonds, without family. In 1982 there had been a fall down a flight of stairs, a broken hip, hospitals, the return to America.

But China remained vivid and immediate. He described a land where railway platforms were known as "moon-viewing verandas" because nothing nearer could be thought of in the Chinese world, where connoisseurs placed tea overnight in lotus flowers to imbibe their aroma, where trained pigeons wheeled overhead in aerial orchestras with flutes attached to their tails, to produce strange melodies of surpassing grace. The grandeur of "gentle Peking," as he called it, suffused the everyday manners of even its humblest citizens. "Lend me light!" (by getting out of the way) rickshawmen would cry, with the utmost politeness, in order to clear a path through the crowd. "It was an agreeable time."

He reminded me of a frescoed Buddha from some desert oasis, serene, idiosyncratic, a sojourner in the world of conventional men. The impression was not of something transcendental in the religious sense. It was, rather, one of limpid ease, of a personality at rest, having found its level.

He was born in 1895, fought in France during World War I, and went on to study at Harvard and Oxford. Chronically restless, he commuted between academe and Hollywood, where he packaged the films of Mary Pickford, Pola Negri, and Clara Bow for European distributors. There were lunches at Pickfair. "Maurice Chevalier's wife kept a pet turtle in her muff and was always pushing lettuce up her sleeve. It was most entertaining." Hollywood's charms eventually paled, and he began to long for another kind of life, without quite knowing what it would be. The catalyst was Tang-dynasty poetry, a casual interest that ultimately became a kind of redemption, "something that relieved me, gratefully returned me to a better self." In 1933 he decided, almost on a whim, to travel to China. He left Beijing only reluctantly, when the Japanese occupation had made it impossible for Americans to stay.

At first unknowingly, and then consciously, he re-created the vanished setting of the scholar class, the old literati. He "went native," as more stiff-necked foreigners disparagingly called it, dressing in a silken gown, taking up his abode in a Chinese house, and applying himself with exhaustive vigor to the study of the Chinese language. He had an operation performed on his tongue to make it more mobile for the correct articulation of Chinese sounds.

"Let us drink tea," he said. A nurse was rung for and deputed to inquire from the kitchen if tea could be had at this unaccustomed hour. She returned after a while with Lipton's in plastic cups. I thought of the aromatic Guan Yin tea, the robust Long Jing, that he must once have been accustomed to. But he drank with aplomb.

"Do you know China, Mr. Bordewich?"

"No," I said. "I can't say that I do."

For a year in the early 1980s I was a small piece of software in China's modernization program, imported and gingerly used rather like a piece of equipment whose function was only uncertainly grasped and more than a little feared by the people who operated it. I had been invited by a Chinese news agency in Beijing to teach "Western-style journalism" to its feature news staff. The middle-aged Chinese writers in my "work unit" knew quite well that only a few years before they would have been sent to hard labor, or worse, for practicing the sort of curiosity and skepticism that I tried to teach. No fools, they diligently ignored most of what I had to say.

China had disappointed. The glamor of the revolution had faded long before. The idealists of the 1940s and 1950s had become feeble and suspicious old men, jealous of their power. The habitat of the "new Socialist man" that once held out such promise had proved to be a depressing world of surveillance, numbed indifference, and wary self-preservation. Officialdom continued to stroke a faith that had gone flaccid.

A new China, of sorts, was being invented. A new "pragmatism" had been proclaimed. After more than thirty years of self-imposed isolation, the Chinese were stumbling over themselves to attract the same multinational corporations that they had long denounced. The rural communes that had so long been touted as the models of Communist life were about to be dismantled. Almost daily, news photos showed Chinese looking vaguely uncomfortable in ties and business suits, swigging Coca Cola and buying television sets, a curiously reassuring image of our own habits and values; a picture, perhaps, of what we wished China to be. Beneath that picture was the equally incomplete palimpsest of Maoist China, grim, gritty, and xenophobic, the bleak cityscape of identical dwellings and factories that seemed to echo the moral emptiness of men and women who had endured decades of punishing political campaigns. Still deeper lay the traces of yet another China, this one more sensed than seen.

Things hinted at a more beautiful, subtler world. I began to recognize beneath the gloomy warrens of brick shacks and lean-to kitchens below my office window ("Don't think those are slums," the chief editor said. "The people there are just waiting for good housing."), the buried courtyards and upswept eaves of an older city. Cycling home I began to notice the gray stalk of a pagoda that rose with pristine grace amid the smokestacks of a factory, where it now served as a storage bin for coal. In a cardboard box in a government shop, I came upon carved pewter sheaths that once protected the inches-long fingernails of some Manchu *grande dame,* embossed to their blue-glazed tips with the runic devices of forgotten fancy. In the crumbled rockeries and lotus-choked ponds of an imperial pleasure park I recognized the ruins of the earth itself turned into art. In the smile of a Buddhist monk I seemed to see the rarest of all possessions in the People's China, spiritual independence.

My feelings were complicated. The Chinese past tantalized, but it was impossible to misunderstand the determination of twentieth-century China to escape it. The destruction of the old world began when the Middle Kingdom collided with the outer world a century ago and discovered that its thousands of years of culture were power-less before Western gunboats and business acumen. Communism set out to finish the job. Mao told the Red Guards who gathered in Tiananmen Square at the start of the Cultural Revolution, in 1966, that it was their duty to eliminate once and for all "old thinking, old culture, old beliefs, and old behavior." They obeyed him with a ruthlessness unmatched in Chinese history.

As Garbo tells the handsome Spanish ambassador in *Queen Christina,* "One can feel nostalgia for places one has never seen." What seduced me, half-consciously, was Cathay, the land of Con-fucius and Lao Tze, of Mi Fei's mesmerizing landscapes and Du Fu's poetry, a world shaped by mandarins and scholar-poets and geo-mancers, where ubiquitous dragons embodied the forces of nature, where travelers swayed in shrouded litters on coolies' shoulders and the emperor's court lived a fairyland existence behind the walls-within-walls that were the imperial palace, a land of moat-girt cities where men believed a wisp of mist might be a sage's spirit incarnate and nurtured an immersion in the past so profound that it constituted a philosophy of life itself.

I recognized a danger in all this. Cathay might be merely a China of the mind, as real as a chinoiserie print or a willowware plate. Old China was also a cruel land, whose dwellers bartered their children for food, deliberately crippled women's feet to please the eye of connoisseurs, and endured a conformity so tacit that a man might be arrested for wearing odd-colored clothes. "Inequalities are in the nature of things," as the philosopher Mencius blandly expressed it. "Those who are governed feed the others; those who govern are the fed." Only a few generations ago, women could be seen every day dropping starving babies from a certain spot on the city wall of Beijing.

Nevertheless, I felt that something crucial had been lost, or at least hidden, deliberately obscured. Like any denial of the past or of reality, it had bred sickness and depression.

NOW, SEVERAL years later, what had been a matter of sentiment, a private escape, had taken on a larger dimension. Communism itself seemed to be disintegrating. The communes had been abolished. A stock market had opened in Shanghai. The deadening Maoist grip on religion and art had relaxed. The Chinese seemed less ill at ease in their Western suits, and a Kentucky Fried Chicken outlet had been opened, like a thumbed nose, across the street from Mao's mausoleum. Restrictions on travel had also eased; it had become feasible for the first time to discover how much of Old China had survived behind the blank mask of communism, and to ask how much of a post-Communist China might be a reincarnation of the old.

One Saturday afternoon I stepped into a secondhand bookstore to escape the blustery rain that rolled through the oily streets of lower Manhattan. A peculiar title took my fancy: *The Years That Were Fat*. It proved to be a luminous memoir of life during the 1930s in what the author stunningly called "gentle Peking." The book had been out of print for years, and I leaned against a bookshelf out of the dank crowd and opened it at random. The author, a man named George N. Kates, was describing an encounter in a curio shop where he had gone to admire an antique that he knew he could not afford.

The shop's owner, he wrote, "saw me thus smitten with desire, unable to extricate myself, between a sudden longing and the ability to gratify it. As we sat in his back room, quietly drinking steaming tea at a table covered with a stretch of fine Chinese carpet, he deftly helped me to help myself. 'Take this object home with you now,' he said, referring to the quite unnecessary object that at that moment completely held my fancy—it was an old, plain, deep-yellow ivory scepter—'and then, when you have loved it sufficiently, bring it back to me again!' "

I was deeply touched by the sheer humaneness of the gesture, by the unspoken communion over a thing of beauty. I envied Kates the world he had known. To someone who had lived in the Beijing of the 1980s, the world he described seemed as remote and unreal as some traveler's tale of medieval Cathay; it was difficult to believe that barely a few decades ago it was the only China that anyone knew.

Kates wrote with mesmerizing intimacy of the lost China that I had sensed. I became almost obsessed with him. He seemed to have disappeared after the publication of his book in 1952, but I surmised that he must have left archives somewhere, letters. A Harvard professor who had met Kates in China thought he had died sometime in the 1960s. I tracked down a former college classmate, now in his late eighties, who remembered Kates as self-involved and alone, in the uneasy position of being a brilliant and cultivated Jew at Harvard in the 1920s. He gave me the phone number of another classmate, a New Hampshire doctor who, he said, had "put Kates away."

I telephoned the doctor and asked him whether he knew where I might find any papers that Kates might have left behind.

"Why don't you just ask George?" he replied.

"I NEVER THOUGHT of myself as something unusual, but I must have been," Kates reflected, basking in the hard light of the New England winter. "I got along very well with the Chinese because I didn't try to change them. I thought they were just fine as they were."

The dignified reserve of the Chinese must have appealed to him from the start. Perhaps he had found in China an echo of the Edwardian world in which he had grown up, and which was lost to him in America. I sensed a man who perhaps always shied away from intimacy, who had cleaved to a way of life that was opulent in the symbolism of affection but kept passion always at a distance.

"The Chinese had a great deal of savoir faire. Good will was so easy. Warmth of heart was displayed immediately. When you entered a home, you were immediately greeted with hospitality. We weren't very self-conscious about it."

As he talked, I saw in my mind's eye Kates's courtyard home, the handsome lines of its well-proportioned inner court, the great gate carved intricately with auspicious inscriptions, the oleanders and pomegranates that graced the facade of the main hall, the interior furnished with a "sober range of dignified furniture," a little ivory, much red leather, finely colored rugs from Chinese Turkestan, scrolls and inscriptions and handsome lacquerware. He rented the house from a court eunuch, who had received it as a gift from the Dowager Empress Cixi. As a mark of special esteem, the dowager had also given the eunuch one of her own handmaids as a wife. This odd couple dwelled in the courtyard adjoining Kates's, and even after nearly fifty years Kates still chuckled at their poignant antics.

"The eunuch was unchanging in eunuch disposition," he said with a catlike smile. "Above all, he was polite, and I was grateful for it. He was ashamed of being a eunuch, and he was uneasy about continuing any conversation which touched upon that subject. He never talked about his days in the palace. That would have been considered undignified. But every so often the poor wife would climb onto the roof and cry to the entire neighborhood the wrong that had been done to her by having been married to a man who could never be a proper husband. Like most Chinese, my servants found eunuchs somewhat obscene, and they were most amused."

Each day, a teacher whose title translated quaintly as the "Elder Born" arrived to help Kates practice his Chinese. "When he appeared at the gate, my servant would ask, 'Does the Elder Born wish to have special tea?' I would reply, 'Whatever you consider appropriate.' These were formulas of graciousness, and they were always repeated in precisely the same way. The servant would bring us jasmine tea and we would sip it as we studied. When the Elder Born spoke of Confucius, and it was often, he would always begin by saying, 'A certain man says . . .' It would have been impolite to have referred to the sage by name. In return, I told him about Tennyson."

He took a bit of salve from a diminutive Chinese jar and daubed it on his temples. He insisted that I try some, too. It had a chilly, menthol effect.

"Isn't that agreeable?"

We sat in silence for a while. Kates seemed not to want to talk. I supposed he felt tired and asked if he would like me to leave. He looked at me opaquely, but kindly. His face was as hard to read as a Chinese face.

"Now I am ninety-two. I have the past but not the future to deal with. The present is so terribly limited. But it can't be changed."

He wheeled himself to a cabinet and with small, plump, sensitive fingers, he extracted from a drawer a procession of objects that were smooth and lustrous from much handling. *"Les petites bijoux,"* he said, lighter-than-air. "Perhaps they will give you some pleasure." Settling them in his lap, he wheeled himself back across the room and spread the objects out on the Formica stand that stood next to his bed.

He handled each one gravely and gently. Each had once no doubt had a story attached to it. There was a small ivory needle case, a brass seal with a grinning mandarin carved on the end, an ivory box carved in the shape of a lotus blossom, in which he kept paper clips. There was a black lacquer box with crescent-shaped compartments that slid out on a hinge to form the yin-yang symbol of primal polarities. A jade dragon writhed and coiled on the lid of a minute lacquerware box that was shaped like a stylized cloud; the golden ring inside it had bats and the ideographs for "happiness" and "longevity" engraved on each side. *Fu,* the word for "bat," Kates explained, had the same sound as the one that meant "happiness." "Simply to think the word *fu,* simply to see the word *fu,* was an auspicious act, you see." He remembered buying the ring in a pawn shop at the Great Wall. His eyes wandered as he fished quietly for a memory of the day; it came close, almost within his grasp, then slipped away.

There was a square brass inkwell with ideographs inscribed on its lid. I wondered what they said. Kates stared at the columns that he must once have known by heart. "It is a poem," he said at last. I asked him to read it to me. He scrutinized the inkwell. "I can see *mountain,"* he said. "I can see *moon.* I can see *drop,* and *brilliant."* He stared a while longer and then looked up and smiled gracefully at me. The rest of the ideographs had been lost in the vacuum of memory.

A handful of objects was all that remained. I wished that more of the China he had loved had been spared for him, and I began to tell him so. But he caught me up.

"Don't think of me as being desirous of going back to China, Mr. Bordewich. The China I knew is no longer there. But the West I knew is no longer there either. The Harvard I knew is no longer there. Nor is the Hollywood I knew. I have no longing or homesickness for a world that's gone. It's gone for everybody. I could make a life of nostalgia for myself, but I regard that with distrust. We have a duty to live in the present, and I want to live on pleasant terms with it."

I remembered his words as I drove south through the hard, vertical New England twilight, and as I prepared to leave for China, and Cathay.

CHAPTER ONE

The Outer Gate

E ARE the oldest people in the world," Amir Khan said matter-of-factly. "It is a well-known fact, sir! Some live to one hundred twenty-five, some to one hundred fifty, some maybe two hundred."

He shrugged as if it were a trifling achievement.

"One hundred is the normal, sir, the normal!"

The morning light revealed an amphitheater of snowy crags, and at its foot a serpentine valley along whose floor the Hunza River tumbled with a deafening roar. Glaciers prowled over distant peaks. Emerald streams caromed from the cliffs and sizzled down through forests of yellow poplars toward terraced orchards that were swollen with apricots and apples, peaches, walnuts, and pomegranates. Here and there, girls in raspberry and violet bloomers were harvesting corn, like figures in a Flemish tapestry.

"We are peaceful people, sir!" Amir's speech seemed lodged in a permanent groove of polite exclamation. "There is no beating, sir! There is no raping! There is no thieving! There is no killing! There is no creating of small nuisances, sir!"

I must have looked skeptical.

"It is a well-known fact, sir!"

"How do they do it?"

"No smoking, eating all the time healthy food, sir."

I waited expectantly.

"Apricots," said Amir Khan at last.

"Apricots?"

"Apricot soup. Every morning eating apricot soup."

Amir Khan was home on holiday from his university in the Punjab. He was widely traveled for a child of the valley. He had been to the capital at Islamabad, and to Lahore, and to Karachi on the coast; he was one of the few people in Hunza who had seen the sea. He hoped to become a newspaperman someday, and he bubbled with talk of the new Chinese-built highway that had opened the valley for the first time to the outer world. We had met the night before, on my arrival in Hunza.

I stood at the very nexus of one of the world's great cultural watersheds. Afghanistan lay a few miles to the west, and beyond it the Muslim Middle East. Southward over the mountains lay India. And to the north, so close now that I could almost smell it, was China. It was here at Hunza that the Chinese borderlands traditionally began; in the seventh century, a Tang army had marched as far south as Gilgit, and as recently as the 1890s Hunza still paid tribute to the Chinese governor two hundred miles north over the passes, in Kashgar.

I HAD DRIVEN up from Peshawar. The picturesque old frontier town had become squalid and dangerous. Hundreds of thousands of Afghan refugees crammed tent colonies on the city's outskirts. Crippled mujahedin hobbled through the bazaars on artificial legs hand-made from bits of scrap iron and automobile tire. Almost every day a bomb went off somewhere in the suburbs; a courtly man I used to know who ran a refugee news service had recently been blown up in his home a few blocks from the American Club.

I hired a rickety Fiat and set off north through mud-walled towns where open-front stalls offered submachine guns for sale and block-houses guarded the turreted homes of smugglers and drug runners. The mountains began at the Malakand Pass, springing abruptly from the hazy plain. The road levered up nearly sheer slopes and around hairpin bends, and finally emerged into an alpine realm of stony fields where wheat grew a luminous green. Huge teetering lorries shot past like bullets; they were phantasmagoric vehicles, hemorrhaging great black gouts of exhaust and ariot with paintings of swooping parrots, leaping tigers, jet planes, railroad engines, thatched cottages, the Ka'aba, and dead Pakistani dictators. Pathans raced them on Hondas, their black beards and the tails of their turbans whipping behind them like streamers. Later, the road snaked alongside the Indus for nearly three hundred miles, and then along the Hunza; night had fallen by then, but I could already sense the twenty thousand-foot peaks all around me in the darkness, like inner certainties.

It was pitch-dark when I reached Hunza. A town lay somewhere nearby, but I could see nothing on the road except an inauspicious clump of wobbly stalls.

"Car can't go, sir! Too much up, sir!"

I peered through the Fiat's window at a cheerful, bushy-browed face. Its owner pointed ambiguously into the darkness.

"Amir Khan, sir! At your service!"

Somewhere he found an antique jeep. We piled into it and plunged up a mountainside that was all but invisible from the road. Soon we were bouncing up a pitted track so steep that I found myself lying almost on my back in the rear, feet in the air and gazing past the driver's profile at the stars.

I kept hearing what I took to be a badly tuned radio that seemed to be coming from behind the jeep. Amir wagged his finger at me.

"Not radio, sir! Boss of jeep talking, sir!"

I looked through the rear window. A man in pajamas was clinging to the back of the jeep. As we lurched around a yet-steeper turn, he darted forward and threw himself spread-eagled over the hood to prevent the jeep from toppling backward. He clung there, grinning shyly at us through the windshield as the jeep bucked disobligingly upward. Amir smiled reassuringly.

"Holding down front end, sir!"

Several tense minutes later we arrived at an inn that was wedged into the side of the mountain. Promising to return in the morning, Amir Khan saw to it that before the hour was out I was dining gratefully on boiled mutton and cabbage, and sweet black tea.

Hunza lay seven thousand feet above sea level; before the highway was built, it might take weeks to reach the district capital at Gilgit. Winter snows still cut the valley off for weeks at a time. But

5

inside the valley the air was thin and sweet, and the balmy sun seemed to infuse the Hunzakuts with a temperament as mild and generous as the rich, fruit-laden terraces of mid-September.

The Hunzakuts are a mysterious people. Most, including Amir Khan, are olive-skinned and almond-eyed. But many others are startlingly European in appearance; some have blond hair and blue eyes, while others are red-haired and hatchet-faced, like Irish cops or Galician rabbinical students. They maintain that they are the descendants of Greek soldiers stationed here by Alexander the Great.

"He left them here when he marched to China," Amir said.

When I said politely that I doubted that Alexander had gone to China, Amir replied, "Are we not here to prove it?"

The Hunza that Amir Khan described bore an uncanny resemblance to Shangri La, the Himalayan paradise that James Hilton invented in his 1933 novel *Lost Horizon*: A group of Europeans is mysteriously kidnapped and taken to a secret valley whose inhabitants know nothing of fear, greed, or anger; they enjoy prolonged youth under the rule of philosopher-lamas whose benign aristocracy rather suggests Plato's republic togged in Tibetan robes. Conway, a jaded diplomat, finds Shangri La to be the answer to his spiritual malaise, and its philosophy of moderation the antidote to the futility and danger of twentieth-century life. He is informed that wisdom and longevity will be his, if he agrees to forsake the outer world forever. Conway's young protégé Malleson, however, determines to escape with a Chinese girl whom the lamas warn is actually a well-preserved ninety-seven. Rather than abandon them to certain death in the mountains, Conway attempts to lead them to safety. Malleson dies after all. Conway arrives half-dead at a mission, accompanied by a withered hag. The story closes with Conway struggling to find his way back to Shangri La.

I supposed that Hilton had heard the stories about the fabulously long-lived Hunzakuts and their serene existence in their remote mountain valley, and then embellished them with the even more exotic ambience of Buddhist Tibet. But something else about the tale tantalized; there was a connection of some kind that I couldn't quite make. Eventually I gave up trying and turned to Amir Khan. I said that

I didn't see many old people, for a place where they were said to live to such remarkable age.

"Naturally they are working, sir! Hunza people are hard-working people."

Could I meet one of these extraordinary old folks?

"Why not, sir!" Amir waggled his head from side to side in the Indian fashion. "You may meet my great-grandfather. He is the family knowledge fountain, sir, knowing every truth and lie."

"How old is he?"

"He is one hundred eighteen, and still working, sir!"

THE VALLEY seduced. I had planned to pass through quickly, but I stayed one day, and then another, and then another. The squalor of Peshawar seemed far away, an irrelevancy in the gentle fastness of the Karakorams. The valley was a complete world, like an island in a sea of stone. Everything existed in miniature: the single road, the tiny capital, the sturdy little people, the even smaller former principality of Nagar that lay across the river.

It was easy to let the days slip by. I spent them hiking up to the glaciers, or across the plateau to the village of Altit, or idling in the little bazaar where there were stalls selling Lipton's tea, Mao caps, plastic sandals, pink Chinese toilet paper, and ambiguous slabs of sinewy meat; there was a shop named "Martyr Ice and Voice" that sold block ice and music tapes, and a hotel that advertised "Flesh System Room." The glacial runoff tumbled off the hills through labyrinths of irrigation channels and racketed down alongside the lanes, and through tunnels under the flat-roofed homes, and finally down in swarming green torrents to the valley floor. The mud walls were plastered with pictures of the country's most recent dictator, who had been blown up in his plane a few weeks before; his eyes were upraised so that the whites showed, lending them an odd transcendental quality, like that of an ancient bodhisattva, while behind him the jet was drawn with the simplicity of a child's hand, so that it resembled a fat cigar exploding in midair. "Peace be with you!"

7

people said when I approached them, and if I greeted them first they responded, "And with you be peace!"

Sometimes I climbed to the small mud fort that clung to a precipitous crag above the town; the kings lived there until Pakistan began exercising suzerainty over the valley in the 1960s, when (probably gratefully) they retired to a more modern dwelling with indoor plumbing, down the mountain. I liked to sit there in the shade of a ramshackle kiosk from which I could look out across the valley and the highway, and the arc of stupendous peaks.

I had chosen this route to China deliberately. The new highway that snaked through the valley below followed one of the world's most ancient routes, the southern branch of the great Silk Road, which for more than two thousand years had tenuously linked China with India and the Mediterranean. The highway was bringing the ancient trade back to life; at a certain hour of the morning, I could see the daily northbound bus careening up the road, filled with lowland Pakistanis on their way to trade for silk across the border in Kashgar.

I had another reason for coming this way. I might have flown from New York to Beijing in twenty-two hours, or from Hong Kong in four. But the speed of air travel fused distant places, blurred distinctions. I wanted to approach the Chinese heartland more slowly; I wanted to feel China coming gradually into focus, the way travelers had in earlier times as they crossed the Karakorams and the two thousand miles of desert that lay between them and the terminus of the old Silk Road at Xian.

AMIR KHAN appeared suddenly at my door.
"Meeting my great-grandfather, sir!"

Shaitam Khan was not easy to find. He moved constantly among the homes of his fifteen sons, as the mood took him; we hired a jeep and drove up and down the valley, inquiring at their mud-walled compounds. Finally, after we had stopped at four or five of these places, Amir Khan returned to the jeep with a smile.

"Great-grandfather is in the fields, sir! Coming soon!"

A great-grandnephew was sent to fetch him. We waited for him nearby, in a willow grove. Across the road, women in pillbox caps with gauze veils drawn over their heads like medieval wimples were harvesting maize with primitive scythes. Pakistani show music squalled from ghetto blasters set out in the fields. Tiny filthy children gawked at me and shouted, "Hi, guy!" Beyond them, the tangled branches of peach trees lay against the sky like the strokes of Chinese calligraphy.

"Why are you going to China?" Amir Khan asked me.

I thought of mist-wreathed mountains, of Taoist hermits laughing in the wilderness, of Confucian gentlemen, the enigmatic seclusion of walled courtyards and intricate gardens; I thought of George Kates and of a way of seeing and of living that was capable of turning even the smallest gestures into things of beauty.

Finally I just said, "I'm looking for what's left of Old China."

"There is nothing left, sir! Everything has changed."

I wondered how much of what I thought of as "Cathay" had ever really been there at all. How much was just my imagination, wishful thinking?

"China is ugly," Amir said, making a face. "Too many factories, too many people. Not friendly people, not like Hunza people. I know. My uncle has written it."

Like many Hunzakuts, Amir had family across the border, near Kashgar. Amir had never met the uncle, but there had been letters. The uncle had suffered badly during the Cultural Revolution; he had been stripped of his property and abused somehow by Red Guards.

"But later they gave back his wives," Amir said.

"Ugliness doesn't matter," I said. "I want to see things the way they are."

A crowd of Shaitam's curious sons and cousins and grandchildren had gathered; they stood around amiably, watching us talk. Milky tea was brought on a battered brass tray. Then after a while a small solemn boy arrived tugging a plastic bag. He picked ripe peaches out of it and handed one to me, and then another, and another until I told him to stop. But he shook his head solemnly and kept on piling them into my hands until they spilled onto the ground and the bag was empty.

Fumbling at the peaches, and looking across the road at the peach trees framed against the sky, I suddenly made the connection that had been teasing at me for the last several days. I finally recognized the ancient myth that was buried inside the fantasy of Shangri La. Hilton's novel, I realized, was a retelling of the Chinese tale of the Peach Blossom Spring. It was one of the best-known myths in all Chinese civilization; its symbols were repeated so pervasively in paintings and poems, on carved jade and on porcelain vases, that the merest reference to peach blossoms, or the sketch of a fisherman's skiff moored near a cave, was sufficient to suggest a safe and secret land that lay just beyond man's grasp. The story went like this:

A fisherman one day follows an unfamiliar stream to a cavern; entering it, he soon finds himself in a hidden valley, "a peach orchard beyond the world," where simple farmers enjoy a life of profound peace and harmony. They explain that their ancestors fled to the valley centuries ago from the anarchy and suffering that attended the fall of the Han dynasty and that they have never ventured out since. They welcome the fisherman into their homes and invite him to live with them forever. But he eventually decides that he must see his home once again; promising never to divulge their existence, he makes his way back through the cavern, and eventually to the city, where he immediately informs the imperial governor of what he has found. The governor sends soldiers with him to invade the Peach Blossom Spring, but even though he had carefully memorized the landmarks, the fisherman is never able to find his way back again.

Chinese imagined the Peach Blossom Spring sometimes as the abode of the Immortals, and always as the spirit's ultimate refuge from the rigidly ordered Confucian world. Some of the tale's elements were quintessentially Chinese: the fisherman's instinctive loyalty to authority, the farmers' fear of chaos in the outer world, the notion of paradise as a small, hidden place. But the tale had a haunting, universal quality, too, that strangely echoed the Christian myth of paradise found, lost, and eternally sought. But to me it also hinted at the lure of Cathay itself; Cathay was the ultimate Land Beyond.

When Shaitam finally appeared I saw that he was cruelly crippled by curvature of the spine. He crept crablike toward us across the road, oblivious to an approaching bus that nearly terminated his long life on the spot. He was dressed in a threadbare pinstripe jacket, rust-colored pantaloons, and green corduroy Chinese slippers; his face was a beaky wreckage punctuated by tufts of silvery bristle.

Shaitam was born in 1870; in that year, the Celestial Empire of China was ruled by the Dowager Empress Cixi, Queen Victoria sat in Buckingham Palace, and Ulysses S. Grant was president of the United States. Hunza was an independent principality; even British India was little more than a rumor far away in the south.

Shaitam spoke only Burushaski, the Hunzakuts' daunting language which accommodates no fewer than four genders and twenty-four declensions. Amir Khan translated for me.

First I asked Shaitam to tell me what he knew about the valley's contact with the outside world.

He told me about the Chinese army that had marched to Gilgit. Then he recounted a vague story about two Persian brothers who had come from the West and had converted the valley from Buddhism to Islam.

"When did that happen?" I asked.

"Long ago," Shaitam said. "We didn't have centuries then."

I said, "Tell me about great men you remember."

He searched his memory.

"There was Safdar Ali."

In his own youth, Shaitam said, Safdar Ali had led the Hunzakuts against Nagar, the minuscule state that lay on the other side of the Hunza River.

Amir Khan narrowed his eyes fiercely. He momentarily lost his poise.

"The Nagar people are nasty people, sir!" he hissed. "They are all thieves. Even they know it!"

Shaitam had swum the river with a crowd of young warriors; they had encircled the main village of Nagar. He made a feeble creeping motion with his knobbly hands.

"We had bows and arrows, and muskets. We crept up on them in the dark. We killed a lot of them!"

He cackled hilariously.

"When did all that happen?" I asked.

"In the old times," Shaitam replied vaguely.

Shaitam clearly remembered the arrival of the British troops who had claimed the valley for the Raj. The Hunzakuts had killed dozens of them, he said, before the British artillery was able to force the entrance to the valley.

"The year 1892," Shaitam said.

Safdar Ali fled across the border to seek the protection of the Chinese governor in Kashgar; the war against Nagar, I reasoned, must therefore have taken place some time in the 1880s. The raid against Nagar, like the Persian brothers and the Chinese invasion, lay in the time of legend. The British had brought chronology along with them in their knapsacks. Until that moment, Hunza had existed outside time, untouched by the currents of history that swarmed beyond the mountains.

Later I came across a small book that told me more about the great Safdar Ali. It was written by a Major General S. Shahid Hamid of the Pakistan Army and was humbly titled *The Land of Just Enough.* The general recounted an almost unbroken history of murder and pillage, and described in gruesome detail an economy that since time immemorial was based on slave trading and the plunder of China-bound caravans. Safdar Ali, in his quest for the throne, first assassinated his father, the ruling mir; he then put his five brothers to death and rolled another rival off a cliff. Later he had his mother murdered as well. Before he fled to China, he boasted, "Potentates like myself and Alexander of Macedonia answer no summonses and acknowledge no rule."

Amir Khan must have known most of this. But the Hunza that he had described so lovingly a few days before was really the fiction of Shangri La. Hilton's fantasy had worked its way back into local folklore and superimposed itself on the valley's blood-soaked history. Education was already transforming Amir; his life, I was sure, would ultimately be made beyond the valley, in the larger world. But I could see that the myth was important to him; it was the clinging of someone for whom the real past had slipped away into irrelevancy.

I asked Shaitam if there were many people older than himself.

He waggled his head feebly.

"A few," he said.

Shaitam had a friend in the next village who was one hundred nineteen. He thought there was another man who lived down the valley, who might be one hundred thirty-five or thirty-six.

"But great-grandfather Shaitam says he hasn't seen him in ten or fifteen years," Amir said apologetically.

I wondered what Shaitam thought of the new highway. I supposed he regretted its rupture of the valley's ancient solitude.

"Anyone who doesn't like the road is a fool," he said. "You used to have to ride for weeks if you wanted to go anyplace. The horses used to fall off the cliffs. It was a big problem."

He nodded happily.

"Now you go in a Suzuki van and you're there in a couple of hours. You can visit anybody you want. Best of all, the highway sends us foreigners who spend their money here and make us rich."

Shaitam said that the road also made it possible for trucks to bring fresh ghee, flour, and rice up from the lowlands. You could buy cheap cotton suits and caps from China and porcelain tea sets that only rich people used to be able to afford.

I asked Shaitam if he still ate apricot soup every morning. He made a face.

"We don't have to anymore. Now we can get corn flakes!"

THE WEATHER made it easier to leave Hunza. Clouds hung low over the valley and leaked an icy drizzle onto the village, which now seemed suddenly poor and forlorn in the half-light; the great peaks had disappeared completely in the clouds, as if they never had been there at all.

Amir Khan packed me off in a Land Rover.

"I think you don't like us," he said gloomily.

I was taken aback.

"I like it here very much, indeed," I said.

"You want to leave us."

I realized with relief that Amir had finally stopped addressing me as "sir."

"I don't feel much like going," I said truthfully.

"Then stay here with us!" Amir said warmly. "You will live in my house. You will eat apricots with us. You will live to be two hundred!"

It was the sort of thing that I couldn't help secretly wishing were so, that in one tiny corner of the world the implausible was absolutely true, that the laws of science could be confounded by something as simple as apricot soup.

The road was a tunnel between sheer rock walls and the low, dirty sky. As I rode out through the northern end of the valley, I thought of the fisherman of the Peach Blossom Spring, wondering how he had felt as he passed out through the mysterious cave, back to the world of ordinary men.

It was a short distance to the Pakistani border station at Sust. Buses loitered amid a sprawl of flophouses, police barracks, and vast heaps of trade goods that were spread around a muddy yard. Traveling merchants shivered mournfully in threes and fours, watching the venal eyes of the customs agents play appraisingly over their goods. The traders were mostly dark, shiny-skinned men from the Punjab, and with hardly an exception they wore mufflers tied lengthwise around their heads, as if they were suffering from a plague of toothaches.

I wandered around the yard, curious to see what the traders were bringing back from China. There were tangles of Chinese bicycles, and cartons of the shoddy tea sets that the Pakistanis loved, and unreliable Chinese radios and televisions. But in the midst of all the cheaply made rubbish was silk, rolls and bundles and bales of it; it was hard to take it in at first—that after all these centuries the luminescent product of the looms of Hangzhou and Suzhou was still traveling over the Silk Road much as it had since the days of Marco Polo, and for a thousand years and more before him.

I struck up a conversation with a man with the apt name of Muhammed Muslim. He was sleek and low-slung, and wore blue jeans and a slash-sleeved Japanese denim jacket, and a baseball cap with "LEE" printed in big letters across the front. He said that he and several friends were traveling to Kashgar to trade for silk. The Chinese, he added deprecatingly, only allowed Pakistanis to bring in a pitifully small amount of trade goods.

"Not to worry!"

He patted the apparently false bottom of his Naugahyde shoulder bag.

"If we have more, we put it in the bottom. Or we give $10 US to the driver and he puts it under his seat."

He leaned close to me and winked.

"These are businessmen's tricks, sir, businessmen's tricks!"

On this trip, Muslim and his companions planned to swap wristwatches and Japanese suits for silk, which they then expected to sell for fabulous profits in the Gilgit bazaar. If you were clever, he said, and lucky, you could make a profit of sixty thousand rupees on an investment of eighty thousand.

"It all depends on the customs chap who is here when you come back. If it happens to be a cousin, maybe you will give him a piece of silk."

The merchant waved his hand airily.

"If you are unlucky, you might pay ten thousand rupees, or thirty thousand."

"I hope you are not unlucky very often," I said.

He smiled.

"I have many cousins."

I looked at the freezing Punjabis. A sense of awesome historical continuity overcame the mud and the freezing rain, and my impatience to get started. These men, with their mournful faces and ridiculous mufflers, were the heirs to countless generations of merchants who had traveled the Silk Road since the days of ancient Rome. The Silk Road was really a web of routes that spanned the ancient and medieval worlds, linking China with India, Persia, and the Mediterranean. The main stem ran from the basin of the Yellow River westward through the great oasis cities of Central Asia to the Levant. The names of its landfalls still thrilled: Changan, Dunhuang, Turpan, Kashgar, Khotan, Bukhara, Samarkand, Baghdad, Palmyra, Tyre, Antioch. The route traversed five thousand inhospitable miles of barren mountains, waterless deserts where sandstorms swallowed whole caravans, and vast plains plagued by marauding barbarians.

The great road arose in response to the insatiable Roman appetite for silk. In China, silk was so common that it served as currency;

15

wealth was measured in silk, and even taxes reckoned and soldiers' wages paid out in it. To the Romans it was a rare and wondrous stuff. So costly was it that in A.D. 14 the Emperor Tiberius attempted to ban its use; but a century later the Silk Road was able to supply it so liberally that Pliny complained that its importation was draining the empire of 100 million sesterces every year. The Romans knew its producers only as the mysterious *Seres,* or "silk-folk," who lived somewhere far to the east and were said to grow to gigantic size and to live for centuries. So successful were the Chinese at guarding the secret of silk's manufacture that it was not until the sixth century A.D., when two Nestorian monks brought the first silkworms to the West in their hollowed-out staffs, that Westerners realized that it did not grow on bushes like cotton.

Much more than silk traveled the great highway. Paper and porcelain, gunpowder, the crossbow, and the art of printing traveled westward; so did roses, peonies, oranges, peaches, and pears, all of which were indigenous to China. China-bound merchants brought glass and wool from Rome, lapis lazuli from Afghanistan, coral from the Indian Ocean, Persian wine and figs, sacred jade from the Kun Lun Mountains, ivory and spices from India, and the powerful Sogdian steeds that the Chinese called "heavenly horses." New religions seeped along the caravan routes, too; Manichaeanism from Persia, Nestorian Christianity from further west, and from India, Buddhism, the only foreign vision to capture the imagination of China until the challenge of the modern West in the present day.

The Silk Road continued to prosper until the age of European exploration opened up safer and more profitable sea routes to China, in the sixteenth century. In the meantime, its fortunes rose and fell with those of the empires that lay at either end and with the flux of the nomadic peoples who prowled eternally in between. In all its long history, there was only one brief period when the entire route lay under the sway of a single power and it became possible for individual travelers to contemplate a round trip between the Mediterranean and China. It was this Pax Mongolica of the thirteenth and fourteenth centuries that enabled Marco Polo to make his epic journey, following in the footsteps, no doubt, of many other brave travelers who had not the luck to be jailed in later life with a literary cell mate with a mind to put their fantastic experiences on paper.

I watched the Punjabis haggling deftly with the customs agents. The traders struck me as clever, plain men of something less than perfect honesty, but something more than average determination. They were probably not very different, I suspected, from the intrepid Venetian who crossed into China not far west of here in the winter of 1298, and who would one day introduce the idea of Cathay to the Western imagination.

There was the blast of an airhorn. The merchants suddenly burst into motion. I was pushed and tugged, and finally wedged with six of the Punjabis into a bone-hard seat that was designed to hold only four. For an hour, the bus zigzagged upward through a desolation of red scree toward the eighteen thousand-foot Khunjerab Pass; the name meant "pass of blood," a reminder of the Hunzakut bandits who until just a few decades ago profitably scoured its slopes for unwary travelers. Far below, the Hunza River roared through a gorge that was littered with shattered stone, like the debris of some primeval ecological cannonade. There was the promise of new races in the flat triangular faces, the tilted eyes of the mountainmen who now and then appeared strangely alongside the road, miles from any sign of habitation. The smothering clouds added to the sense of strangeness, to the impression of one world slipping away and another waiting to be revealed.

The Chinese pilgrim Xuan Zhuang passed this way in A.D. 643, on his way home from his twenty-year sojourn in India; he left a description of the landscape, but it seemed bizarre and implausible: "There was not a trace of vegetation, only a mass of crazily piled rock on rock, and everywhere slender stone pinnacles looking like a forest of trees without leaves." But when the clouds cracked open they revealed a wild dreamscape of weird snow-crested pagodas and cathedrals, and Gothic ruins that spired high into a crepuscular sky.

The Chinese knew Xuan Zhuang as the greatest of the intrepid pilgrims who quite literally carried Buddhism from India to China on their backs. China was remote from the source of the faith, and news of the religion seeped only unreliably along the caravan routes. Translations were often incoherent, and Chinese theologians were perennially perplexed; every time a traveler arrived with a bundle of new manuscripts, fresh conundrums arose. How did you reconcile the notion of the Buddha as a simple teacher with scriptures that spoke of limitless heavens filled with tens of thousands of buddhas? Was the monk to bow to the emperor, or the emperor to the monk? How did you get hold of a living Buddha to help you reach Enlightenment? Xuan Zhuang, an early chronicle recorded, was "afflicted at heart, and fearing lest he should be unable to find out completely the errors of translation"; he set out for India to get it all straight.

A long while later, in Xian, I saw an engraved stele that portrayed him on the march; the monk's face was plain and innocent, his step was firm, and in a backpack that towered over his shaven head loomed the scrolls that he had carried all the way from the banks of the Ganges. His tale strained credibility, but it was well attested. Horses died beneath him, guides abandoned him, travelers warned him repeatedly that the way was beset by demons and fiery winds. Driven by faith, he persisted. He walked to Afghanistan, and from there over the Hindu Kush to India; eventually, he traveled as far east as Bengal, living in monasteries, learning Sanskrit, and collecting manuscripts. After twenty years in India, he walked home again.

I crossed Xuan Zhuang's path often in the weeks to come. I had nothing like his idealism or faith to propel me, just a driving curiosity (such a modern thing, so un-Chinese). But I came to think of him as a fellow-traveler, of sorts, a companion on the road to Cathay.

THE CHINESE border post at Pirali was a slum of concrete sheds inhabited by policemen swathed in antique greatcoats that made them look as if they had been mustered for the siege of Sebastopol. I stamped my feet against the cold while the customs officials gloomily poked and prodded at the Pakistanis' luggage; I was relieved for Muhammed Muslim to see his Naugahyde bag pass through without a hitch.

Finally a boxy silver Chinese bus arrived. A woman in swirling Indian garb bustled on at the last minute with a pair of small, very blond children in tow. She carried a dog-eared volume of *Practical Astrology* and announced cheerily to everyone that she was from Honolulu, had lost her passport, and had been trying to get out of China for days; the Chinese kept refusing to let her out without a visa. She and the kids went up to the border every day, in the hope that the Chinese would give in and let them through. She said they had been traveling around Asia for two years.

"We're free spirits. We wanted to travel and I knew that if we stayed home I'd just blame the kids for it, so here we all are!"

She beamed at them. The kids looked grim.

We passed the night in Taxkorgan and then set off at dawn for Kashgar. A Pakistani torch singer shrilled heart-stopping quarter-tones from Muhammed Muslim's tape deck as we spun slowly down through alpine pastures where fat-tailed yaks grazed on a fizz of yellow grass. There were yurts in the distance, and herds of double-humped camels tended by robed men with wispy Confucian beards. The Free Spirit went on unstoppably about mandalas and sun signs, and star signs, and Indian fakirs who made ashes spring from their palms.

At midday we halted for lunch among a cluster of mud-brick huts. Flat-faced Tajiks in robes and skullcaps swarmed over the road, followed by rakish women in bead-crusted caps. The traders pulled nylons and plastic bangles and whole woolen overcoats from their bundles; Muhammed Muslim extracted clumps of smuggled wrist-watches from his Naugahyde bag and threw them to partners down the road. Hawk-faced Punjabis strutted like models on a Parisian runway, with their coats flung open and arms spread wide to show off the half-dozen vests that each had put on to conceal them from the Chinese customs agents.

"Only the poorest people wear that stuff in Pakistan," said Muhammed Muslim. "Here it is high fashion."

Bargaining raged in a babel of Urdu, Chinese, and Uighur, as vendors and customers swirled in a bedlam back and forth across the ice-flecked prairie. Prices were scrawled across palms in Pakistani rupees, rubbed out, reduced, switched to Chinese yuan and back, raised, and then slashed again. Just so, I thought, must the merchants of Samarkand and Isfahan, and the canny Polos, have done their business on the way to the great entrepôts further east.

The Free Spirit was a warehouse of dangly Indian jewelery; perhaps the Tajiks mistook her for a merchant's wife. The blond children cowered against the bus as a frenzied scrum of women in scarlet leggings and bead-crusted caps snatched at her chest and plucked her wrists.

Muhammed Muslim was transformed.

"Make me your agent!" he shrilled at the Free Spirit. "Sell! Sell!"

He fairly danced over the prairie, tugging the Free Spirit along with him in a virtuoso performance of elementary capitalism. At every step, he sold off another piece: The earrings went first, then the brass bracelets, a turquoise ring, a necklace that might have been silver.

The two children looked terrified. I wondered if they feared she was going to sell them off too.

The market ended as suddenly as it had begun. The air horn blared, and the Tajiks were soon left behind waving bouquets of nylons and huge Seiko watches in the silence of the infinite prairie.

I N T H E days of the great caravans, Kashgar must have seemed like an ethereal vision to merchants who had spent months on the desert roads from Balkh or Lanzhou. Its plenitude was thrilling even now. We bounced and rumbled past earthen farmsteads, beyond whose thick mud walls I could see rich orchards of apple and peach trees, and vineyards fat with ripening grapes. Doors bossed with iron knobs gave onto balconied courtyards where parakeets chuddered in domed bamboo cages. The lofty colonnades of poplars that flanked the road lent the entire landscape an air of sedate civility that contrasted sharply with the wild emptiness of the Karakorams; in the space of a few miles, we had crossed the ancient divide between barbarism and civilization, between the free and the governed.

To Chinese, it was at Kashgar that the outer world began. It was from here that Gan Ying set out in A.D. 97, on his famous journey in search of the West. The Chinese had recently conquered the vast emptiness that is now Xinjiang, and they had hopes of winning control of the lucrative westbound trade routes, if they could only find out where they went. Gan Ying traveled in the company of the Parthians, whose merchants profited most as intermediaries in the silk trade. He reached the Parthian capital of Hecatompylos, and then a land of rhinoceroses and peacocks that was probably Mesopotamia. The annals say that he arrived at last in Diaozhi, "on the coast of the great sea." Sailors told him that it took up to two years to cross. According to the *Hou Han Shu*, they told him, " 'There is something in the sea which is apt to make man homesick, and many have thus lost their lives.' When Gan Ying heard this, he stopped."

One can imagine this man, a soldier bred among the cramped fields of Shanxi or Shandong, further away from home than any Chinese had ever been before, standing amidst the lateen-rigged ships, staring across an unknown sea, knowing that he ought to go on, giving in at last to his fear.

The "great sea" was only the Persian Gulf. Gan Ying was just a few weeks short of his destination. The Parthians had hoaxed him. They apparently never told him that there was a land route to the West. What might have happened if the Chinese had discovered the splendors of Alexandria and Antioch, or of Rome herself, and the cantankerous individualism of Greece? But Rome remained undiscovered. Gan Ying returned home instead with tales of a country far to the west called Daqin, where lambs grew from the ground, gold was plentiful, and the inhabitants were "tall and well-proportioned, somewhat like the Chinese." Daqin was the Roman Empire. A few more details were added as time went on. But Daqin remained a staple of Chinese geographies until modern times, the Chinese imagination's counterpart of Cathay.

Few cities on earth have been touched so feebly by the twentieth century as has Kashgar; its dimensions, even now, are marked out by the ruins of the towering mud battlements that for centuries fended off the nomads of the Taklamakan. The city's dusty lanes are filled with the sounds of an earlier age: the clop of a donkey's hoof, the ring of the smith's hammer, the whir of the spindle, the chuff of the carpenter's adz and, above all, the human voice, an undulating susurrus that rises with the morning market, ebbs in the heat of afternoon, and swells again as men gather for evening prayer.

Most of Kashgar's people are Muslim Uighurs, the human silt

left behind by the great Turkic migration that swept across Asia a thousand years ago and never stopped until it reached the gates of Vienna. The Uighurs look toward Mecca (and perhaps secretly to Ankara) for their identity, not to Beijing, and they regard the Chinese as interlopers; as recently as 1935, they massacred the city's entire Chinese population at a stroke.

I sat one afternoon on a carpeted platform in the *chaikhana* across the street from the Id Gah Mosque, drinking thin green tea from a battered tin pot. My neighbor was an elderly Uighur gentleman, split-whiskered like a playing-card king. A boy in a Mao cap was fanning a grill full of kebabs, bathing us with a cloud of meaty grease. In the street, a crowd of uproarious nomads was watching a magician produce chopsticks from a bottomless tin coffeepot and eggs from his backside.

The old man spoke to me politely in Uighur. I could tell that he was pronouncing the names of countries.

"American," I said.

I tried to reply in Chinese, but it was clear that he barely understood. Chinese was the conqueror's tongue.

The old man struggled to express himself in murky, flat-toned Chinese. He repeated himself until I grasped the question.

Laboriously, the old man was asking me the name of my city.

"Brooklyn," I said.

He repeated the word, turning it over on his tongue, testing it against his knowledge of the known world, finally making it his own, a new part of the Uighur cosmos.

Straining, he got out another question.

"Who is your khan?" he asked.

"Reagan khan."

"Ray-gun khan." The old man tried it out. "Is he a good khan?"

"A not-so-good khan."

The old man nodded sagely and sighed. He knew about khans.

ONE EVENING I hired a donkey cart to take me to the government guest house, where I planned to have dinner. It lay, inconveniently, a couple of miles outside town. I rode out through the crumbled battlements in a twilight of dust, amid fleets of ghostly cyclists who veered away with a jingling of bells in the haze.

The guest house seemed deserted. I wandered among concrete halls the size of airplane hangers until I found the dining room. Two dozen tables were neatly laid for a meal, but the place was dead empty. Behind a screen I found a half-dozen waitresses with their feet propped on chairs, sucking noodles. They were plainly put off at the sight of a customer.

"No food," one declared, leaping up to shoo me away. "This is a restaurant. Dinner is at seven."

I showed her my watch. It read 7:20.

"Beijing time," she repeated. "No food."

She returned to her noodles and made it clear that she had no interest in me. After several more attempts to attract her attention, I capitulated to the obvious hopelessness of my situation and the sheer gloom of the place.

On my way out I noticed the clock. It said 9:20.

Beijing time.

It was 9:20 in the capital, two thousand miles to the east, as the crow flies. Dinner had been served two hours ago, when it was dinnertime in Beijing.

The hotel was a Chinese island, a colonial outpost in the sea of Turkestan. Even time bent itself to the dictates of the imperial court.

The only places still open when I got back to the city were the kebab stalls in front of the mosque. Crowds of turbaned Uighurs were staring gravely at greasy televisions that the vendors had propped on benches and tuned to Kashgar's only channel. On half a hundred sets, Jennifer Jones was making love in Chinese to Joseph Cotton in *Duel in the Sun*.

I WENT ONE day to the site of a monastery a few miles outside the city, where the peripatetic Xuan Zhuang had put up on his way home in 643. The chronicles said that he had liked Kashgar, whose wealth sustained hundreds of Buddhist institutions and no fewer than ten thousand monks. Buddhism then flourished in all the oases that lay like stepping-stones along the Silk Road. They accumulated fabulous wealth from the caravan trade, and spawned, in turn, a civilization of surpassing grandeur whose remarkable Buddhist art fused the styles of India, China, and Persia. But most of the oases had withered, Buddhism had been superseded by Islam, an entire civilization shriveled away.

Three of the monastery's cells were left; they were caves really, cut high in a cliff that lay perhaps a mile from the road, beyond a river that meandered across the gravelly plain. Buildings had once stood against the cliff, with hundreds, perhaps even thousands, of rooms. But all that remained were the holes in the yellow cliff, beneath the cloudless cobalt sky. Frescoes still survived in the caves; looking up, I could barely see a rust-colored buddha, a flaming aureole.

I was hot, and muddy from scrambling through the river. The atmosphere of desolation was overwhelming. I felt suddenly depressed. The old world seemed remote and alien; like the buddhas high overhead, faint and beyond reach.

I watched a cloud of dust coming toward me across the plain. After a while I could see that inside the cloud there was a minibus. It maneuvered precariously through the water, around boulders and up the crumbly bank, and finally bounced to a stop where I stood.

Twenty or thirty Japanese piled out. They were mostly elderly and wore golf hats and neckties, and tailored leisure suits. They set out neat rows of folding chairs that they had brought in the minibus and settled themselves sedately facing the cliff.

Three Buddhist priests in violet robes busied themselves with a collection of silk boxes. First they unfurled a piece of silk illustrated with an ink rubbing of some kind; they attached the banner to a pole which they then erected over a makeshift altar. I could see that the rubbing was of a bald-headed figure in antique dress. With a start, I realized that it was Xuan Zhuang.

A lady wearing a T-shirt that said "Silk Road" told me that they were from the Medicine King Temple in Nara and that each year they organized a pilgrimage to a different place on Xuan Zhuang's route.

"We want to feel a little of what it was like for him."

She tittered with Japanese embarrassment.

24

In previous years, she said, they had traveled to Hunza, Xian, and Xuan Zhuang's original home of Luoyang. Next year they hoped to visit Turpan and Dunhuang.

The priests spread a piece of red silk in front of the banner. On the red silk they laid a pewter pot of tea on a bamboo tray, and then sprinkled salt and sake from a waxed milk carton on the gravel around it. Then they extracted a bolt of purple velvet from a silk box, and from the velvet a fragment of bone in a glass bowl.

"Xuan Zhuang," the woman said. "Maybe his head, maybe his foot. Who knows?" She explained that they carried the bone with them wherever they traveled.

The chief priest tapped a bronze bowl with a metal wand. The three priests cried, "*Doi!*" They repeated the cry three times.

The pilgrims began to chant. Their voices resonated in unison, echoing throatily across the plain.

I felt unexpectedly privileged, touched by the past. For the men and women in their golf hats and leisure suits the monk was not an artifact but a living presence. I needed the caves and the frescoes in order to get a grip on the old world. But listening to the ancient, throaty drone of the Heart Sutra (for that was what the Japanese were chanting), I felt that a hidden passage into the inner courtyards of the past must still exist within the hearts of men and women, and that it would be there that I might discover what really survived of Cathay.

I became aware of a second minibus slowly approaching across the plain. I expected more Japanese. But this time a troupe of Uighurs dressed in bead-crusted caps and gowns piled out in a tumble of accordions, tambors, pipes, and long-necked stringed instruments. I had seen them performing a day or two before at a hotel in Kashgar, and I guessed that the pilgrims had hired them as part of their tour.

When the priests brought the ceremony to a close, the Uighurs burst into motion, flinging themselves through the air like Cossacks. The pilgrims hopped among them, photographing each other in giddy poses. The priests pulled Nikons from their robes and snapped the pilgrims. The pilgrims snapped the priests. The priests snapped each other. I snapped the priests, the pilgrims, and the Uighurs. Only the Uighurs had no cameras. They tootled away wildly on their frail pipes, beneath the unscaleable cliff and that wonderful cobalt sky.

25

CHAPTER
TWO

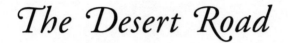

The Desert Road

HE DESERT'S name was a Turkish word: Taklamakan. It meant "Go in and you won't come out." Its sands were treacherous. Whole cities had disappeared into them. Even hardened travelers were driven mad by the buran, a kind of dust storm that produced terrifying clashing sounds and the scream of the invisible "spirit eagle," which confused men and made them rush blindly into the desert. Xuan Zhuang found his way across by following the bleached bones of caravans that didn't survive. Mirages tormented him. He saw, "here camels and horses with splendid harnesses, there glittering lances and gleaming standards. Soon these became new shapes, new figures; each instant it changed, this teeming scene, offering one by one a thousand metamorphoses."

I skirted the desert along the pitted band of asphalt that the Communist government built in the 1950s to replace the camel track of earlier times. The desert spread away to the south in a sea of yellow-gray dust and gravel. The Celestial Mountains marched along the northern horizon; they seemed forlorn at the start, ground down and naked, a succession of crumbly massifs pigmented in honky-tonk tints of salmon, tangerine, ocher, and olive. Later, after Kucha, they were a mass of snow-covered peaks in a fog of dust.

There was little traffic except for the long-snouted Liberation trucks that haul cotton, fodder, and oil between the oases. In the back of one I saw a crowd of women shrouded in gaily colored veils, swaying with every swerve and bump like a field of oversized wildflowers; in another, an elderly man in owlish spectacles perched atop a chaos of bicycles, poring over a dog-eared Koran. Men in blue boiler suits squatted behind pyramids of watermelons and then ran at the passing trucks with the lovely green fruit outstretched in desperate hands. Finally the road dropped down into the Turpan Depression through a netherworld of dust-drenched canyons, and debouched into a fairyland of dunes that seemed weightless and gently suspended in the last rose light of sunset. The driver cut the engine and we coasted, silent except for the wind, down into the pink-blue infinity.

The seeming gentleness of the sands was deceptive. Over the centuries, the oasis cities that Polo and Xuan Zhuang knew had succumbed either to the drying up of the rivers on which they depended for their water supply or to the depredations of Muslim and Mongol. One by one, they slipped under the sands, to be rediscovered only in the early twentieth century.

Sir Aurel Stein was the first to present irrefutable proof that they had ever existed. Stein was an intense, enigmatic man who dismissed the crossing of the Khunjerab as "an outing for the ladies." His coldness hid the suppressed conflicts of a Jew who had been raised as an Anglican, a Hungarian who had become a Briton, and a foreigner struggling to succeed in the bureaucracy of the Raj, which employed him on the staff of its archaeological survey.

Stein's perennial rival was a gentlemanly German of Huguenot extraction named Albert von Le Coq. The two were brilliant scholars and courageous men, but they traveled the Taklamakan as predators, who regarded China's past as free for the taking. In 1907 von Le Coq and Stein almost simultaneously heard that huge quantities of manuscripts had been discovered at the Thousand Buddha Caves of Dunhuang. Stein was far to the west at Khotan; von Le Coq was much closer, at Turpan, but he was expected at Kashgar, where he was to join the official head of his expedition, a tiresome hypochondriac named Albert Grunwedel, who was traveling overland from Germany. Von Le Coq flipped a coin. It came down heads. He returned to Kashgar, unknowingly ceding to Stein the greatest single discovery that anyone was ever to make in Central Asia.

But von Le Coq also had his successes. In the summer of 1907 peasants told him that strange manuscripts had been found at Turpan. When he began to dig amid the mud ruins known as Karakhoja, he found the capital of a forgotten Uighur kingdom that in the eighth century had held sway over Xinjiang and, perhaps alone among the world's civilizations, had embraced Manichaeanism as its state religion.

Mani was born at Ctesiphon in Mesopotamia around A.D. 250 and wandered through Persia, Turkestan, and India, proclaiming the revelation he had received from a supernatural "King of the Paradise of Light." The Zoroastrian priesthood incited the public against him and crucified him as the price for his defeat in a theological debate. His followers suffered equally cruel persecution. Refugees fled to the oases of the Silk Road, where they exercised an improbable puritanism among the arbors and vineyards, and grew wealthy from the silk, spices, and jade that passed through on camelback.

Mani's vision was essentially tragic. He believed that although the material world was inherently evil, Light had mingled with Darkness to create Heaven and Earth, and men and women. He was convinced that Light was endlessly subdivided and weakened by human births; procreation and all sexual union were therefore proscribed for the Perfecti, whose ascetic lives embodied the uttermost expression of the faith. The great mass of followers, known as Auditori, who remained in the world of dust, were forbidden lying, murder, adultery, theft, slackness in good deeds, and religious doubt.

Karakhoja's ruins suggest something dreamed or invented, a sketch for a city never built. The city was still prosperous in Polo's day; he remembered the inhabitants as "keen students of the liberal arts," who told him that their king's line had sprung from a tuber. The only people about now were dusty boys who tried to sell me worthless coins embossed with the pinched face of Chiang Kaishek. I walked among towers that had eroded into teetering pinnacles, rooms that had been carved into caves, walls that had been gouged and polished into smooth hillocks—a phantom city that spread for mile after mile in silence across the plain, until it blended almost imperceptibly into the walled, low adobe homes of the present-day oasis, suggesting, if only for a moment, that the great city still lived.

A fleet of doves whirled over my head, diving, circling, and spinning in lunatic arcs. Beneath my feet, I felt an invisible world—shrines, homes, palaces, markets where men from every corner of Asia had traded—tantalizingly near yet almost painfully beyond my grasp. The pregnant hillocks of rubble evoked a sense not only of the whole lost Central Asian world but of the incessant falling away of all time; of minutes, hours, years sifting away from the world's history and from my own life in a soft poignant cloud and disappearing into the yellow mud and rubble.

Von Le Coq found what he was looking for at Karakhoja. He discovered the first known Manichaean manuscripts packed two feet deep in a ruined chapel and soaked from top to bottom with water by farmers who had cultivated the land on top of them. He painstakingly dried the manuscripts out, only to find that in the summer heat they crumbled to fragments "on which the remains of beautifully written lines, intermingled with traces of miniatures executed in gold, blue, red, yellow, and green were still to be seen." Von Le Coq wept as he watched them disintegrate in his hands.

I found the large mud-brick building next to the western wall where Von Le Coq came upon the piled-up corpses of a hundred murdered men, apparently monks. The "frightful wounds" that had caused their deaths were still visible when the German uncovered them. One skull had been split from the top of the head to the teeth by a saber. Von Le Coq speculated that the carnage had occurred in the mid-ninth century, when, in a curious foreshadowing of the Cultural Revolution of the 1960s, the Chinese government ordered monks of all sects to return to civil life, do practical work, marry, produce children, and pay taxes. Pious men preferred death to conformity.

In the summer of 1907 von Le Coq shipped hundreds of cases of frescoes back to the Berlin Ethnological Museum. They were carried by cart to Kashgar and then lashed to camels and sent over the Pamirs to the nearest railhead in Russian Tajikstan, and from there three thousand miles by rail to Berlin. Remarkably, they arrived without a single loss. The museum immediately recognized their importance and displayed them prominently in concrete frames that could not be removed. Three hundred frescoes that had survived a thousand years of abandonment in the Taklamakan were thus turned to dust by Allied bombs during World War II.

THE LOUDSPEAKER at the railroad station at Dehe was blaring "God Save the Queen." I arrived at 6:30 P.M. in order to catch the 9:30 P.M. train, but the clerk at the ticket window would only sell tickets to foreigners for a train that was due at 1:00 A.M. When it arrived every seat had already been taken. Solemn Chinese in blue boiler suits were squeezed four and five to each wooden bench and curled asleep on scraps of paper that they had spread over the sludge of melon seeds, banana peels, spilled rice, mucus, and sputum that covered the floor. An elderly peasant made room for me to sit on part of his bundle. He kept tentatively touching the blond hair on my forearm with a calloused forefinger, clearly amazed that it was real. I dozed for a few minutes at a time, bent over my knees. The radio system played the same four bars of xylophone music all night.

At dawn I stopped trying to sleep. I found myself sitting next to a nervous young man in denims whose card identified him as Zhou Xiao, the director of the Communist Youth League in Shanghai. He said he was on a "personal research tour" of the western regions. He had a harried look and kept a voluminous diary which he scribbled in from time to time as we talked.

Morning was a cacophony of hawking, spitting, nose blowing and picking, and coughing. A surf of cigarette smoke rolled down the car. Uighur babies were stuffing plastic bags in their mouths. Old men with imperial whiskers and stovepipe karakul hats sucked at bowls of cold noodles. The desert outside was a fiery red plain.

"My job is very hard," Zhou sighed.

The League had traditionally been the proving ground for up-and-coming young commissars. Zhou was supposed to drum up support among young people for the Party's policies. He grimaced forlornly.

"Nobody wants to join anymore."

33

The slogans and ideological appeals that had once moved millions didn't work anymore. The Chinese had become a more cynical people. Without quite saying so, even the Party leadership had abandoned orthodox communism and was preaching shamelessly the advantages of shareholding, bankruptcies, and privatization.

Zhou told me that he had just been accepted by the University of Wisconsin. He was planning to study for an MBA. I listened for a hint of irony, but there wasn't any.

"Once they get abroad, Chinese students don't seem to want to come home," I said.

"I won't be like them!" Zhou declared vehemently. "I shall return to China to help my country develop and become a great nation."

He was reciting an official formula. I wondered if he was afraid for his faith.

"Why do you think people don't want to join the Youth League?" I asked.

But whenever I mentioned the Party Zhou skittered away, coughing, smiling, clearing his throat.

After a long while he said, "It is very difficult to explain."

It was a quintessential Chinese conversation, filled with blank spaces, like the places on medieval maps that are marked "Here be monsters."

I REACHED DUNHUANG in the evening. Podgy women in caps that looked like colonial farthingales had created a Lilliput of eateries in the town square. Patrons sat on elfin stools at miniature tables, drinking diminutive bottles of *mao tai* and shoveling down tofu and pork from clay pots that were plucked from an open fire and served with a pair of mechanic's pliers.

For the first time, the majority of people I saw were Chinese. There was less body language; the faces were stiller and the expressions more guarded, less easy to read.

For millenia it was at Dunhuang that guides were hired, supplies taken on, new camels purchased, and wills written before caravans embarked into the fatal nothingness of the Taklamakan. East lay civilization, China; and to the west, myth.

From the fourth century until the beginning of the twentieth, Buddhist monks occupied a vast honeycomb of rock-cut monasteries at the desert's edge. The Thousand Buddha Caves were an ecumenical, multilingual community that included Tibetans, Indians, Turkis, Khotanese, and Mongols, as well as Chinese. They were famous for the quality of their scholarship, and the scriptures they translated were treasured as far away as Japan. The monks also ran a lucrative spiritual security service, praying for the souls of travelers about to set off across the desert and (prepaid, one assumes) for those who never returned.

I RENTED A bicycle and pedaled out an arrow-straight road colonnaded with poplars that glowed a brilliant gold in the thin, chill autumn light. Dunes rolled and billowed away to the west in an undulating chiaroscuro of yellow-gray sand. The caves, four hundred of them, lay in a crack in angular hills that resembled a torn sheet of rusty tin. Painted buddhas by the hundreds and thousands peered from the caves' walls. It was too much at first, an aesthetic short-circuit. Fire-breathing skeletons, fanged gargoyles, popeyed demons, and cow-headed phantoms swarmed at imperturbable Siddharthas. Bosomy flautists peered down from *trompe l'oeil* balconies. Robed mandarins rode blue-crested birds. Buddhas swarmed up lotus stalks like transcendental Jacks-and-the-Beanstalk. Celestial sprites dove like Stukas over lotus gardens populated by musicians and half-naked houris. None of this had much to do with the simple teacher who had walked the plains of northern India in the sixth century B.C. Over the centuries, Siddhartha's austere moral lessons had grown jungly with an infinitude of nirvanas, buddhas, and bodhisattvas, who had foresworn redemption to minister to the sufferings of man. Chinese pilgrims had no way of knowing how vastly Buddhism had changed. The Buddhism that Xuan Zhuang brought home maintained, for instance, that the world was pure consciousness; his interpreters postulated multiple paradises that the adept could enter through the inner tunnel of meditation. In the Western Heaven, it was said, everyone would live to be 4,800,000 years old. Every man would have five hundred wives. Clothes would grow on trees. The dead would leap from their graves. The frescoes showed these wistful hopes with a quaint literalness.

Visitors are not allowed to wander at will through the caves. I was assigned as a guide a former art student named Guan Jinfong, who had lived her entire life in the valley except for four years that she had spent at the university in Lanzhou. She wore her hair in a stiff bouffant puff and had the quality of brittle virginity that Chinese girls often preserve well into their twenties.

IN 1900 an illiterate monk named Wang (a Taoist, curiously enough) who had made his home in the caves chanced upon a hidden chamber that had been sealed and forgotten almost a thousand years before. Inside he found a cache of nearly eleven thousand manuscripts written on parchment in half a dozen languages. Some were original translations from Sanskrit by Xuan Zhuang. Wang offered them to the provincial government, but the authorities decided they were not worth the expense of the bullock carts that would be needed to ship them to Lanzhou. It was the monk's discovery that had piqued the curiosity of both Stein and von Le Coq.

Arriving with his caravan at Dunhuang in February of 1908, Stein found that the trove surpassed his wildest dreams. He recognized immediately that the manuscripts comprised one of the greatest finds in the history of archaeology.

"Would the resident priests be sufficiently good-natured—and mindful of material interests—to close their eyes to the removal of any sacred objects?" Stein wondered. Stein's Chinese secretary did his best to persuade the suspicious Wang that the removal of the manuscripts to a "temple of learning" in "Ta Ying-guo," as the Chinese called Great Britain, would in fact be an act that the Buddha would approve. Stein would of course be glad to "propitiate" the pious monk with "an appropriate offering." As it happened, Wang had been struggling for years to collect money with which to restore the caves' idols and frescoes to their former glory. "With many a sigh and remonstrance," Wang began hauling out bundles of manuscripts. One night he panicked and shifted the entire heap back to a locked chamber. But finally brought around by "our suavest manners," Stein wrote in his diary, the monk allowed Stein to take what he wished. The one thousand manuscripts and scroll paintings that he shipped back to the British Museum provided Western scholars with one of the most extensive archives of information on early Buddhism outside Asia.

Guan's flashlight picked out a rank of bejeweled bodhisattvas marching along the cave's wall. Where the seventh should have been, there was a small door.

"This is where the manuscripts were found," she declared indignantly. "Then they were stolen by the British so-called explorer Stein."

She had obviously been trained to present the caves as a textbook study of the destruction that Western imperialists had wrought upon China. She made no mention of the Cyrillic names carved into frescoes by Russian mercenaries who were quartered here in the 1920s or of the Islamic zealots who had hacked away the eyes and faces of scores of buddhas, probably during the Tungan rebellions of the 1870s and 1930s. There were Chinese graffiti everywhere.

"After Stein, more foreigners came and stole more national treasures. They only gave trinkets in return."

According to his own report, Stein had paid Wang 130 pounds for one thousand manuscripts and scroll paintings. Later, I recognized some of the plaster buddhas that the monk had had made with Stein's "donations." They were cartoon caricatures of the Buddha and his disciples, torpid and earthy, painted with a flea-market aesthetic of ghostly white flesh, blue hair, and brick-colored robes.

"The monks were ignorant men," Guan declared. "They didn't know the value of what they were giving away."

I asked Guan if she was a Buddhist.

She giggled. "Of course not," she said with an evasive smirk.

"What are you then?"

"It's hard to say."

In another cave, Guan angrily pointed out a scabrous patch where in 1926 the "so-called scholar" Langdon Warner of Harvard had attempted, and failed, to remove a piece of the Western Heaven, severely damaging the original fresco in the process. He had managed to buy a seated bodhisattva, which today rests in the Fogg Museum in Cambridge.

"What nationality are you?" she asked.

When I told her American, she apologized profusely.

"We don't like to embarrass foreigners by showing them the damage that was done by their countrymen."

We entered another cave. Row upon row of terra-cotta bodhisattvas smiled their enigmatic smile from the walls. Many of them had been broken away. The damage looked relatively recent.

"They fell over and broke," Guan said.

A few minutes later, I heard another guide tell a group of Hongkongese that the statues had been stolen by foreigners.

"Did the Red Guards destroy them?" I asked Guan.

"It's hard to say."

I pressed her.

"Maybe," she said. "Maybe they fell over then."

We went into another cave through a wooden gallery. Inside, a colossal Buddha rose a hundred feet into the gloom. Twelve hundred years ago, the monks had carved it from the living rock in an act of monstrous piety. It was meant to be the Maitreya Buddha, the "Merciful One," the messiah. But there was no mercy to be gotten here. The figure was overbearing and imperial, and it reminded me of the gargantuan Mao statues that until a few years ago loomed gracelessly over the main square of every Chinese city.

The Buddha's hands were huge slabs eighteen feet long, the right one upraised in a gesture that might as easily have been one of refusal as of benediction. The face was a vast white moon. It was an emperor's face, the eyes mere slits, the lips fixed in the smirk of power; it was the face of Mao in the airbrushed pictures of the 1960s, omniscient, idealized, and dangerous.

I was grateful to escape into the daylight, to birdsong, the mutter of chickens, the cry of a baby from some peasant home hidden amid the apple trees and yellowing poplars. A souvenir stand calling itself the "Bodhi Shady Painted Corridor" was selling black-currant juice, plaster Taoist immortals with heads like hard-boiled Easter eggs, fat babies blowing trumpets, and Santa Clauses playing the electric guitar.

I PASSED WITHIN the Great Wall at Jiayuguan, where the westernmost gate of the Celestial Kingdom brooded forbiddingly over the plain. The Chinese used to believe that a man who had traveled beyond the wall had died a kind of death. Passing within it didn't imply rebirth, however. Rather, a man who returned to China was viewed as a kind of pariah, tainted by his experience of the world beyond.

There were, as usual, no seats to be found on the train, but a lantern-jawed man let me sit on the edge of his bench and showed me his collection of switchblades. When he curled up under the seat to sleep, his wife gave me rock candy and pickled string beans to eat.

The bus I took from Lanzhou to Labrang climbed into a steep corrugated land populated entirely by Muslims. The men wore identical white cotton caps that stood up on their heads; it was market day and the entire countryside looked like a vast convention of chefs tugging handcarts heaped with pears and garlic, piloting spindly tractors, haggling over cotton and sheep, spreading wheat on the pavement to be threshed by the traffic. The roofs of their mud-walled homes had upturned corners, like the prows of ancient biremes.

I slept for a while. When I woke it was as if I had fallen through a cultural trapdoor. The chefs had completely disappeared. The bus was now packed with fantastic Tibetans in brass-studded boots, and robes trimmed with lynx and snow leopard, who managed to suggest swaggering panache even stuffed four and five to a bench. The mountains had swung shut like iron doors, and clumps of prayer flags fluttered from the tumbling scree. Hunched pilgrims plodded the road spinning prayer wheels in filthy hands.

Labrang lay at six thousand feet amid snow-dusted yellowish hills studded with evergreens. It was a holy city, a Tibetan Assisi, of cells and temples that tapered from the ground to the top in Tibetan fashion, creating a curious impression of loftiness even though none was more than three stories high.

From the roof of the Prayer Hall, a monk bent back taut as a bowstring and let out a thunderous groan: "Om!" Another lifted a conch to his lips and blew it resoundingly across the valley. I tagged after monks in running shoes who flooded the muddy alleys, hitching fuscia robes over their ankles as they ran to prayer. Mustard-yellow hats were slung like spare coxcombs over their shoulders.

Kham nomads with half-shaved scalps and quick, bandits' eyes clogged the door of the Prayer Hall. Butternut-brown women in bush hats were flinging across the threshold scraps of paper on which the names of dead relatives had been scrawled. Inside, half a thousand monks sat cross-legged in facing ranks, their pates gleaming in the thin wintery light. The abbot sat like a brass idol at their head, calling out the names of the dead to the thud of a muffled drum and the clash of cymbals. The prayers rumbled primevally, rhythmic and numbing. The Communist authorities regulated the number of monks allowed to attend prayer, and scores of young monks huddled among the Khams, bent sinuously as frescoed saints, straining to hear, their naked shoulders prickling in the cold.

Labrang's monks had once presided over forty-seven other monasteries, as far away as Beijing and Inner Mongolia, and had operated one of the handful of printing presses in Tibet. As recently as the 1950s, four thousand monks had inhabited its warrens of cells. But that was, as they say, in another incarnation.

"I will tell you whatever I saw, whatever I know," the monk said. "I want to speak."

The monk might have been fifty, or seventy. It was impossible to say. He had a broad face and a knobbly Byzantine brow, and he was curled on a raised wooden platform, writing out the names of the dead on scraps of paper. Later the monks would pray for them at the afternoon service.

Huge prayer wheels were mounted in the next room and their sound kept intruding on us. There were hundreds of them, copper cylinders three or four feet high and as thick as tree trunks, each of them stuffed with scrawled prayers. Pilgrims trotted at breakneck speed along the rows, pushing the wheels faster and faster until they creaked and whirred and rumbled and whined, launching their prayers in clouds and flotillas to the heavens; I imagined them soaring over the roofs of the monastery, over the mud alleys and gray concrete blockhouses of the Chinese town and the unsuspecting heads of the commissars, over the wintry uplands and the tents of the nomads, over the reek of Shanghai and across the seas and the Siberian tundra, cruising through space and time to sift down over the humid jungles of the Amazon, over the oblivious Bedouin of the Sahara, over house-wives grilling steaks in American backyards, to detonate their benefi-cence in generations yet to come.

The monk told me that in 1959 the monks of Labrang had risen against Chinese occupation, as Tibetans everywhere had that year. The People's Liberation Army easily overran Tibetan troops armed with matchlocks. The Dalai Lama fled to India, and Tibet's tenuous independence came to an end. Sixty of Labrang's monks died when the library burned to the ground. Most of its ten thousand manu-scripts also perished.

"Eight of every ten monks were arrested. The rest ran away."

The monk poured shallow bowls of cloudy green tea from a thermos. He wrote for a while in silence. Then he said, "They labeled me a 'class enemy.' " He spent the next two years in a labor camp.

"I was never free after that. Sometimes they sent me to do road work, sometimes farming, sometimes herding cattle. Belief wasn't allowed, but when I was alone with myself on the grasslands, I recited the prayers."

He took a sooty piece of cloth from a bag and handed me the two plastic-covered notebooks that were inside.

"I carried them all those years. I hid them in my clothes."

In an elegant spiky hand, he had copied from memory all the prayers he could remember. The pages had been thumbed so often that the corners were worn away.

"I was caught once. I could have been killed, since prayer was quite illegal. But they let me go."

During the Cultural Revolution, the Red Guards smashed fres-coes, pillaged reliquaries, and demolished hundreds of prayer wheels. They installed a butcher shop in one of the temples. Seventy percent of the monastery was leveled and the valley repopulated mostly with

Chinese. A slum of factories and concrete dormitories for the Chinese colonists was built where the monks' cells had been.

The monk managed a brief visit to Labrang after Mao's death in 1976.

"I knew I was witnessing the Wheel of Life. Everything here had been alive, and now it was all dead. I thought, 'Man must be born, and so he must die.' Labrang had died."

But now there was a fragile recovery underway. The authorities had allowed the monastery to reopen in 1980. Gutted shrines and cells were being rebuilt. Masons were swabbing new walls with chocolate-brown paint. Craftsmen were carving fanged dragons, leaping deer, and swirling clouds on new pinewood doors. Monks who had survived the Cultural Revolution were allowed to return. Young men were beginning to flow down as they had for generations from the highlands of Qinghai and inner Tibet, in hope of becoming monks. There was talk of building an airport. The new market-minded Chinese administration thought the monastery had excellent prospects for tourism.

"This used to be our home," the monk said. "But now we are only guests here."

I TRIED TO read the future in Kesang. He was a sparrow-frail man of twenty-five who ran a stall that sold boots and leather goods, in the town that had grown up outside the monastery's gates. His father had been abbot of a monastery that was destroyed by the Chinese in 1959. He fled to India, where he got work on construction crews. India was full of monks without monasteries in those days; eventually he forgot his vows and married another refugee. In 1983 the father began to sense death approaching and decided to come home.

"It was his idea to die in the place where they were born," Kesang said with a gloomy smile. "It was a very powerful thing."

Kesang's father had died last year. Now Kesang was waiting for his mother to die. I could see that he wanted to go back to India.

"It is a problem," he sighed.

Kesang favored tight jeans and the kind of billowing jacket that was popular with young people in Hong Kong. They marked him as someone from the outside, and I sensed they were important to him for that reason.

He had been born in India and educated in English. The language was his last link to the larger world.

"Can you understand me?" he kept asking, needlessly I thought, for his grammar was still good. Then I realized that he felt it gradually slipping away, and it scared him.

I wondered why he had not tried to go to Beijing or Shanghai, where he could put his education to use.

He shrugged. China was not his country.

Kesang was devoted to the idea of Tibet, but he was more Indian than Tibetan. ("It's so cold here!") He was a permanent outsider, a foreigner among his own people, an anachronism from the future.

India's secularism and his father's apostasy had worked at him, and he seemed embarrassed by the idols and the forests of prayer wheels, the altars reeking of rancid butter.

"The old people don't understand me and I don't understand them," he giggled humorlessly. His tiny sparrow's frame shook.

I wondered which way he would turn, back to the beloved world beyond the mountains that receded further with the passage of every year, or toward the ancient world of his parents, which was perhaps already an anachronism, a tourist attraction in the making, an exercise in solipsism? For that matter, was there a past to return to anymore? The Chinese hadn't left very much. Or would he sink into sterile and bitter isolation, or even suicide?

The bus back to Lanzhou left at dawn. Kesang was already awake, fussing at his stall. We stood together for a while, waiting for a horsecart to take me to the station. The mountains were gloomy shadows in the frigid night, ghostly where they were crusted with snow.

"You know, during the Cultural Revolution, the Chinese tried to force Tibetans to smash the statues," Kesang was saying. "But many of those who tried, died. It is a scientific fact. The power of the statues killed them before they could strike. Many of the Chinese who attacked the temples and abused the Living Buddha got fatal diseases or committed suicide. You know, it is just possible that the gods have not gone away completely."

The events of twenty years past were already beginning to slip into myth.

I TOOK THE bus back to Lanzhou and boarded a train bound for Xian. I traveled through fog all the next day. Scraps of snow hung from invisible mountains. Then the land tightened like a muscle. There were fields wedged together like cloisonné against rust-colored hills, and then coal yards and brick kilns, railway sidings and factories that gushed Day-Glo green and orange pollution. Then the battlements of the last walled city in China loomed through the muck, pacing the train like an urgent message from the medieval past. A spiky-haired Tibetan in a sport jacket snatched a guitar from a soldier and played "Red River Valley" as the train pulled into the station.

Xian was China's capital for most of the empire's first thousand years, since the First Emperor built a palace here in 212 B.C. (it was known then as Changan), on what was then the western rim of the Chinese world. But the city reached its most glorious heights when it served as the capital of the Tang dynasty, which ruled China from A.D. 618 to 907. The Changan to which Xuan Zhuang returned in 645 was the richest city in the world; the Tai Zong emperor could claim, without bombast, "Taking my three-foot sword in hand, I have subjugated the two hundred kingdoms and made quiet all within the four seas, while the far-off barbarians have come one after another to make their submission."

Two million people lived within Changan's thirty square miles of walls. The outer city was divided like a chessboard by right-angled streets flanked with elms and locust trees; in their shade, markets and workshops traded briskly in Khotanese jade, African ivory, the spices of Southeast Asia, Tibetan furs, the "heavenly horses" of the Scythian steppes, and the newly popular drink known as tea, as well as the countless necessities of daily life that were demanded by an affluent and sophisticated urban population. Mongolian nomads and Indian mendicants rubbed elbows in Changan's streets with Arabs, Malays, Japanese, Persians, Sogdians, and the gawking citizens of a dozen other now-forgotten nations.

At the city's heart, the emperor lived attended by an army of eunuchs in a walled city of his own, graced with hosts of elegant pavilions, multitudes of courtyards that opened out one from the other like Chinese boxes, and gardens whose intricate construction was meant to evoke the ephemeral isles of the immortals.

Xuan Zhuang's fame had already spread through the city, and as he approached through the western suburbs, an immense throng waited to greet him. "The inhabitants of the capital, scholars and magistrates lined both sides of the street, standing in postures redolent of both love and wonder." So dense were the crowds that the monk was unable to get through and wound up spending the night on a boat moored in the city canal.

A few days later, Xuan Zhuang was granted the extraordinary privilege of entering the imperial palace. The emperor listened to his tales of the lands beyond; he pressed the monk to join his personal advisors. But Xuan Zhuang had not walked all the way to India and back for the sake of power. With the emperor's reluctant blessing, he retired with his manuscripts to the solitude of a monastery near the south wall; but sometimes, it was said, an imperial sedan chair could be seen carrying him through the palace gates, where he presumably did his best to answer the Son of Heaven's queries about Sassanian ambitions in the Pamirs, or the climate of the distant Punjab. I tried to imagine the doughty monk, sighing to himself as the bearers jogged through the bustling lanes, grudging every hour lost from the pressing job of translating the scriptures of the True Faith.

The Tang city disappeared long ago; imposing though they are, the walls that now loom over Xian were built by the Manchus in the seventeenth century and enclose only a fraction of the ancient city. I cycled past miles of indistinguishable beige and gray-brown apartment blocks to a pagoda that once lay in the heart of the Tang city but now stands in discrete solitude on a hill in the southern suburbs. It was a simple building, a sort of ziggurat of seven diminishing stories piled one atop the other. It was unassuming in every respect but one:

It was erected by imperial order for Xuan Zhuang himself, and it was here that he sat until the end of his days, translating the manuscripts that he had carried on his back all the way from India.

I stood on a high floor of the pagoda, gazing out over the factories and boulevards of Xian. Hunza and the Khunjerab, Kashgar and the Taklamakan seemed almost unimaginable now; this was the Silk Road's end and China's beginning. The streets lay beneath me in a grid that I imagined might still preserve a part of the old Tang checkerboard. But it was difficult to see much. Smog hung heavy over the city; my eyes smarted from it. I counted twenty-six smoking chimneys before I gave up.

It was hard to put it all together, the smog, the gloomy apartment blocks, the smokestacks, and the dream of Cathay. I thought of what I had said to Amir Khan, in Hunza, weeks before: "Ugliness doesn't matter." But it did, after all. The ugliness defied penetration, like the walls of red, yellow-gray, and salmon-colored brick that surrounded every office compound, apartment block, and factory and stood inside every gate to block the eye, like the spirit walls of Old China that were erected to deflect the malignant demons that the Chinese believed swarmed everywhere through the air.

I thought of something the American traveler E. R. Scidmore wrote at the turn of the century, when an emperor still ruled in the Forbidden City at Beijing and his mandarins still traveled in sedan chairs as they had in ancient Changan: "Defying age and time and progress and the harsh impact of Western civilization, China continues, and will continue, to be China. One may see now the same ancient, original China, the same conditions as in the Middle Ages." That world had, at least on the surface, largely disappeared. What I saw spread out in the smog was a product of a twentieth-century (or at least a nineteenth-century) industrial civilization; Xian resembled a Dickensian Coketown more than it did brash, quick-step cities like Hong Kong and Taipei. But somehow China must continue to "be China," I thought. The Maoists had attempted to abolish history, to wipe out the past completely, but it could not be done so simply as that. The monks flooding back to Labrang Monastery hinted at the seismic power of tradition that might still lie buried beneath the gloomy surface of things.

The other thing I said to Amir Khan was, "What matters is to see things as they are." In the end, the ugliness was part of whatever truth there was to be seen; perhaps a good deal more of it stained the reality of Old China than the imagination wished to know. Fantasies of the past could obscure one's sight as much as the acrid smog of the present. I would try, as I had promised Amir Khan, to see things as they were.

CHAPTER
THREE

Vibrato

FIRST RAN into Rui, quite literally, in the elevator of my hotel, a mammoth confection erected by the Russians to house their advisors in the 1950s. He stumbled out of the elevator in a welter of tweeds, near-sightedness, and incipient hysteria.

"Did you see the Taiwanese? Where have the Taiwanese got to?"

I thought for a moment he might be mad. But he blurted, all in an apologetic mouthful, that he was looking for a family of Taiwanese relatives who were on their first visit to the mainland since 1949 and that his dream was to study violin at the University of Oklahoma.

He pointed me toward the China Travel Service office and went hurtling off down the hall.

"Taiwanese!"

MISS LI'S cylinder of permed hair tilted regretfully up from her knitting when I entered the CTS office. I showed her a list of temples that I had copied from an old Nagel's Guide. Miss Li stared at the list.

"I must call my director."

Mr. Lu was probably in his late thirties. He was dressed in a black leather jacket and skintight slit-sided leather jeans.

51

"You go to the Great Mosque," he said with a starchy smile.

I had been there. The mosque was a curious place, with its stumpy minaret and lulling, secluded courts that owed more to the hide-and-seek architecture of China than to the democratic openness of Islam. It had been laid out in the eighth century, and handsomely rebuilt many times since then. But is was ultimately a Potemkin village, a polemical artifact that the regime had preserved in an effort to prove its respect for culture and religion to tourists, as well as to ambassadors from the Middle East.

I said, "I want to find the Five Western Terraces."

Miss Li looked blank.

Mr. Lu scratched his head.

"There was something," Mr. Lu said finally. "Where we are putting up the new hotel. It is a multiservice hotel. You will like it."

"The Temple of Goodwill?" I asked.

They pored over the map, grimacing politely.

"We are very young," Mr. Lu said.

Then I asked about the Temple of the Recumbent Dragon.

Mr. Lu smiled vaguely. Miss Li looked longingly at her knitting.

Surely they could help me find the Taishan Temple. According to the Nagel's it was the largest Taoist establishment in Xian.

"Maybe disappeared," said Miss Li.

There is a strange flatness, a blankness to Maoist cities. It is hard to get a visual grip on them. Partly it is the sheer gloominess of the too-wide avenues, and partly the instant shabbiness of the gray-brick and concrete buildings that were erected at a time when even the slightest embellishment was a crime. But beneath the monotony there is something else, a basic fear of distinguishing; a distrust, a hatred even, for idiosyncrasy.

The Nagel's told me that I would find the Temple of the City God a few hundred yards past the Drum Tower. But I passed what had been its entrance three times before I managed to identify it.

The City God's temple was the symbolic heart of every Chinese city. The god was the city's protector, chief of the celestial bureaucracy that administered the community's supernatural affairs. The whole population took part in his annual feast. Heralds cleared the streets with gongs and drums. Men costumed as the god's steed, attendants, and staff executioners paraded his idol on a palanquin through the streets. Boys dressed as demons drove troops of penitents loaded with chains and fetters. Awe changed quickly to contempt when it was felt that the god had failed in his duty. In years of plague and famine they dragged his idol into the street and beat it with sticks.

An old man pointed me down a sort of tunnel flanked by brick sheds and roofed with plastic tarps. Tiny stalls sold cigarette lighters, sequins, thread, socks, pipestems, and shoe soles. Like fish swimming around an obstruction, the mob of shoppers instinctively parted to let me through. Astonished tots murmured "outlander" as I passed.

I could see the temple's colossal maroon doors at the end of the bazaar. I tried to slip through, but half a dozen young men who were playing cards in the gatehouse leaped up and violently waved me away.

"Can't look!"

I asked if I couldn't just take a walk around the courtyard.

"*Bu xing*!" they barked. "Impossible!"

I smiled.

"Go away!"

A teenager who sold thumbtacks in the bazaar told me that the temple was now a factory.

"There's nothing to see. They make trinkets."

I FOUND THE Temple of Great Goodwill wedged into the northwest corner of the city wall, behind a sprawl of makeshift workshops. I was about to give up looking when I saw a battered stone lion propped unsteadily on a heap of bricks at the dormitory gate. Inside, hysterical chickens were dodging an implacable housewife beneath feet-long squash that dangled from a trellis.

Nagel's described "a vast series of buildings." I looked for them in vain.

A man with a tired, friendly face and padded clothes of old-fashioned cut was amusing himself by kicking a German shepherd puppy chained to a post.

"*Puodaole*," he said. "All smashed up."

Elderly couples were living in several of the half-dozen halls that remained. I had an impression of ruin that had recently been tidied up. There were piles of freshly hewn lumber and newly cut stone. But there wasn't much left to restore.

The old man pushed open a pair of crimson doors. I didn't expect much and was taken aback when the gray light fell upon the Buddha of Transcendental Wisdom, broad-shouldered and slim-waisted, and graced with the smile of a child of unearthly innocence. He seemed so weightless that I imagined he might slip from the altar and waft to the heavens like a gust of joss. The gilding seemed new.

"Things must be nice for the tourists," the old man said.

Faded ideographs of the Cultural Revolution were still legible on a wall, strident and runic.

I CYCLED THROUGH warrens of tree-lined lanes, between rows of decrepit mansions where the Manchu nobility once lived. Through studded doors that stood ajar I saw courtyards crowded with brick huts, piles of lumber and coal, spare tins, caged birds dangling from lofty and fissured eaves, doorposts carved with flaking bats and lions, rusty bicycles, the cramped quarters of the poor in the husk of a bygone world.

The Eight Immortals Temple was flickering feebly back to life. A factory was being peeled away from it like the rind of a fruit, where it had been built up around the old columned halls. Carpenters were fitting new doors, hammering lintels, laying new roofs. There were also new idols, vivid pink, like kewpie dolls with wispy beards, wearing orange, lime-green, and yellow robes.

I was repelled by the newness of things and wished for the graceful patina, the handsomely faded fresco. I had to remind myself that this was no ruin sculpted gently by time. It was a battlefield. The walking wounded were all around me, a handful of survivors who to this day didn't know whether they had won or lost.

Three or four young novices stood out of the drizzle under an upturned eave, snickering at some private joke. I wondered what had driven these children of Mao to seek shelter in the conundrums of

Taoism. What had convinced the woman in worker's blues, burning clumps of incense, to confide her hopes to hidden powers that the commissars thought they had dispelled decades ago? What cruelties of history might have befallen the shriveled monk who sat with his face pressed almost to the desk, writing spells on scraps of yellow paper?

He told me that the monastery now had twenty-five monks.

"So many!" I exclaimed.

"So few. We used to be two hundred."

He got up and shuffled around the altar for a few minutes, rearranging the offerings of apples and oranges. I thought he had forgotten me.

Then he said, *"Puodaole."*

The drizzle had become a steady downpour. The route to the hotel took me past the former Taishan Temple, which had been dedicated to the great primeval mountain deity of Shandong and the seventy-two hells over which he presided. At the gate, a wary woman with a tight, unchallengeable smile sent me to another entrance several blocks away. There, a sign announced that the complex had become the "Foreign Languages Evening Institute." I could see that its colonnades had been bricked up and that what must have been a majestic composition of halls had been colonized by a mess of modern structures.

I was too wet and tired to bear being turned away from another gate. I decided to leave with a last glimpse of the roofs, enormous and green-tiled, floating above a scum of ironmongers' sheds and dingy apartment blocks. I joined the stoic, sopping stream of cyclists and allowed myself to be borne away, chilled to the bone, into the gray, foggy heart of the city.

I RAN INTO Rui again at the Pottery Army, playing host to his Taiwanese cousins. They might have been Americans, festooned with cameras and stuffed into hip-hugging designer jeans. They were tense and polite, and clumped beneath the fierce suzerainty of the family patriarch, Rui's uncle, a retired air force officer. Rui fluttered back and forth among them like a wren on a branch.

There was something restless and unsatisfied about Rui, but I couldn't quite get a handle on it. I sensed that he was pleased to have a foreign acquaintance to show off to his cousins.

We walked for a while along the wooden catwalks that have been erected over the trenches where the warriors were found. The army was disquietingly spectacular. In the third century B.C., the First Emperor, Qinshihuangdi, buried seven thousand life-sized clay soldiers for acres around his tomb, to escort him on his journey after death. They stretched away in rank upon terra-cotta rank beneath an arched tin roof that could have covered a football field, memorializing to eternity China's first totalitarian.

Qinshihuangdi was profoundly influenced by the school of political philosophers known as Legalists. The most famous of them, Han Fei, wrote, "In an entire state you could not find ten men who can be trusted to do good of themselves, but if you make it impossible for the people to do wrong the whole state can nevertheless be kept in order." He blamed "useless scholars" for wasting time in discussion and denounced literature altogether. "In the state of an intelligent ruler there are no books. The laws serve as teachings."

The First Emperor put Han Fei's teachings into practice. He forbade all praising of the past and criticism of the present and ordered all books burned except those on medicine, divination, and agriculture. Four hundred and sixty scholars were put to death for "spreading doubt and disorder." There was no possibility of clemency, no matter how extenuating the circumstances. He also took to heart the earlier Legalist Shang Yang's dictum: "Make the ordinary people's life so hard that they will welcome war as a release from it." He spent the lives of an estimated million laborers in building the Great Wall and then sent his armies sweeping across China, to unify it for the first time in history and found the imperial system that would survive until 1911.

I didn't want to embarrass Rui by talking about dictatorship. So I asked him how he had learned to play the violin.

"My parents were afraid I would disappear during the Cultural Revolution so they kept me at home, for ten years. There was nothing for me to do. They had burned all their books except Mao Zedong's.

Then one of the neighbors gave me a violin. He was afraid to keep it because it was foreign."

Rui said his parents were "workers," but I sensed an evasion of some kind.

For a decade, Rui did nothing but practice the violin. He was so proficient by the time the radical Maoists fell from power with the Gang of Four that he was invited to play for Isaac Stern when he toured China in 1978.

We stared for a while at the clay soldiers. There were young braves, fierce and resolute, veterans with trimmed moustaches, expectant commanders awaiting orders, cavalrymen poised with their mounts, no two alike, each sculpted with riveting grace and inspiration, the face of a man who once lived and breathed upon the earth. I wondered how a monarch so contemptuous of men could portray man with such remarkable sensitivity. Was it possible after all to have humanism without humanity?

"Actually, you could say that my family was part of the nobility before 1949," Rui said abruptly.

His grandparents had been financiers and were forced to surrender all their property after the revolution. Because of their "bad class background," Rui's parents were not allowed to go to university and were taught to think themselves fortunate to have been permitted to do factory work.

I thought of the lugubrious Shang Yang, who in the fourth century B.C. demanded that everyone be compelled to work at the "fundamental occupations" of farming and weaving, and that those who sought gain through trade be made slaves along with the lazy and indigent.

"Now they say 'heartfelt thanks' to Nancy Reagan."

"Excuse me?"

"My parents. She inspired them. They took up turkey raising and became rich overnight."

When the Reagans visited China in 1980, the president's wife gave several California turkeys to Deng Xiaoping as a symbol of Sino-American friendship. Suddenly turkeys became icons of modernization. All over China, people began breeding them.

"Now we have three color televisions, three Yamaha motorcycles, and three telephones."

Before we parted, Rui asked if I would like to go to the ballet. A work based on Bai Juyi's great eighth-century poem, "Endless Sorrow," was to premier in a couple of days.

"It is very avant garde."

"Of course I'll come," I said.

BOTH BALLET and poem recount the haunting story of Yang Guifei, the beloved concubine of the Tang emperor Ming Huang and reputedly the greatest beauty of Chinese history. Tradition cast Yang Guifei as China's Helen of Troy, as played by Elizabeth Taylor: magnetic, mythic, a bit sluttish. For 1,200 years she has served as a universal Chinese symbol of the hopelessness of erotic love.

The story is essentially tragedy. "There were three thousand beauties in the inner apartments, but of all these three thousand he loved only one." Ming Huang forsook his duties for Yang Guifei's "warm bed netted with hibiscus." Rebels rose, the "mandate of heaven" slipped away, the emperor fled. His troops demanded Yang Guifei's death. At last, wrote Bai:

Knitting her moth eyebrows, death caught her among the horses,
Her hairpins scattered over the earth

Ming Huang was restored to a ruined empire. Still obsessed with Yang Guifei, he lived on in the "Palace of Endless Days," discovering her face even in the hibiscus and her brows in the curve of willow twigs. In desperation, he dispatched Taoist sorcerers to seek her spirit in the realms of the dead. One found her at last in the Isles of the Blest. She had become immortal but was denied for eternity the sight of Changan, which remained forever obscured in dust. She gave the Taoist a message to take back to the emperor:

Heaven is enduring, earth long lasting, but they will perish,
The everlasting sorrow will come to an end.

The poem's superficial message is that love is eternal. The subtext is that it may lead not only to insanity but to the destruction of the state and of the immutable order of things that was the Confucian ideal.

After they came to power, the Communists systematically discouraged sexuality. Maoist literature fairly pululated with men and women who deliberately rejected love in order to "build socialism." In the early 1980s, Communist intellectuals could still be found claiming that sexual intercourse was dangerous to mental and physical health.

In 1982 I knew an American who taught literature at Beijing University. Before his girl friend's arrival from the United States, he was advised that he would have to obtain a doctor's prescription in order to buy condoms. The doctor who interviewed him at Capitol Hospital asked how many he would need.

He told her a year's supply.

"Will ten do?" she asked.

Panic-stricken, he replied, "I was thinking of a few more than that."

"Well, how many will you need then?"

"How about one hundred?"

The doctor leaped up, flung open the door of the consultation room, and shouted down the hall.

"The foreigner wants a hundred condoms!"

In a moment, the door was filled with doctors, nurses, orderlies, and patients, staring wide-eyed at the American where he sat hunched on a stool.

"A hundred!" they murmured among themselves.

The doctor nevertheless wrote out the prescription. The teacher walked down the hall to the dispensary, where he handed it through the sliding window to a nurse to be filled. She reached beneath the counter, counted out fifty condoms, barked "that's enough!" and slammed the window in his face.

THE HALL was a bare concrete barn of the sort that was erected by the thousands during the Cultural Revolution, when conventional theater was banned and propaganda performances proliferated. "All Xian is here," said Rui. He meant the city's artistic elite. There were whole rows of men in berets and mufflers, and hundreds of girls in black woolen tights.

As the curtain opened, Yang Guifei unfolded from a wire lotus in a wreath of green gauze. She led a dozen attendants across the stage in kaleidoscopic June Taylor routines until she erupted into the arms of the goateed emperor in a flood of ecstasy so blatantly sexual that it would have been utterly unimaginable a few years ago, when the police were still raiding disco parties as "obscene."

The music had a florid, Russian quality—not surprisingly, since for the generation of composers now in their maturity, "modern" music means mostly what they heard as students in the concert halls of Moscow in the 1950s. Yang Guifei pirouetted fruitlessly for her life as Tchaikovskian brass surged and rolled in oceanic cascades. Drums thundered as soldiers swung her aloft to be crucified on streamers of gauze flung across the stage.

During the intermission I asked Rui what he had learned from Isaac Stern.

"He told me that many Chinese have excellent technique, but no inspiration. It's true. Chinese practice, practice, practice all the time. There is no time for inspiration. Isaac Stern told me to forget about technique and to think about what I loved. He told me about the vibrato."

Rui played upon the veins on the back of his hand as if they were strings.

"The vibrato. It's very fine, very beautiful, very feeling, but very difficult."

He seemed to be talking of emotional release, but when I asked him why the vibrato was so hard he replied, "It's difficult to say." He looked away and seemed to blush. Instinctively, he retreated to the physical and concrete. It was as if he had no vocabulary for the intimate and emotional.

"It's easier for Westerners," he said. "You are so big. We are so small and weak, and thin."

The next act opened in the Isles of the Immortals. Girls in bridal gowns and sequined tiaras paraded in a tableau that could only have been copied from the Miss America Pageant. When the lovelorn emperor begged Yang Guifei to appear, I thought of Bai Juyi's fragile lines:

Rivers of stars dimly scatter their light, pretending at dawn.
Who will share the kingfisher quilts of old?

On the stage, Yang Guifei shimmered up from beneath a billowing wave of silk amid a steam of dry ice, to couple with the emperor in a tangle of pumping thighs. But it was only Ming Huang's fantasy. She disappeared once more into artificial steam and the ruined emperor spun away, accompanied by a crescendo so deafening that the walls shuddered.

"Very Shostakovich," said Rui.

Shostakovich was something new.

As we left the theater and walked past the long blocks of Maoist hulks, along the too-wide, oppressive avenues, I had the depressing sensation of wandering through a great city a century after its fall. To be sure, there was an air of prosperity. Even at this late hour, private stores were selling television sets and stereos, and the sort of bargain-basement couture that passed for high fashion in post-Maoist China. But I couldn't escape the feeling that one might have had wandering through sixth-century Rome or fifteenth-century Constantinople, whose citizens had turned their temples and their history into quarries for a lesser civilization.

Despite the gaudy costumes and the attempt at being up-to-date, the ballet only reminded me of the temples I had seen, a jerry-built effort to make use of a past that had slipped beyond reach. Myth had become mere novelty. Rui said that few young people had even heard of Yang Guifei, or even of Bai Juyi's poem, for that matter. Like so much else, it had been torn out of their consciousness like the core of the City God's temple.

We heard the cacophonic strains of Chinese opera and dogged them through darkened lanes until we found their source, where a corner of the old battlements loomed over a ragged troupe of actors in turquoise and scarlet robes and a half-dozen musicians who sat under a corrugated tin canopy. Two men in Mao suits sawed bowl-bottomed fiddles. Others hammered at wooden clappers and cymbals, and played bamboo mouth organs that were like clumps of miniature

61

smokestacks bound together with hoops. But the soul of the orchestra was a gaunt young man with greased, unkempt hair and a stubby, wide-mouthed trumpet jammed in his lips. He wrung music from the battered brass tube like a Chinese Louis Armstrong, dragging it out by main force, twisting it like macaroni, spitting it out, and then begging it to come back.

Forty or fifty people stood in a semicircle around the musicians. There were bow-legged ladies with clumsy, once-bound feet, square-fisted workers with woolen jackets buttoned to their chins, a few stylish boys and girls in jeans. An actor pushed through with a bucket, calling for money. Small boys leaped up and down like frogs, bleating imaginary horns into the night.

The curtain was a sooty sheet. The actors' costumes were torn at the hems and sagged in the sleeves; the dragons that adorned them were unraveled and the phoenixes decapitated. A young woman disguised in a scholar's garb journeyed over the makeshift stage, flicking her hands with meaningful and obscure grace. With a simple pole, she brought to life the languid rocking of a countryman's boat, a lonely night on the water, an entire river. Her voice shrilled and soared, pinging and sliding, careering and leaping like an immortal among the mist-wreathed pinnacles of fantastic mountains.

"I hate the opera," Rui said. "Art must be fast and hard, as fast as a Toyota or a jumbo jet."

I wished him well in America.

"In Oklahoma," he said, "I hope to learn the vibrato."

A FEW MILES east of Xian there is an ancient spring that is associated with Yang Guifei. Tradition holds that she bathed in one of the pools. Bai Juyi visualized her there "washed smooth as curd." I had hoped to find a place where I might read in silence, but it was hopeless. Guides were marshaling battalions of Chinese and Taiwanese tourists and driving them forward in flying wedges with battle flags and police whistles, like the generals of Chinese opera. I was swept along with them as they lunged and ebbed, eddied for a moment around crimson kiosks, and then swept all before them in pincers movements around the pools. Archaeologists had recently uncovered the floor of a Tang-dynasty bath, and the guides were making the most of very slender evidence. Phalanxes of tourists were shoving relentlessly forward to photograph a heap of broken clay tiles.

A small girl attached herself to me, as the only foreigner in sight, and tried to sell me persimmons at an exorbitant price.

"I don't want any," I said.

"You are not a good person."

"Why?"

"You must buy."

"No, thank you."

"You are not a good person."

I followed stairs up the hillside, but the crowds surged up behind me. Everywhere, tape players shrilled an Armageddon of Taiwanese disco.

"A flower won't keep its blush forever," wailed a Taiwanese siren. "If you love me, tell me now!"

A teenage boy in a blue boiler suit joined the girl and held out a handful of phony ancient coins.

"But they're fakes," I said.

"You are not a good person."

I outran them at last. Abandoned hermitages clung like aeries to the cliffs. The tiled roofs of what I took to be a disused temple rose over a copse of pines. A peasant family had occupied the front court-yard. A woman in a gray smock was husking corn and I asked her if I could take a look inside.

Where huge idols must once have been, the farmer had stored spare tins, and lumber and sacking. In the corner there was an altar built of bricks, where joss sticks burned in a plastic cup in front of a rotogravure of the Jade Emperor. I was grateful for the silence. The altar was primitive, but I admired its innocence and its implication of private worlds.

Just at that moment, an ancient creature in a monk's ragged leggings and a wispy topknot ran, or more nearly hopped, into the room. Laying a claw on my arm, he pulled me down with surprising strength and, cheerily waving away my protests, took pieces of stale candy from the altar and popped them into my mouth by way of hospitality.

I had difficulty understanding him, but he managed to make clear that he first came to the mountain in 1935. After the revolution, Communists came and told him that he was part of "old culture" and had to be remolded. He was put to work on a commune. In 1979 he was allowed to return. As far as I could gather, he had never been down the mountain since.

He punctuated each remark with a gust of laughter. Finally, he looked me in the face and laughed louder and longer than anyone I had ever heard laugh in China. It was laughter utterly free from irony or contempt or resignation. His eyes danced. Somehow he had survived, frail, ancient, crippled, and a little mad. I couldn't stop myself. I began to laugh too. The monk grabbed hold of me with his bony claw, and we held onto each other and shook. Our laughter caromed around the filthy chamber and echoed wildly in our ears.

At last I got up to leave. The monk paused at the door. "I like good company!" he cried. As I descended the mountain, I seemed to hear his airy laughter still flickering through the trees.

CHAPTER
FOUR

The Mermaid's Tear

IN TIMES of peril, desperate emperors fled to Sichuan. It was like a hidden garden or an inner courtyard, protected by mountain walls and narrow passes, which imperial armies closed behind them like palace gates. It was on the road to Sichuan that the fleeing Ming Huang emperor murdered his beloved Yang Guifei. And it was to Sichuan that Chiang Kaishek fled from the Japanese in 1937, under the illusion that he was still the ruler of China.

I had come to Chengdu intending to climb the great sacred mountain of Emeishan, but the entire province was socked in with fog. I asked the desk clerk in my hotel when it might lift. "Maybe five months," he said. The fog seethed along the broad Maoist boulevards, ferreted in the kinked lanes of the old town, lapped at the hotel's glass facade like a vaporous sea, hung as a backdrop to every encounter. I have memories of cyclists evaporating like wraiths a few yards in front of my eyes, of buildings that slowly coalesced from the mist and then suddenly disintegrated, of muffled cries and stygian dimness.

WHEN THE indefatigable traveler Isabella Bird visited Chengdu in 1898, she found it "a very prepossessing city." Its noble walls were in good repair, and within them commerce was carried on along canals and streams that were crowded with boats of all sizes. Fine shops specialized in silver filigree and Himalayan lambskin, and the strange, wild figures of Tibetan traders roamed the streets.

I liked Chengdu. Despite the fog, life had an almost Mediterranean lilt. People were smaller and livelier, more alert. There were teahouses everywhere, and jungly undergrowth nibbled at any neglected bit of land. The battlements had disappeared, and the canals, and the fancy stores. But the Tibetans were still there; every day I passed a row of them camped in front of my hotel selling bear paws, monkeys' skulls, and tigers' toes from mats spread on the street.

Even the Maoists seemed to have capitulated to the slower pace and grown haphazard. Broad avenues plowed through ramshackle suburbs and then petered out in the middle of a field. The old city had survived in tenacious fragments; medieval clumps of half-timbered buildings canted over bustling markets where vendors hawked flattened ducks, tripe kebab, blue-tailed parrots, and goldfish with tumorous eyes and tails like pleated chiffon.

A monstrous statue of the Great Helmsman still dominated the center of town. When people gave you directions, they always told you, "Go to Mao and turn," and smirked.

CHENGDU'S DAIMON was the great Tang poet Du Fu; "the famous city," he called it, "full of the sound of flutes and reeds." Du was born near Changan in A.D. 713, during the halcyon years of the dynasty, which Chinese even today regard nostalgically as a Golden Age, their Periclean Athens and Renaissance Florence combined. Du's life, like the empire itself, was irrevocably disrupted by the same cataclysmic rebellion that sent Ming Huang scurrying south. Du was captured by the rebels and spent a year in captivity. In his absence, his family was reduced to penury and one of his sons died of starvation. Du was given up for dead. He recorded the moment of his homecoming in one of the most beloved poems in the Chinese language:

I was drifting sand in the wind of the world's anger.
It is just fate that has brought me back alive.

The fence gate is filled with neighbors' faces,
Sighing and shedding a few tears.

In the deep night we light a new candle
And see each other face to face as in a dream.

Chinese usually paired Du with his rumbustious contemporary and friend Li Bo. Li seduced with exuberance; Du with compassion. Du was a moral man who craved peace but was determined to bear witness to the horrors of his time. I envied Li's escapism, but I admired Du's depth of feeling more.

In his poems, the spirit voices of newly killed soldiers mingled with the whispering of those who died long ago. Recruiting officers carried off old women when young men could no longer be found. Tax collectors bled those who survived.

> From the South Sea
> did a guest appear
> And give to me
> a mermaid's tear
>
> And in that Pearl
> there were cloudy signs:
> I tried to unfurl
> what lay in those lines;
>
> Wrapped it away
> in a little box,
> Kept it to pay
> the Government Tax:
>
> Opened and saw
> it had turned to blood—
> Alas, today
> I have nothing else!

As a young man, Du seemed destined for success. But he repeatedly and embarrassingly failed the imperial examinations; only in old age was he finally appointed to a sinecure among the "ducks and snowy herons" of the bureaucratic rank and file. Artists traditionally gave him an emaciated face that was meant to embody the hardships he had endured. He was also an almost obsessive traveler; he envisioned himself as an old fisherman "wandering through all the lakes and rivers of the earth."

In 759 he fled over the mountains to Chengdu, where he built a cottage on the bank of the Brocade River. He grew flowers, drank tea, read the Buddhist classics:

> My wife rules the squares for a game of chess.
> My young son hammers a fish-hook out of wire.
> I, who am ill so often, want only to plant flowers—
> My humble body desires nothing more.

The alleged site of Du's cottage lay on the city's eastern outskirts. I hired a bicycle and cycled out through suburbs where farmers were deftly lathering fields with night soil from long-handled buckets. I passed young men selling radishes the size of hand grenades, and then a woman pinning lettuce leaves on a plastic line like laundry, and then another woman walking along with a pair of severed pig's testicles dangling daintily from her fingers. Pork was a big thing that day; I kept seeing shoppers with pigs' carcasses swaddled like human infants and slung over their bikes, and with alps of trotters in barrows attached behind.

I found the "cottage" in a bamboo forest next to an emerald brook. The place was much visited. Streams of Chinese tourists shuffled through exhibits on Du's life that had been set out in halls whose eaves curled up in the shape of dragons' snouts. The site has been famous since at least the eleventh century, but the cottage was pure fabrication. It was really more a gazebo than a house, barely large enough to shelter the poet's tablet beneath its conical thatched roof. Young couples posed in front of it and giggled, and snapped each other's photos.

I sat on a stone and read some of the poems that Du had written here. They were amused and gentle; it was astonishing that they had come from the same brush as the poems of war and suffering. Catkins were "mad" to follow the breezes, peach blossoms "silly" to ride the spring spate; it was "so like the wind" to steal his neighbor's plum blossoms. "Wandering breezes," the translator called these poems of Du's halcyon days. Du had been happy here, by the measure of his troublous age.

The cottage was an imaginary retreat in a stylized wilderness; I had seen its archetype in a thousand paintings. Ultimately, I realized, it memorialized less a man than a mood, a dream of escape that was buried in the psyche of every Chinese, the hut of the man of nature who has grasped the futility of earthly struggle, who has resigned and found peace. I sat in silence for a long time, watching the fog sift through the bamboo. Hilarious infants swarmed around me, whirling sticks with papier-mâché birds tied to the end, that whizzed and whirred gaily in the viscous air.

There were revolts in Sichuan. Du was forced to flee again and spent the last five years of his life on the open road; aged, ill, weary, full of grace. He wrote, inimitably:

Oh, from the ancient days always there have been travelers
So why should I grieve?

I WANDERED ONE afternoon into a temple in a southern district of the city. Outside the gate, crones in velvet tams were hunkered behind battlements of fireworks, selling tangerine-colored incense and tinfoil ingots to be burned for the dead. I gave a few cents' donation to the monk at the door and stepped through into a fog of incense. The temple's vitality was startling after the decrepit establishments I had seen in Xian; it was my first sight of the vast religious awakening that was taking place across China. Communism was palpably dying. Old gods were being rediscovered, new ones shyly explored.

A tablet inside the gate proclaimed, "Grow not proud from what you must do; act in silence." Gilded buddhas stared from smoky altars, blessing the pious with their transcendental hand jive of upturned fingers and outstretched palms. In front of each one, grandmothers were teaching tots in miniature shakos and mandarin caps to pray.

"Hands together, then kneel."

"I want to do Guanyin!"

Guanyin was the thousand-armed Goddess of Mercy.

"First kneel."

"I want to do Guanyin!"

(Sighing)

"Like this."

"Guanyin! Guanyin! Guanyin!"

The most precious object in the temple was a diminutive Buddha made of alabaster. Pilgrims too poor to give anything else borrowed flowers and held them near the buddha for a moment, as proof of their piety.

"A monk walked to Burma to get it."

I turned. Two young men were standing behind me. The speaker said his name was Yang. He was lean and humorous and had a thick brush of black hair that stood up straight on his head. His companion blinked at me through thick spectacles.

"Huang," said Yang. "A bashful boy."

A doglike monster was painted on a wooden screen behind the Buddha.

"Its eyes are so bright because they can see through everything in the world," said Yang.

"It's not real," Huang murmured reassuringly.

Yang taught English and Huang physics at a local college. I asked if they were Buddhists.

"No, but we think its theories are very good," said Yang.

"Which ones in particular?"

Yang said, "That life is empty."

"That life undulates," said Huang.

We made our way to a back courtyard of the temple, where the monks ran a teahouse in a timbered hall furnished with hewn wooden tables and bamboo chairs. Hundreds of old folks guzzled jasmine tea and chattered deafeningly in slurry Sichuanese while a bedlam of pet larks in bamboo cages trilled and whistled and chirruped overhead. Yang and Huang introduced me to a fragile young man in blue jeans.

"I am a poet!" he declared.

They peppered me with questions. What did I think of Balzac, of Hemingway, of Rambo, of Mark Twain, of Robert De Niro?

"And *Remorse*?" Huang asked.

"Sorry?"

"The famous book," said the poet.

"We have all read it," said Yang.

Huang said, "It's about a man who runs a prostitution house and how he makes use of teenage girls."

China was bursting open. Anything at all might fly in through what the Chinese always called the "open door," to alight on minds that had been parched of Western culture for almost forty years.

The poet's name was Zhou, but he preferred the pen name of "Zyz," which was an acronym formed of the first letters of his names in English.

He said, "Maybe you can take something from my imagination."

"I hope so," I said.

"Good! Then I will recite to you my latest poem. I wrote it fifteen minutes ago."

He stood up and placed his hands on the table. He recited:

Character
It seems as thousands of stars.
Universe
It seems like the sole of your shoe.

" 'Thousands of stars' is the mind," said Zyz. "It means that you forget yourself. 'Universe' is the imagination."

" 'Soul of your shoe'?" I said.

"Eh? Maybe I should say 'a small-sized field' instead."

"See my bird," said Yang.

He brandished a small gray creature in a bamboo cage.

I was surprised. Bird-fancying was an old man's pastime. "Only losers keep birds," a friend of mine in Beijing once told me. "Parents get hysterical if you bring a bird home. It means you're on your way to ruin."

"I just bought him, but I'm going to let him go," Yang said. "I can't stand to see things caged. I know how they feel without freedom."

He put the bird back in its cage under the table, where it gazed longingly at a panorama of melon seeds, peanut shells, and orange peels.

73

"How do you know?" I asked, expecting to hear a heartbreaking story of the Cultural Revolution.

Yang took out a cassette player from a canvas bag and turned it on. Suddenly Joan Baez's voice rang out:

"I've got a ham-mer! I'll ring it in the mor-ning. I'll ring it in the eve-ning, all over this land!"

"From Joanie!" Yang said.

Yang had paid six yuan for the bird, a sizable sum. He planned to release it later in the afternoon.

"For six yuan, I think I can enjoy him a little. Then he will fly away into the trees and eat insects until he is fat."

Releasing birds was an old Buddhist tradition. In the past, clever vendors stationed themselves outside temples and sold worshipers birds that were trained to return home to their cages. The pious gained credit in heaven, the vendor retained his capital, and the hard-working bird was assured of a permanent roof over his head. It was a happy system.

"The Buddhist heaven is not someplace far off, in another world, but right here where we are now, in this city, in this teahouse, in any decision we make any day, today, now," Huang murmured. "Heaven is in choosing to be kind and generous and loving, and acting with a pure heart. The Buddhist hell exists, too. It is also a real place, with all kinds of torments, but it is not in some other world either, but right here now."

Joanie was singing: "Michael, row the boat a-shore, hallelu-jah!"

The poetry, the bohemianism, the spiritualizing reminded me of Greenwich Village twenty-five years ago. But I was underestimating Yang and his friends. They were rediscovering the truths that lay behind the gilded buddha faces, and beginning to look for their own answer to the eternal question: How do I live my life? Even ten years ago they would have looked for the answer in the Marxist gospel. But that had died for them. They were the survivors of a revolution, and they were fairly boiling with the need to speak and be heard.

"Listen! Listen!"

It was Zyz.

He stood up and flung back his hair. He declaimed:

Character
It seems as thousands of stars.
Universe
It seems like a vegetable field.

He waited. I smiled. He sighed with relief.

The fog had grown still thicker. I cycled all the way back to my hotel with my heart in my throat, dodging the huge articulated buses that fishtailed through the murk; school had just ended for the day, and hosts of small children stood motionless on the rear fenders of bicycles, lashed to their parents' backs and peering over their shoulders like ships' captains in a storm. The colossal Mao at the center of town stretched out his arm in ghostly benediction as I passed.

I FINALLY GAVE up on Emeishan. I ran into a Colorado mountaineer who had just climbed it in spite of the fog. "Go ahead," she said. "Die." But when the sky cleared for a few hours one day, I raced to the bus station and found a minibus traveling to Qingchengshan, which lay in the Himalayan foothills a few dozen miles to the north.

Strange tales clung to the mountain. During Emperor Ming Huang's flight from Changan, the ghost of the great alchemist Sun Simo appeared to him in a dream and asked him to send a lump of sulfur to Qingchengshan for use in a potion. The emperor was bewildered, but he was a superstitious man and he did as he was bidden. When his courier reached the mountain he was met by a hermit with a flowing beard and preternaturally bright eyes. No sooner had the hermit taken hold of the sulfur than he vanished; rumors spread far and wide that Sun Simo had never died at all, but still dwelt on Qingchengshan at the age of two hundred.

There was another story set some centuries later. In it, a monk was called to the mountain to chant a sutra for an ailing hermit. Arriving there, he found a ragged creature with matted locks and earlobes that hung to his shoulders. After the sutras had brought him around, the patient told his servant to offer the monk a cup of tea by way of payment. "It's just something poor that we grow here," he apologized. But when the monk tasted it he felt as if he had been "caressed by a spring wind," and before he knew it, he found himself at the bottom of the mountain as if he had flown. "What is your good master's name?" the monk asked. The servant sketched three ideographs on the palm of his hand: "Sun Simo."

For centuries, connoisseurs had come to Qingchengshan to taste this legendary "fairy tea." The tea performed no such miracles for me. But it led me to Peng.

Qingchengshan resembled some eighteenth-century chinoiserie fantasy more than it did a real place. I followed a steep trail that hopped over diminutive bridges and emerald rills and finally swerved up through misty jungle to a crag that hung in the clouds. In the distance, the Himalayas rose and fell like the strokes of a calligrapher's brush.

Three men ahead of me on the trail were arguing furiously about sacred mountains. They were dressed in Mao suits made of some shiny synthetic material and lugging sacks of food. I guessed they were workers on holiday.

"You've got the two Hengshans," ruminated the one in dark glasses. "Then Wutaishan. Then Songshan."

"Don't forget Taishan, it's the most important of all," interrupted the skinny one.

"And Qingchengshan," the stocky one said truculently.

"Qingchengshan's not sacred," the one in dark glasses retorted condescendingly.

"Of course it is, you dog fart," said the stocky one.

"It is not, you turtle's egg."

"So you've got the two Hengshans," the skinny one said soothingly. "And Taishan, and Songshan, and . . ."

"And Qingchengshan," the stocky one persisted.

"I won't give you Qingchengshan, no sir!" erupted the one with dark glasses.

"It is."

"Isn't."

"Is!"

"Isn't!"

"Turtle's egg!"

"Dog fart!"

There was a Taoist monastery tucked into a fold in the hills. I got to it just as the late-afternoon prayer was beginning. Bells were clanging, and suddenly everywhere around me topknotted monks in blue smocks were hustling to their devotions amid galleried courtyards that swarmed through the forest. I found a teahouse wedged onto a rear veranda and ordered "fairy tea" from a novice who fairly leapt with astonishment at the sight of what might have been his first foreigner.

The teahouse was peculiarly sited, and the view seemed cramped and oppressive at first. I could see almost nothing except an ooze of mist coagulating against a sheer slope a few dozen yards away. After a while the novice returned with a small cup with a few leaves of tea in the bottom. It was thin and almost flavorless, and disappointment must have showed on my face, for the man at the next table leaned over and said, "Expect more from the second cup."

He had a pruned and fastidious quality, and I surmised that he was in his early sixties. His clothes marked him as an intellectual of some sort: a tie and a black leather jacket, pinstripe trousers. His hands were tiny and light, and his flat, spade-shaped face bore a disconcerting resemblance (as so many of his fellow Sichuanese did) to Deng Xiaoping. He told the novice to bring me more hot water. This time the tea fairly detonated on my tongue and radiated through my mouth. The flavor was extraordinary, smoky and floral, oddly like the aroma of rhododendron.

"The third cup is also good, but not quite so perfect," said my neighbor.

When I had finished it, I called to the novice to give me fresh tea. I drank cup after cup, nearly paralyzed with pleasure, until I was dizzy from it.

My neighbor told me that his name was Peng. He taught art at a college in Chengdu, and he had come to Qingchengshan to appreciate a pine tree that a friend had painted.

"It's a shame you can't see more," I said, gesturing toward the forested slope.

"Perhaps you haven't looked properly."

Peng made me look carefully at the forest. Within the mist, I began to see that it was comprised of strange feathery trees that were quivering faintly in an almost imperceptible breeze. Gradually I realized that the mist was not stagnant at all, but was roiling and surging through the forest in wild foamy currents. Suddenly I understood that it was the sheer quivering density of nature that was the intended spectacle.

Peng was watching the mist too, with obvious enjoyment.

"How like a stage," he said.

I thought at that moment of someone who had taught me to love the opera years before, in Beijing. Every week or so, we would climb on bicycles and journey to some far corner of the city to huddle in a drafty hall where one or another of those great hieratic dramas of ancient days was being performed. She taught me to read the emptiness of the stage as if it were the mist in a classical painting, which contained within it the seed of all form. From her, I learned to interpret the symbols that could instantly invent a state of mind or an entire landscape; to feel the distress signaled by a turn of the finger, to see the mountain suggested by a chair, the torrent implied by an oar. "You drink tea but there is no tea; you climb stairs, but there are no stairs," she once said to me. "As much as possible is left to the imagination. Art that kisses reality on the mouth is never very good."

I told Peng something of those nights in Beijing. He was plainly taken aback. It was an article of faith among Chinese that foreigners were constitutionally incapable of enjoying their opera. Peng, it turned out, was an aficionado. Every Friday afternoon, he said, members of the amateur opera society performed their favorite selections at the Jinjiang teahouse in Chengdu.

"Come," he said. "You must come."

ON THE way back from Qingchengshan there was a dead man in the road. At first I thought something had fallen off a truck. Then I realized that it was a corpse spread-eagled in the middle of the lane. I watched a car and then a stream of cyclists, and then another car, and then a truck make deliberate arcs around the body. No one slowed. Then we were passing him, and I looked down. It was a middle-aged man. I could tell from his clothes that he was a peasant.

Had he been hit by a car? Fallen off his bicycle? Had a heart attack? Been dumped there by someone? No one else on the bus seemed to notice. Then we were past. It only took a few seconds. I looked back. More cyclists were maneuvering around him. Now he looked again like a sack that had slipped from a truck, and then I couldn't see him anymore in the yellowish fog.

I FINALLY FOUND the Jinjiang at the end of an alley that opened off a busy downtown lane. It was really just an open courtyard; scarlet columns formed an arcade around the atrium and lent it a Grecian quality that begged for hard sunlight and the smell of the sea. But instead fog seeped outlandishly in damp tentacles around the columns and among us where we perched on rickety straw chairs. Women with faces like bronze masks slouched among the tables, pouring tea from battered tin pots.

The Jinjiang was officially called a "cultural center." Curtains had been hung across one side of the courtyard, and behind them pool sharks played at billiards. Young couples danced to a disco beat in a cavernous hall on the other side.

Peng seemed remote. I worried that my tardiness had offended him or, worse, that I had intruded, having mistaken a merely polite invitation for a gesture of friendship.

Two middle-aged men sat on a dais with their hands shoved into their sleeves. They sat utterly still while the fog crept around them as if they were pieces of some strange anthropomorphic landscape. From musicians seated off to the side came the plaintive wail of an *erhu*'s strings, the whack of clappers, the shuddering tremor of a gong.

"Help, help me to raise the emperor!" the man on the left sang in a careening falsetto.

He wore fuschia gloves and a sharkskin raincoat, and bore a startling resemblance to Walter Matthau.

"That's the empress," Peng said.

Before the revolution, women almost never appeared on the stage; puritan Communists blanched at the louche reputation of the men who specialized in female roles. But the taste for female impersonation had survived among working-class enthusiasts who were otherwise as masculine as the Sicilian navvies of an earlier day who might come to blows over the resonance of a Caruso.

The action, like that of most opera, was taking place in mythical time, the Chinese equivalent of eighteenth-century Seville, say, or Bourbon Naples. The "empress," Peng explained, was charged with rearing the infant emperor, but she had injudiciously offended the mandarin upon whom his safety depended.

"Poor thing's just a tyke," a tipsy man with horny workman's hands leaned over and kibbitzed.

The "mandarin" was hunkered deep in a trenchcoat, and square-jawed and handsome, except for his ears, which were very small and curled peculiarly inward, like Brussels sprouts. His baritone swelled, roamed over the scale, suddenly jabbed upward, and then snapped into silence.

"How foolish you were to ignore me!" he sang.

"Oh, she's stuck!" the drunk said. "She's stuck all right!"

"If you protect the emperor, you'll stand shoulder to shoulder, his venerable next of kin!" the "empress's" falsetto wheedled.

"Well sung! Well sung!" bellowed the drunk.

"I'll do my duty to the emperor," the "mandarin" sang. "But do you repent your discourtesy?"

"So risky!" Peng exclaimed. "He wants an apology, but asking for it straightaway verges on disrespect for the emperor. Offend the emperor, immediate execution!"

He made an abrupt chopping gesture with his hand.

As the performance went on, Peng was loosening up. The music had hooked him. He was fairly hopping with it, tapping out the clapper's rhythm on his knee, and with his feet, and with his spade-sharp chin bobbing against his chest as he spoke.

I looked around me at the audience. There must have been two hundred people, giddily cracking melon seeds, knitting, spitting, guzzling tea, and puffing hurricanes of smoke from homemade stogies stuck upright in slim brass pipes as they listened.

"Look at them carefully," Peng said.

I saw a Tibetan panhandler pleading at a table nearby, and an itinerant ear cleaner working at a client's ear with a horrific succession of wires, brushes, and tweezers.

"All old," said Peng.

I looked again. There was no one who looked less than sixty.

Peng fretted about the opera's future. It had managed to survive the Cultural Revolution, when performers were reviled, and sometimes killed, for practicing a "feudal" art. Ironically, it was the recent liberalization of culture that threatened to administer the coup de grace; the opera now had to compete with film and television, and the unpredictable cornucopia of Western culture.

"The youngsters are only interested in disco and kung fu," Peng said glumly.

Even as we spoke, Michael Jackson's androgynous tenor resonated from the dance hall behind us.

"I'm bad . . . I'm bad . . . I'm bad . . ."

Yet another door was closing on the past. Stock opera figures like the judicious Bao Gong, the sly Zhuge Liang, and the cruel Cao Cao were for half a millenium the very poles of Chinese morality, as familiar as Nestor, Odysseus, and Agamemnon once were to the classically educated West. They had been superseded by Mao and Zhu De, and the demonized Lin Biao and Jiang Qing. The idols of the coming generation were Taiwanese pop stars and Madonna.

"I'm bad . . . I'm bad . . . I'm bad . . ."

"It's not very artistic, but I hear that disco is good for the health," Peng said with an unconvinced smile.

By now a new performance was underway. Walter Matthau remained, but the "mandarin" had been replaced by a woman of Wagnerian dimensions who was dressed in a silk jacket embroidered with chrysanthemums.

Their voices sculpted a world of miraculous grace. I sat rapt. The ear cleaner's hand poised in midair. The Tibetan paused in his fawning round. The drunk subsided into glazed beatitude. Together, we were inexorably drawn into a courtyard of the old world, secluded and remote, a place of profound unspoken passions, of an entire emotional realm sublimated in diaphanous metaphor.

The story began as a sort of Shakespearean farce of confused identity and missed cues, and wound up as tragedy. It recounted the fate of an aristocratic young woman who disguised herself as a man in order to study the Confucian classics in the capital; there she fell in love with a handsome scholar, who failed to realize that she was actually a woman. "Breeding" constrained her from divulging the truth until it was too late, when her parents informed her that she had been betrothed to a landlord.

"This is Old China," Peng said with a connoisseur's smile. "There is no possible resolution."

Walter Matthau sang the role of the young scholar. His voice plodded hollowly to the crack of the clapper:

"Cruel woman! You've spurned me for another who has more money!"

She retorted in a piercing contralto, "Every night I wait with a lantern next to the bridge built in my dreams, but you never cross."

"That's what I like, something elegant and refined!" the drunk burbled.

"Listen!" Peng commanded.

The Wagnerian sang, "The sun has fallen behind the clouds. Ducks are coming in for the night."

Her voice strained and trembled, and shrilled through the fog. It was breathtaking.

"Her heart has closed now," said Peng. "It is all over."

"What happens to them?" I asked.

"They die, naturally."

As we rose to leave, the drunk bent and shook his own hands, in the antique gesture of parting.

I WAS SURPRISED when Peng invited me home. The banality of it was disconcerting, and a measure of how fast things in China were changing; when I lived in Beijing, it was six months before a colleague ventured to have me over, and then she had to bribe the doorkeeper not to report my presence to the block committee.

Peng and his wife lived in a concrete-slab tower owned by his college. The apartment was luxurious, by Chinese standards; there was a small bedroom and a living room, and space for a hot plate and table in the hall. Fog lapped at the windows, and when I looked out I could see that underwear hung in lurid festoons from the concrete balconies across the alley. Somewhere further away, slabs of metal were slamming rhythmically against each other in a factory.

Somehow Peng had gotten hold of wall-to-wall carpeting, and he had filled the walls with scroll paintings. The effect was stunning in a country where decoration of any sort had for so long been denounced as "bourgeois" and even the apartments of officials were often little more than bare concrete cubicles. An African mask with puckered lips hung over the table, with a metal crucifix draped over its brow.

"It looked like a Christian, so I bought the cross to go with it," Peng said blandly.

There was also a photo of Peng rouged and powdered in the garb of a stage emperor.

"It's only for fun," Peng said. "I have a Rightist voice."

Peng's wife floated in and out of the room, but so unobtrusively that I was hardly aware that she was there, plying me with fragrant tea, and plates of fried peanuts, and salted plums that had somehow been kept moist and succulent inside little twists of colored paper. She was a teacher, and I tried to talk to her, but she sifted vaporously away whenever I addressed her.

I walked around the apartment enjoying the paintings. I was sure that Peng had done some of them himself, but he wouldn't tell me which. None was antique, but nearly all of them portrayed the old world of vibrant nature that the Taoists had loved. In one, a white pine burst eerily through the roof of a mountain pavilion.

"This one?" I asked.

In another, a rustic hamlet teetered amid mountains that rippled like shock waves.

"This one?"

Peng was too gracious, too Chinese, to say either yes or no, or even "don't ask." It was difficult to find the man behind the wall of gentle cordiality. It was always happening with Chinese; you groped through the outer courtyards of the personality, and then found doors unexpectedly shut, the inhabitants out. The paintings were signposts, hints, but no more.

Peng pulled a pile of rolled-up scrolls from a closet and extracted from it a painting of a fat-bellied lohan who was all curves and bulges, and then one of a roly-poly panda playing with a piece of bamboo in its paws.

"*Guai,*" he said. "Cute."

I saw kitsch; but Peng saw the essential quality of innocence, of childlike curiosity. Only in China, it struck me, could serious art be "cute."

"Now something modern," he said.

There was a floating cow, an unsteady cottage, a disembodied peasant with a market basket, the suggestion of a fragmented world where things did not quite hang together. In China, such things whispered in a dangerous undertone.

"It's unorthodox," Peng said, with a twinkling smile. "Many traditionalists don't like this painter, but I do. I don't like other people to tell me what to like. I like to find my own meaning in things."

That was what had gotten him into trouble. I understood now the joke he had made when I arrived. A "Rightist" voice was one that didn't fit.

As a young man, Peng had won a certain amount of attention by writing occasional articles and reviews. But the simple fact that he wrote about classical art was enough to taint him as a "passive counterrevolutionary" during the Cultural Revolution.

The Red Guards had stuck posters all over the college, declaring that Peng's reviews had "put a gun to the head of the revolution." His face collapsed at the memory. He was ordered to surrender his art books to the Red Guards. He destroyed his calligraphy and paintings rather than hand them over. He was sent to a reform camp for a year.

He said, "I was condemned because I loved what was beautiful and old."

I knew that one year of punishment wasn't long, by the standards of the day. I sensed something unsaid. I wondered, had he done something to shorten his term, informed on someone, perhaps? It was a cruel thought, but it nagged.

"The 'chen' stroke is the shape of a mountain," he said, suddenly didactic, drawing a parabola with a pale, feminine finger. "The 'ran'

84

stroke is this deep wash. 'Dian' is the short stroke that shapes the leaves on these trees."

The non sequitur was a rebuff. I was being told to ask nothing more. The door shut again. I found myself abruptly back in the outer courtyard. We had come close to some kind of intimacy, but the moment had passed.

Peng pulled still more scrolls from the closet and, squatting on his heels like a peasant come to town, unfurled them across the floor and over the bed until the whole small room became a carpet of wild gorges, misty pines, crags and clefts, sampans and hazy seas, a world utterly free of politics and pain, where fishermen traced trails of peach blossoms toward secret caverns, and hermits wandered peaks where, perhaps, one might still encounter the unaging Sun Simo.

The paintings were the painstaking accumulation of a dozen years; Peng was oblivious now to anything but them. In the play of his limpid smile, I saw something that I had last seen in George Kates's face in the hard vertical light of that New England afternoon: a faith in the beautiful that was so deep and self-confident that the frigid air around us seemed almost to tremble with his joy.

As I watched him, I thought of Du Fu, who had lived so happily in his bamboo forest east of town. One night a storm tore the roof off Du's cottage and scattered the straw along the riverbank. Boys ran off with it and laughed at the poet when he pursued them. Like a premonition, rain poured in torrents onto his family. He shivered and wrote:

Now I dream of an immense mansion, tens of thousands of rooms,
Where all the cold creatures can take shelter, their faces alight.

Peng had found his warm room, his Peach Blossom Spring, in the scrolls that lay about us, in the chasms and lotuses, the *guai* pandas and potbellied lohans. The paintings and the opera had freed him, at least a little, from history, from the dull clangor of the factory across the alley, from a world where a man's corpse might still be left on a public road like a hunk of carrion.

Peng was still on his haunches. Scrolls were still flying from closets, from beneath beds. He slid one from the pile. In it, winter-bare lotuses were bold swatches of ink.

"Everything is black," he said. "But there is nothing depressing. Look."

Peng pointed to a small patch of white that was barely discernible among the leaves. It was the only blank space in the painting. He called it the "breathing space."

"A painting must breathe," he said. "Just like a man."

CHAPTER
FIVE

Riverine

LUXURIATED IN my good fortune; not only had I managed to get a sleeper on the overnight express to Chongqing, but, miraculously, no one else was assigned to the compartment. A new city, new landscapes waited for me in the darkness. In a day or two I would be on the Yangzi, the greatest highway of the old empire, which drew into itself all the waters of central China, streaming eastward in a mighty flood for twelve hundred miles through cities and towns whose names leaped and bounded over the tongue, half-forgotten names that once sang with siren magic in the imagination of the travelers of an earlier time: Wanxian, Yichang, Hankou, Jiujiang.

I knew instinctively, even before I opened my eyes the next morning, that my passport was gone. For a long time, I kept my eyes closed and tried to convince myself that it wasn't so. Then I gave up and felt through the bedclothes, then on the floor around the seat, then on the table, and finally in my breast pocket, where I always carried it.

I was numb with panic by the time the train reached Chongqing. I had travelers' checks, but they couldn't be cashed without my passport; I had enough cash to fly back to Chengdu, but unless I showed a passport I wouldn't be allowed to buy a ticket. I could return to Chengdu on the night train. But what would I do when I got there? If my pocket had been picked, what was the point?

I took a taxi to the People's Hotel, a sprawling Stalinist palace whose centerpiece was a gargantuan replica of the Temple of Heaven

at Beijing. I gritted my teeth and lied to the clerk, who was a cadaverous young man in his twenties.

"My passport is on its way from Chengdu," I said.

He squinted distastefully; in China, without documents, you
were nothing. But he registered me without it, against regulations.

I phoned the American consul in Chengdu. I might have left the
passport at the hotel, I told him, or possibly where I had rented my
bicycle; they had required it as security.

"You'll have to go to Beijing to get a new one," the consul said.

Beijing was one thousand miles away.

"But I'll see what I can do," he promised.

Three hours later the phone rang.

"I've got it!" the consul announced.

I had left the passport at the bicycle shed. Fortunately, it was
located just down the street from the consulate.

I said, "I feel like an idiot."

"Forget it," he said. "We're sending it express. You'll have it in
the morning."

Later I ran into a British businessman who was living in Chongqing. I told him what had happened.

"What a relief!" I said.

"How are they sending it?" he asked.

"Express mail."

"Ah," he said. "That takes longer."

THERE WAS nothing for me in the morning mail. The post
office was located on a traffic circle fifteen minutes' walk away.
There I found two young women hunkered behind a window that
opened onto the sidewalk; they stared at me hard, with the uncom-
prehending look of Chinese who find it so implausible that a stranger
might be speaking their language that they assume that what sounds
like Chinese must in fact be some foreign tongue. Finally one of them,
a chubby girl in a salmon-colored jacket, succeeded in parsing my
words. Suddenly her face lit up.

"Express mail! That's me!"

The airport was closed because of the weather, she cheerfully explained.

I looked up. The sky was soupy with fog.

"They have no instruments," she chirped. "Fly by eye."

"When is the next plane?"

"Maybe tomorrow."

When I returned the next morning, she gave me a tall, lidded cup of jasmine tea and made me sit in her own chair. Her name was Xiang, she told me; she might have been twenty or twenty-one, and I could see that she took delight in practicing her schoolroom English.

"At your service!" she said.

There were six people in Xiang's section, seated at a double row of desks that were wedged into a small concrete room. I asked Xiang how many express letters they handled each day.

"Oh, it's never the same," Xiang said perkily.

"But how many?" I said.

"Sometimes one, sometimes ten. You just never know!"

Then the mail arrived in a canvas sack emblazoned with a logo that had obviously been copied from the one used by Federal Express.

"Oh, so sorry!" said Xiang. "Nothing from Chengdu."

"Please tell me where my letter is," I said.

I was fighting down hysteria.

"It will come," said Guan, an intense man with bad teeth who appeared to be in charge of the office.

"I want my letter," I said.

"Please be patient," Guan said. "It is express mail."

"Find my letter!" I shouted.

Guan phoned the airport, then the railway station, and then Chengdu. He put down the phone and smiled with evident relief.

"We found your letter," he said.

"Where is it?"

"The weather is very bad. The plane has not left Chengdu."

"I know," I said. "Fly by eye."

"Exactly!" Guan replied.

"Then when will it leave?"

"Maybe tomorrow," said Guan.

"Tell them to put it on the train!" I shouted. "It will be here in the morning!"

Guan took on a pained look. He fiddled with his teacup.

"It's an express letter," Xiang explained patiently. "Express goes by plane."

WHEN I got back to the hotel the clerk watched me expectantly, but I pretended I hadn't seen him. I sat in my room and read, trying to fight off a gathering depression. After a while, the phone rang. It was Xiang.

"Guess what?" she said.

"I can't guess."

"I called Chengdu. Your passport is on the train. You'll have it in the morning."

"Thank you," I said. "Thank you. Thank you!"

I found a taxi, rushed to the ferry office, and bought a ticket for the next day's steamer to Wuhan, and then celebrated with an indulgent meal at the old hotel near the docks. Then I had a massage that went on for forty minutes until the masseur begged me to let him stop.

In the morning I packed my bag and phoned Xiang, and said I would be coming by for my letter.

"So sorry," she said.

"But it was on the train."

"Maybe not," she said.

"Where is it then?"

"It's hard to say."

I phoned the consul in Chengdu.

"What am I supposed to do?"

"Hope for the best," he said.

I SLIPPED INTO a funk of helplessness. Whenever he saw me now, the cadaverous clerk said, "Your passport, Mr. Bordewich!" As the days went on, the "mister" grew fainter. I prowled the city from end to end; I came to loathe the place.

Chongqing clung to a rocky promontory that jutted between the Yangzi and Jialing rivers, which joined at its tip. You saw the Great River constantly, a gray-brown flood that loomed beyond the plateaus of gray-tiled roofs, at the ends of the cluttered lanes, below the hills that were still honeycombed with tunnels where the city's population had lived during the wartime bombardment, and at the foot of the bluffs where it wrapped itself around the city like a monstrous, dirty serpent.

Turn-of-the-century travelers often regarded Chongqing as the archetypal city of Old China. The staid Isabella Bird fairly gushed at the sight of such a "noble and most striking spectacle," with towers and temples rising above massive walls, and crowded flights of stone stairs, twenty feet broad, climbing steeply from the river to monumental gates. She wrote: "The harmony between man's work and nature is yet unbroken, and the evil day of foreign inartistic antagonisms, incongruities, and ugliness has not yet dawned."

But the Chongqing she saw was bombed to dust by the Japanese during World War II. What remained was a great gray behemoth of a city; its ugliness was stunning. The city was rebuilt hastily and crudely. I had heard that new buildings were painted black to make them harder to identify during air raids; the painting black was still kept up, it seemed, like a fashion or a neurotic obsession, and it gave the entire city a permanent gloom that was accentuated further by the soot that caked everything and by the fog that hung implacably overhead. The atmosphere seemed to infect the inhabitants. Pedestrians skulked through the sooty streets. Someone tried to pick my pocket in the bus. Taxi drivers demanded outrageous fares and then smirked.

I telephoned Xiang each day after breakfast.

"So foggy!" she would say.

"YOU LIKE break dance," the hotel clerk informed me one afternoon.

"No," I said.

"Yes, you like."

Break dancing was sweeping China, and this was the final night of the First Annual Chongqing Break Dancing Competition. It was also the only live entertainment in town.

I followed a besodden stream of young people, guessing rightly that there was no other place they could be going. Beneath canvas awnings outside the arena vendors were selling flat ducks, tripe, liver, and less distinguishable body parts. The interior was decorated with murals that seemed strangely quaint and antique. In them, robust athletes surged smilingly to victory at track meets and on basketball courts; they were Stalinesque and generic, radiant with joy, icons of the once-virile socialism that had now gone awry.

The contest opened with a bell, like the start of a basketball game. Red, blue, and green strobes splashed over the floor. The inflections of 125th Street and Eastern Parkway suddenly thundered through the arena. Taped voices roared: "Come on and steal it! Come on and get it!" amid erotic chirps and shrieks and gasps.

Two men in silver jumpsuits sprang onto their hands and then onto their backs, undulating across the floor with limb-shuddering ripples. Electric guitars shrieked, and synthesizers dinned like pile drivers. A man in some kind of silver-flaked costume bounced into the spotlight to a deafening sort of subaqueous beat; he dragged himself along a wall, climbed an imaginary ladder, built a room whose four walls began to close upon him inexorably. Then two boys with the ideograph for "Double Happiness" sewn on the back of crinkly suits swam in slow-motion struggle, as if through dense membranes that wouldn't give way.

I guessed that there were five or six thousand people in the arena. The girls mostly wore helmet hairdos and shapeless cotton jackets, the boys Mao suits and soggy greatcoats made of blue, black, or gray cotton. They sat stolidly in folding wooden seats, sipping hawthorne juice from foil containers and gaping impassively at the performers as they tumbled across the floor. What were they really seeing? I wondered.

The music was aggressive and jarring, but the dancing had little of the mechanical, hard angularity that you saw on the New York streets. Instead, it suggested a hybrid, a sort of street-smart tai chi.

Left to themselves, the Chinese were instinctively drawn to the sensual and stylized; all the years of Communist dulling had been unable to eradicate the craving for grace. But the imagery hinted at deeper feelings of confinement and escape, death and rebirth.

A girl in black tights spun out of the shadows, leaped into cartwheels and backflips, swung her elbow like a loose joint, knocked herself over, hauled herself up by an invisible rope. She was slim and handsome; the movements weren't deliberately erotic, but it was impossible not to be aroused as she slithered and writhed across the floor. The music was almost too much. "Let your body take the heat! Your body . . . your body . . . your body . . . ," it thundered.

I looked at the kids in their clumsy hairdos and greatcoats, dressed in the age-old palette of the Chinese countryside, and still soaking from the rain. But they gave nothing away.

ANOTHER DAY, I went to Red Cliff, a suburban compound where the Communist representatives to the Nationalist government lived during the war. The main building was a large gray-brick structure, vaguely Western in shape and still painted black. In the back, wedged into a cleft in the hills, was a pretty, old-fashioned garden with an ornamental bridge that hopped over a stream.

The house had been made into a museum. There were lots of photographs of the young Communists on the walls; I looked into the confident faces of hopeful, ardent young men (there were no women), all of them strikingly well groomed, like American college students of the 1940s. It was hard to accept that a few years later these same men would invent labor camps, produce the terrible famine of the early 1960s, set off the Cultural Revolution, and be its victims too. On the shelves there were yellowing paper-covered copies of Lenin's and Stalin's works in different languages. Mao's office was in a corner; on the wall hung a photo of him incongruously wearing a white colonial topee. The whole place had an odd, *fin de siecle* air to it: the antique radio transmitter, the dusty wicker chairs that looked as if they'd come from some tea planter's veranda in Assam, the old-fashioned double-sided desks. To Chinese, it was a famous place, but there were only four or five other visitors, and two of them were soldiers.

Souvenirs were on sale at a counter. Amid the enameled soup spoons, miniature opera masks, silk purses, mandarin caps, hand-painted fans, clay warriors, jade bracelets, stuffed dragons, and chopsticks there were boxes and boxes of old Mao buttons and stacks of Mao's *Little Red Book*; they had become mere artifacts, tourist kitsch. I bought two pins and a copy of the book.

One of the pins showed Mao on a windswept mountaintop, like a god just arrived from the heavens, an immortal. The other was the familiar official portrait, with the sleek airbrushed skin, the narrowed eyes that were meant to be farseeing but in fact seemed only cold and unfeeling, and the famous mole, his single flaw, polished to a luminescent glow.

The young man who ran the concession at first demanded fifty cents for the lot. I bargained him down eventually to thirty-five cents. We might have been haggling over cucumbers or the price of noodles. Less than twenty years ago, these were sacred symbols, icons; it was as if the Vatican had abandoned the Virgin Mary and was selling off Bibles by the pound, as scrap paper.

LATER THAT afternoon, there was a knock on my door. I opened it to find Xiang with an elfin smile on her face. I could tell that she had rehearsed her message all the way to the hotel, through the rain and traffic.

"I have a surprise for you!" she piped.

She whipped an envelope from her pink tunic.

"Express delivery!"

THE NEXT morning, I slithered down mud-slick steps amid a tumble of travelers and quick-footed coolies to the Yangzi, and then along a shuddering catwalk to a pale-blue and white craft that a sign unpoetically identified as *Number 8* of the Sichuan Provincial

Steamship Line. Fanfares blared from loudspeakers. With a blast from the ship's horn, the *Number 8* slipped out through flotillas of flat-bottomed barges and into the stream, and before long the gray city fell away astern and the land opened up like a breath. The riverbanks were low and red and rocky, and rich fields beyond them lay like crumpled green velvet beneath the inky, drizzly sky. Disused pagodas punctuated the headlands, elegant tools that the Chinese of another age believed held in check the predatory dragons of the Great River.

The river was just a few hundred feet wide in places and made dangerous by reefs that narrowed the channel even more. Something still remained here of the wild torrent that rose far to the west in the wastelands of Tibet, something raw and formidable, and unwelcoming to man. Until the twentieth century, the Yangzi was the only commercial route into Sichuan, and the annual loss of life was fearful in the gorges that lay ahead; an 1896 British consular report estimated that during one three-month period alone, one hundred boats and one thousand lives were lost in the gorges. But the muscular current and the mountain walls that loomed in the distant mist still only hinted at their presence.

Like the Chinese railways, the *Number 8* maintained the Maoist fiction that privilege had been wiped out in the People's Republic. "First class" had in fact been abolished; but another class had been added at the other end of the scale, so that instead of "first-," "second-," and "third-," the steamer had "second-," "third-," and "fourth-" class quarters. All that had actually been eliminated was comfort. My second-class cabin was walled with Formica and lit by a fluorescent tube fitted to the ceiling, and when the cabin attendant swabbed the floor in the morning, she sloshed water over my baggage and shoes and the book I had left on the floor. The second-class lounge was graced with chairs made of some foamy orange material, and with paintings of hydroelectric facilities, and with plastic gladiolas set in pots on a billiard table for which there were no cues or balls. The public address system played the "1812 Overture," Schubert's "Wedding March," "The Blue Danube," and "Funiculi Funicula"; the tape automatically rewound itself and repeated the same tunes again and again, all day, as *Number 8* threaded the reefs of half-submerged rock.

Second class was officialdom's refuge from the less-washed masses astern. There was a flabby, sly-looking man from Beijing, who administered a military dance troupe; an ample bureaucrat from the Tianjin Writer's Union; a physicist from Shanghai, who was on his way home from a conference in Chongqing; and several others whose origins remained shrouded in pompous majesty. Each clung to his foamy orange chair as if to a private island. I tried to talk to the man from Tianjin, but when I said that I was a writer, he turned away. The impresario smiled cordially and put up his hand, and said, in English, "No English"; when I said I could speak a little Chinese, his smile dimmed and he said, "No."

The physicist was easier to talk to, at first. He had a lean, intelligent face and the kind of poise that betrayed a background in the old upper class. He apologized politely for his English, explaining that when he had gone to university in the early 1950s everyone had been told to study Russian. When I asked if he found Russian of much use anymore, he said, "Oh, no, no, no," and laughed.

I had been reading *Dream of the Red Chamber*. The physicist picked it up and mused, with the special affection that older Chinese have for the saga of the Jia clan, "A stone comes to life, becomes a man, falls in love with a girl who is a goddess." Then he unexpectedly became contemptuous.

"The language is old and difficult," he said. "Nowadays people just want to read trash and watch TV."

He seemed about to say something more, when he suddenly became self-conscious. He sensed the others listening, I guessed, and he drew away.

The third- and fourth-class dormitories were teeming warrens redolent of roast duck, tea, and sweat, where young men lay playing cards and smoking gustily in rooms jammed with a dozen or more bunks. Despite the discomfort, or because of it, inhibitions were suspended, and even the slovenliness had a Rabelaisian vigor; food was swapped, uproarious jokes told. I looked for someone to talk to, but I became an instant spectacle, a visual morsel to be appraised and consumed along with the dinners of cold rice, stale duck, and greasy twists of dough.

I stepped out of my cabin the next morning into an astonishing landscape. It was as if the earth had cracked open in the night. The river had become a shadowy alley beneath cliffs that rose two thousand feet from the water and erupted at their tops into cones and spires and pagodas of stone. The cliffs receded for miles ahead, like a succession of monstrous gates, suggesting an infinity of monumental courtyards that opened out each from the one before. High overhead, I could see tiny terraces green with wheat, a rosary of white cottages, an abandoned temple with wildly upturned eaves. From time to time, the cliffs opened out into scree, or coves and beaches fringed with orange groves; and then on the slopes above there would be loquat and pomegranate, bamboo, clematis, maidenhair and cypresses. But for the lulling thud of the ship's engines, there was utter silence.

When Isabella Bird entered the Witches' Mountain Gorge on a February day in 1896, the rock walls echoed with the wild cries of boatmen begging the god of rivers "for a wind, with many vows and promises to pay." Bird was sixty-four years old and famous, having already published popular books about her travels in Japan, Persia, and Hawaii. Only the nineteenth century could have produced such a combination of self-confidence, physical fortitude, and incredible single-mindedness.

Photographs show penetrating eyes and a firm mouth, a face that a vainer woman might have made handsome but that now comes across as rather cold and austere. She was in fact deeply compassionate, and had remarkably liberal convictions for her age; her family somewhat ostentatiously refused to sweeten their tea with West Indian sugar as a protest against the Caribbean slave trade for decades after it had been suppressed. But later life was not kind to her. She was traumatized by the death of a beloved sister, and then in a state of shock married "a pure, saintly, heroic" man, who fell ill and died within months of their wedding.

In 1893 Bird told her London publisher that she was "too old for hardships and great exertions." Having said that, she undertook a journey to parts of China that were still barely known to Europeans and that would eventually subject her to riots, physical attack, and a ghastly ascent of the Yangzi gorges, not to mention a close brush with death in the frozen marches of Tibet.

Bird was a devout Christian and went to China under missionary auspices, but she slipped the traces as soon as she could. "My chief wish on arriving at a foreign settlement or treaty port in the East is to get out of it as soon as possible," she later wrote. She dressed in a specially tailored suit of Chinese clothes whose capacious pockets concealed everything from a revolver to a small gas lamp, and wherever she was she managed to maintain a diet of rigorous Victorian monotony. Each morning, she had tea brewed from "tabloids" and a plate of boiled flour, and at the end of the day, "for 146 days, at seven," an undeviating menu of curried chicken or eggs and rice.

Bird traveled by steamer from Shanghai to Yichang, where she spent several days seeking a vessel to carry her through the gorges. She finally hired a single-masted sampan manned by a pilot, a steersman, and sixteen trackers and oarsmen; from the mat shed in which she slept, she was presented every night with the sight of the pilot and most of the crew "lying on the floor beside their opium lamps, passing into felicity."

Europeans were still rare this far upriver, and anti-foreign sentiment was intense. "The men asserted that with my binoculars and camera I could see the treasures of the mountains; the gold, precious stones, and golden cocks which lie deep down in the earth; that I kept a black devil in the camera, and that I liberated him at night, and that he dug up the golden cocks, and that the reason why my boat was low in the water was that it was ballasted with these auriferous fowls and with the treasures of the hills." Awe mingled with loathing. More than once, Bird underwent "the divertissement of being pelted with mud and with such names as 'foreign devil' and 'foreign dog.'"

In the four hundred miles between Yichang and Chongqing, the Yangzi rose more than ninety feet, through an estimated one hundred cataracts. Before entering the gorges, a functionary boarded Bird's sampan and positioned himself in the prow, waving a flag on which was written: "Powers of the waters, give a lucky star for the journey." The crew butchered a sacrificial cock and sprayed its blood over the ship. Everyone knew that death could come at any moment. The slightest error by a pilot or a snagged bow sweep might spell disaster and mean the loss of hundreds of lives.

The atmosphere in the gorges was primitive and terrifying. Eastbound junks swept downriver broadside, their masts lashed to their sides. The captains frantically yelled and danced; drums and gongs were madly beaten. The whole river echoed with the wild cries of the crews as they fought to maneuver around shoals and whirlpools, ten men to an oar.

Junks bound for Sichuan were hauled upriver by teams of "trackers," who pulled them, literally inches at a time, through whirlpools and rapids, by means of ropes that were attached to the masts and that stretched as much as a quarter-mile to the shore. A quarter-million trackers worked the river during the winter months, when the water was low and most boats made the passage upriver. They clawed their way over boulders, climbed up cliff walls on each other's backs, crept forward on their hands and knees, and clung, sometimes with their fingers and toes, to a narrow track cut into the rock three hundred feet above the river, "holding on with their eyelids," as the Chinese said.

Bird was watching hundreds of trackers maneuver a single large junk through a cataract when the towrope snapped. "Suddenly the junk shivered, the lines of trackers went down on their faces, and in a moment the big craft was spinning down the rapid; and before she could be recovered by the bow sweep she flew up in the air as if she had exploded, a mass of spars and planks with heads bobbing about in the breakers." In all, she counted forty-one wrecked junks in the course of her trip.

Her own flimsy sampan required seventy trackers. They struggled manfully against a current that averaged between seven and twelve miles an hour, slipping back again and again while the sampan hung suspended in the flood. Bird's nerves finally got the better of her, and she asked to be put ashore to hike along with skittish passengers from other ships. "It was piteous to see the women with their bound feet hobbling and tumbling among boulders, where I, who am not a very bad climber, was glad to get the help of two men." Signs of disaster were everywhere. Shattered derelicts were half-submerged in quiet reaches; human skeletons lay on the rocks.

One day, Bird's boatmen callously left her by herself outside a trackers' encampment. "There were unholy sounds of tom-toms, the weather relapsed and the wind howled." Bird sat alone on boulders in

101

a bitterly cold, sunless wind, surrounded by "a repulsive and cease-less" mob of men and boys. "Mud was thrown and stuck; foul and bad names were used all day by successive crowds." She was near despair. "Could these people ever have come 'trailing clouds of glory?' Were they made in the image of God? Have we 'all one Father?' I asked myself."

This was the flip side of Cathay: China as hell. The skeletons on the rocks, the lost souls tugging hopelessly at the towropes, the howling mob, the abandonment; it was the imagery of damnation. For Bird, the ascent of the Yangzi was also a descent into Hades, a self-conscious trial of her humanity and faith, and thus, in a sense, a sacred experience, an archetypal journey toward martyrdom and transcen-dance.

The stupendous landscape offered another sort of redemption. She steadfastly continued to find the gorges a "glorious sight," the villages "captivating to the eye," and the half-hidden vales beyond them "a farming paradise." And in spite of everything, she retained a tenacious faith in the Chinese, "so ingenious a race."

Bird left the river at Wanxian and set out through the mountains toward Chengdu. Determined to get a good look at the countryside, she insisted, against the advice of her guides, upon traveling in an open sedan chair which so offended local custom that it inspired riots in the towns through which she passed.

At Liangshanxian, she was attacked and beaten by an outraged mob that accused her of being a "foreign devil" and "child eater." "There was nothing for it but to sit up stolidly and not to appear hurt, frightened or annoyed, though I was all three." Her coolies managed to push her into an inn, where they locked her, for her own protection, in a pitch-dark shed. Through chinks in the wall, she watched the mob break down the inn's door and then, armed with pieces of it, set about beating at her refuge, howling, "Beat her! Kill her! Burn her!" They tried to set fire to the shed, but the matches were damp. Bird sat on a barrel, drew her revolver, and prepared to shoot. Little by little the door began to give way, and would soon have fallen in. Then there was a sudden rush of feet, soldiers appeared, and in a few minutes the yard was clear; one of her coolies had fortunately informed the local magistrate that a foreigner was about to be murdered. Later the magistrate's wife arrived to console Bird. "If a foreign woman went to your country, you'd kill her, wouldn't you?" the woman asked.

"These riots were unbearably fatiguing after a day's journey," Bird wrote, "and always delayed my dinner unconscionably."

She eventually passed beyond Sichuan altogether and into Tibet. By this time, her clothes were falling apart, her guides recalcitrant, and the local officials obstructive. She was told that there were neither roads nor inns ahead, that the inhabitants were savages, the tribes at war. Bird's life was now constantly in danger. She had no clear reason to continue, but she pressed on unstoppably. She was driven by curiosity, of course, and by a habitual tenacity in the face of danger; but one senses something more. Possibly, she was secretly preparing to die, to permit herself a single indulgence in her austere Christian life, to disappear, to pass away into legend and romance.

The crisis came atop the twelve thousand-foot Zagushan Pass. "The snow deepened, whirled, drifted, stung like pin points." The light was ghastly, the cold numbing, every breath a moan. Bird's guide disappeared in the darkness. She sank in snow up to her neck. Her clothing froze. The coolies refused to carry her any further. At 2:00 A.M., Bird at last stumbled onto a hovel in which she found shelter for the rest of that awful night; perhaps in spite of herself, she survived. Whatever impulse had driven her this far had finally exhausted itself. After regaining her strength, she returned to Chengdu, to Chongqing, and then back down the Yangzi to Shanghai, and finally to England, where she wrote probably the best book of her vivid life, *The Yangtze Valley and Beyond.*

Bird came home from China inspired. From one angle, contemporaries might see the Chinese as a "Yellow Peril," she admitted, but "surely looked at from another they constitute the Yellow Hope, and it may be possible that an empire genuinely Christianised may yet be the dominant power in Asia."

She kept traveling until the end. Her seventieth year found her in Morocco where, she wrote a friend, she rode "astride a superb horse in full blue trousers and a short full skirt with great brass spurs belonging to the generalissimo of the Moorish army."

Thinking of Isabella Bird, I began to understand Du Fu's famous words: "The Great River flows east/endlessly as are a wanderer's days." I always assumed that the old poet had meant to invest the "journey of life" with a sense of a river's calm and majestic flow. That, I saw, was the facile assumption of someone for whom journeys were safe and arrival assured. There was no serenity, no reassuring sense of eternity in the river that Du Fu and Bird knew. But the chaos and terror of the gorges was an apt metaphor for the unending calamity of Du Fu's age, when life and the river alike promised cruelty and danger, and only a hope of survival.

The gorges had now been gutted of their terror. *Number 8* cruised through them at a speedy and untroubled clip. The most dangerous cataracts were blasted away by Red Army engineers in the 1950s. Then, in the 1960s, the government dammed the river at Yichang and turned the gorges into a lake. An even bigger hydro-electric project was being planned, the largest in the world, the regime claimed, and by the turn of the twenty-first century it would lift the water level by another one hundred feet and effectively eliminate the gorges forever.

Pretty white villages perched on crags and outcrops. But my eyes were drawn back again and again to the old trackers' trails; they were still visible in places, mere sketches across the mountainsides, fading, troubling memories that nagged at the eye. All the dehumanizing brutality of Old China seemed written into the shallow steps that crept around hairpin bends and levered themselves up sheer cliffs and across naked scarps as if notched by a sculptor's stylus in the towering rock.

At Yichang, the mountains fell away and the river dropped through the massive locks of the Gezhouba Dam into the brown plains of Hebei. Yichang was famous at one time for the golf course that foreign residents had laid out among the tumuli of a Chinese graveyard; "a course of a thousand bunkers and hazards, with fine drives insured from teeing-grounds fixed on certain superior mandarin mounds," as one turn-of-the-century traveler remarked. The dam had transformed Yichang into a sprawling industrial center, with long rows of concrete apartment blocks flanking the shore, and factories whose assembly lines, I imagined, now employed the children of the men who since the dawn of Chinese time had hauled ships up the cataracts of the Yangzi.

There was more traffic on the river now, mostly flat-bottomed, square-prowed craft, with sooty superstructures and sooty crewmen who peered like troglodytes from their pitchy depths, bearing sand and bricks and coal eastward into the rosy twilight. The countryside was without depth or dimension; the riverbanks were gray threads, the river an opaque brown plate, the sky vague, hardly there at all. The sooty barges drifted insubstantially past in long strings, like motes of dust in a void. After the symphonic crescendo of the gorges, it was hard to get a grip on this silent, motionless epicenter of China.

The next morning, I was standing alone in the prow, straining for a first glimpse of Wuhan. The physicist from Shanghai jogged past me twice, making a circuit of the deck; he passed me a third time. The fourth time he stopped. I said I was sorry that the other passengers hadn't been very friendly.

"Cadres," he said. "They're afraid to be seen talking to a foreigner."

There was no one else in earshot now, and he began to rant.

"Cadres!" he said again, this time contemptuously.

In the early Communist years, the cadres' self-discipline was legendary, the physicist said. Now their greed was ruining the country. Bribery had reached epidemic proportions. He made a gross gesture of greedily scraping heaps of wealth to himself.

"Money, money, money!" he sneered. "It's worse than the old days."

When I asked the physicist if he was a Party member, he was evasive. But he belonged to the generation that had willingly sacrificed.

"When we were young, we didn't want anything for ourselves. It sounds unbelievable, but it's true. We just wanted to build the country and socialism. We never even thought of self-advancement."

I dug in my memory for a poem; it was by Mu Ren, who had been popular in the 1950s:

Put me in place and screw me in tight.
There I shall stay firmly put, my heart at rest.
Perhaps people will not know that I exist
But I know that vibrating in the throbbing of a great machine
Is the life of a tiny screw.

"Yes, like that," the physicist said. "It was a beautiful dream."

Now his students all wanted to go to the United States to do graduate work; none of those who went came back. He missed them, but he sympathized.

"One of them earns $9,000 a year!" he exclaimed. "If I were young, I wouldn't come back either."

The sum clearly stunned him. He earned the equivalent of $50 a month. Occasionally there was a perk, like the second-class ticket on the steamer.

"I have enough to feed myself, to clothe myself, but nothing more, after almost forty years of work," he said.

He kept coming back to the $50 a month, to the $9,000. The figures circled endlessly through his head, like the taped music on the PA system, which was now playing "The Girl from Ipanema" and the "Mexican Hat Dance," over and over. But I felt that the money was just a metaphor, that he was really talking about a life that had lost its value.

"What about the future?" I asked.

"There is no future," he replied.

We stood in silence and stared across the Yangzi. The man-made landscape was so blank that it was difficult for the eye even to register it: rectangular concrete factory blocks and dormitories; verticals of chimneys, and winter-bare poplars, and slipways that dropped abruptly from warehouses to the waterline; horizontals of long, low, brick sheds, and brick walls that went on for miles upon miles, it seemed, shielding the secrets of the heart of China.

The physicist's depression began to infect me. I tried to change the subject.

We began to talk about Chongqing where, as a child, he had spent the war. I told him how I had had to wait for my passport, and then said something obscene about the fog.

He said, "We used to pray for the fog, you know. It meant the Japanese bombers wouldn't come."

He remembered sirens, the tunnels, fear, the smell of corpses.

He was originally from Nanjing. Trackers had pulled his family upriver in 1938, in a sampan crammed with refugees. He had no memory at all of the gorges. He remembered only a feeling of helplessness, and crouching in the belly of the sampan all the way to Chong-qing, scanning the sky for Japanese planes.

For all his pessimism, he knew he was lucky to have survived at all, and to have married and raised a family. I asked him how many children he had.

"Three," he replied with an unexpected edge.

"And what do they do?"

"They're cadres."

He disappeared with an equivocal handshake as we approached the outskirts of Wuhan.

WUHAN LAY athwart the Yangzi like a giant engine room. First came miles of booms and cranes, and then floating docks that stuck out into the river like tentacles. Tugs and lighters dodged among steamers as they swung into the current, churning at the muddy water, smoke charging from their stacks. Long rows of warehouses faced the riverfront; beyond them, I could see cupolas and fluted colonnades that incongruously suggested the Europe of an earlier age, some provincial capital, say, of the Austro-Hungarian Empire.

Wuhan was really three cities. We passed Hanyang first, on the north bank, and then Hankou, and on the south bank Wuchang; it was there, in 1911, that imperial China died. The Republican Revolution was an almost spur-of-the-moment affair. Rebellions had sputtered all over China for a decade; but each time sufficient numbers of heads had been removed, and peace restored. The accidental explosion of a bomb alerted the authorities to the presence of agitators in the imperial garrison. Defying arrest, the ringleaders seized the east gate of Wuchang; the panicked commandant fled, and then the viceroy. Garrisons all over China spontaneously defected.

Within months, most of China south of the Yangzi had proclaimed its independence. Imperial power disintegrated, and Chinese were treated to the spectacle of helpless Manchus straggling feebly back to the northern forests whence their ancestors had come galloping nearly three centuries before. The infant Puyi abdicated, and for the first time in 2,131 years there was no man who called himself the emperor of China. Soon there would be a fragile parliament, a provisional government headed by the idealist Sun Yatsen, and the promise of an only vaguely grasped thing called democracy.

For decades, the modern world had seeped in through the European "concessions" that lined the river at Hankou. Steam engines, basketball, gatling guns, labor unions, fedoras, the notion of democracy; they came willy-nilly, much the way that the Fat Boys and Jean-Paul Sartre, and blue jeans and Freudianism were coming three-quarters of a century later. The British were the first to wrest the right of free trade from the enfeebled Manchu regime, in 1861; the French and the Russians, the Germans and the Japanese followed suit, staking out their tiny enclaves, each with its own hotels and banks, governed by its own laws, and protected from the vast tide of China by its cordon of gendarmes or red-turbaned Sikhs.

Travelers on the Yangzi usually spent at least a few days at Hankou, which has for many centuries been the most important port on the middle Yangzi. At the turn of the century, you could still see junks colored like cockatoos crowded ten deep along the shore, in a vast river-borne market whose every floating shop advertised its trade with a hank of thread, a pair of trousers, wooden buckets, or a barber's bowl and plaited queue dangling from its mast. Slim Hunanese rice boats and weird fiddle-shaped craft from Lake Poyang jockeyed for dock space with Fujianese sampans laden with bamboo, and ponderous Sichuanese junks bound for the China Sea with cargoes of pekoe and keemun.

Matting shaded the narrow lanes of the Chinese city, so that commerce was carried on in a strange tinted twilight punctuated by the gleaming crimson and gold of the long, hanging signboards. So confusing were these warrens, Isabella Bird complained, that it was difficult even for old hands to find their way "without irksome and delaying tergiverisations." I envied her the sight of the human panorama: the jostling coolies, the compradors in brocaded furs, the soldiers with gaudy umbrellas decorated with mythical monsters and Confucian maxims, the robed mandarins in gilded chairs, "nearly always very pale and fat, with a thin moustache of long curved hairs, and that look of unutterable superciliousness and scorn," the lepers with their gaping sores, the children, Bird noted (now wearing her missionary hat), with "precocious depravity written on faces which should be young."

These were all icons of the Old China that to those who saw it less than a century ago seemed eternal and incapable of change, frozen in a permanent, vivid tableau of cruelty and exotic grace. E. R. Scidmore confidently wrote a few years before the Republican Revolution: "One need not assume that this is at all the end, the absolute and final ruin, the last wreck and crash of the old empire, of its curious 4,000-year-old civilization, all because the present parvenu Manchu dynasty happens to fall." But it was; they were all gone now—the coolies, the mandarins, the spectacular lacquered signboards, the exotic junks—as if they had been a figment of the travelers' imagination. Oddly enough, it was the husk of the old concessions that survived.

My hotel was located in the old French Concession. It was a neighborhood of domes and Doric colonnades, Grecian pediments, mansard roofs, bay windows, clerestory windows, and French doors that opened creakily onto boulevards shaded by mottled sycamores. Down the street, there was a fine stone church that might have been transplanted from Caen or St. Lo, and in a bakery window—miracle of miracles!—I saw French bread displayed like an artifact from some ancient, lost civilization.

But the arabesqued balconies were draped with laundered underwear, most of the mansards had been reduced to a tar-paper epiderm, and the Norman church had (perhaps more usefully) been turned into an institute for the handicapped; the shape was all that remained French about the bread, which, when I bought a loaf, tasted disappointingly of lard. Yet even so, after Chongqing's relentless Maoist gloom and the affectless landscape of the last days, it was a relief to walk once again among buildings that sought to charm, surprise, awe, and entertain.

The hotel still preserved traces of imperial grandeur. The halls were lofty and dim, and the old high-ceilinged rooms cavernous. Potted plants brooded on the landings. Massive stairways ascended into a sepulchral gloom, and in dark corners brocaded armchairs disintegrated in silent splendor. There was also no electricity.

The clerk said, "Every week tomorrow no power."

"But it's off today," I said.

"Yes."

There was a burly Chinese in a business suit standing next to the desk.

"The whole city's short of power," he said. "Factories only work a four-day week. Whadda place, huh?"

He took hold of my hand with a huge pumping fist. He said, "Everybody calls me Chuck."

We went in to breakfast. The old furniture had been replaced by aluminum chairs and tables, and the windows were smudged and cracked in their grandiose casements. But elegant bronze gas lamps shaped like human hands still protruded from the walls, and as we ate in the eerie gloom I kept looking up, half expecting them to move. The food was inedible: cold toast, unspreadable butter, rice gruel, pickled radishes. It was hard to get the waitresses' attention. Most of them were bent over a table in the corner, painstakingly separating sheets of two-ply toilet paper for napkins.

Chuck was a Presence. He stood well over six feet, and beamed a big sunny smile in every direction as he spoke. He had grown up in Wuhan, but he had lived in Los Angeles for the last nine years, and he had the picked-up style of southern California. The herringbone jacket, the pullover, and the corduroys that he wore were Ivy League. But the big gold Rolex and the diamond-studded ring were pure L.A. He had three American girl friends, owned a condo in the Valley, and drove an Oldsmobile.

"The Americans," Chuck said. "They're nuts, you know? They all drive these Japanese cars. You can't beat an American car, that's what I say!"

Chuck's father ranked high in the provincial government. After high school, family connections ensured him a seat at a prestigious Beijing college, and then at an elite engineering school when Mao sent the rest of his generation to the countryside. Had he remained in China, he could have risen to a position of some importance. But revolution had left him disillusioned.

"Mao played us for suckers," he said.

When he asked what I was going to see in Wuhan, I said the

110

Temple of Eternal Spring. There was a legend that Lao Tze used to meditate on a terrace there.

Chuck said, "It's not there anymore, I tell you true."

"What happened to it?"

"Cultural Revolution." Chuck spread his hands. "Those were crazy times!"

I said, "You were in Beijing then?"

"Was I there? Was I there?" He spread his huge palms. "I was a Red Guard! I was right in the middle of the whole thing!"

Chuck's natural abilities, and connections, had gotten him a job at the Command Center, which received direct orders from Mao's office and then passed them on to the middle-school students who were the foot soldiers of the Cultural Revolution.

"We were really outta our minds! We knocked down everything!"

Chuck slapped his knee, pummeled the arms of the chair, collapsed into hilarity.

"I stood up in Tiananmen Square waving the *Little Red Book*. I even shook Mao's hand once."

"How did that feel?"

"It left me numb. He wasn't a man to us. He was like a god."

Chuck sent out teams of Red Guards to scour the city for the "old culture" that Mao had condemned. Whatever survived the revolution of 1911, the Japanese war, and the Communist Revolution, they destroyed. They confiscated gold, jewelery, statues, books, ivory, rare furniture, pewter, carpets, scrolls, calligraphy, paintings, and carved jade and brought it all back to the Command Center, to Chuck. Vast warehouses filled up with what was left of Old China.

"Some of you must have gotten rich," I said.

"We never touched any of it," Chuck protested. "We were pure then!"

"Pure?"

"I could have had any girl I wanted. But I never thought, 'This one is a real piece-of-you-know-what'; I only thought, 'Is she revolutionary?' There was a girl once, from a bad political background. She was really beautiful. I mean, I really liked her. But I only thought,

'How can I save her and make her a real revolutionary?' I wanted, well, you know . . . But I put it out of my mind. It really hurt me, you know. But we felt we were there to make revolution, and you couldn't let yourself think about anything else."

Chuck meticulously catalogued everything that had been confiscated and then saw that it was turned over to the State Bank. The bank shipped it to outlets in Hong Kong, whence it was profitably funneled onto the international market.

"How did you feel?"

"Whatever the movement did, that's what you did. You didn't think about it. If you wanted to do something different, you were in deep shit, man."

Chuck was at one point ordered to investigate one of his own professors, who was suspected of being an American spy. The professor owned an American-made radio; it was the chief clue.

"I was ordered to find out if he was using the radio to send coded messages to the CIA. So I took it apart. The fact is, it was just a radio. But I couldn't say that, or I would have been accused of covering up for him. So in my report I wrote, 'As far as I can conclude, it is a radio, but it is possible that something could be added to it to enable the accused to transmit messages.' But it was only an old radio! Whadda riot, huh?"

Chuck now regarded those as wasted years. But he had done well for himself. When Chinese were permitted to study abroad in the late 1970s, Chuck was one of the first to go, to study computer technology. Although he didn't say so, I guessed that his connections had helped once again.

"The Americans hadn't seen mainland Chinese for thirty years," he said. "We were a novelty. They just said, 'Hey, come on!' and gave you a scholarship, just like that."

He laughed uproariously.

"You never know what's going to happen in China," he said. "One day I'm great because I'm a revolutionary. Then I'm down because I belong to the wrong faction. Then I'm up again because I'm an engineer and everyone's supposed to build the country with technology. First it's 'Down with the U.S.!' Then everybody wants to go to the U.S. to study. Whadda riot!"

Chuck had now left computers and gone into business with his brother, who lived in Wuhan. He was here now scouting out deals.

"Import-export," he said. "Anything at all, you name it!"

I ran into Chuck again at lunch.

"Hey, I want you to meet my brother!" he shouted across the dining room. "This is the guy who sacked the Temple of Eternal Spring! My own little brother! I asked him what happened to it, and he said, 'I'm the guy who did it.' How about that!"

The brother was smaller and seedier, and unpoised. He was wearing a leather flight jacket and Calvin Klein jeans, but he seemed ill at ease with Chuck's Americanized flamboyance and splendid English. The brother had never finished high school; the Cultural Revolution had aborted his education.

It was obvious that Chuck was the brain behind the business. Until a few months ago, the brother had been a hospital orderly, but Chuck needed him for his connections with the sons of certain local officials. Several of these were sitting at the table, enveloped in a beery haze. The mounds of gnawed chicken and fish bones betrayed a recent banquet.

"You gotta have an angle on the government, you gotta be plugged in," Chuck sighed.

"That's the way you do business here," the brother said sullenly.

"My brother, the big man!" Chuck said, with obvious sarcasm.

I saw the brother cringe.

"Those guys are all former Red Guards," Chuck said to me. "The same people, twenty years later. When we were Communists everybody cared about the country's reputation and his own. Now all they want to do is sit around and play cards and mah-jongg, and banquet. You're just a piece of meat to them. Everybody just wants to take his slice, that's all."

Chuck and his brother were negotiating to sell disposable syringes to a hospital in Yichang. They were catching a 4:00 P.M. flight.

I began to excuse myself, saying that I was going across the river to Wuchang. I wanted to find the place where the 1911 revolution had begun.

"I'll give you a lift," Chuck said. "I've got my limo."

The car was the fruit of yet another connection. Actually, it belonged to some government bureau, but Chuck's brother had arranged to have it on call all day. A shipment of imported cigarettes was involved in some way that I never got straight. The car was supposed to arrive at 2:30; but soon it was 3:00, and then 3:15, and it still hadn't come.

Chuck said, "They got no concept of time, these people."

More time passed. By now, Chuck was stalking back and forth in front of the hotel.

"That's my brother for you. They only thing he ever did was burn down that goddamn pagoda."

"You'll miss your plane," I said. "I'll take a bus."

"Fuhgedaboutit!"

I could see that Chuck wouldn't let me go. It had become a matter of face. Chuck beamed his sunny southern California smile.

"Don't worry about it. The plane will wait. I've got a connection at the airport."

The brother finally showed up in a new black Toyota. The driver was a middle-aged man, and he was dressed in a Mao suit and white gloves.

We drove to Hanyang, where we turned onto the graceful new bridge that spans the Yangzi to Wuchang, and in a few minutes we were passing beneath a famous pagoda that had been demolished during the Cultural Revolution but that had recently been rebuilt as a tourist attraction. I visited it later on. Inside the pagoda, there was an elevator driven by a girl in a smart uniform, who whisked you up to an observation deck on the top floor. It was popular with Chinese tourists; the past was distant enough now to be treated as entertainment, no longer threatening.

"Brand-new," said Chuck, as we drove past. "Better than before!"

Chuck's self-confidence was stunning. It was like another presence in the car with us, a pristine creature untainted by remorse or self-doubt, handsome and capable of anything. I envied and feared it at the same time.

"How much does it bother you that so much was destroyed?" I asked.

"You're always asking me things like that," Chuck said irritably.

"Isn't it important?"

"It didn't mean anything!" Chuck said. "Nothing! Chinese figure they've got a five thousand-year history. They've got more history than they need, more than they know what to do with. What are a few statues and temples? Nothing. Who cares? Nobody cared. They still don't care, if you want to know the truth."

Chuck pointed up a lane.

"Hey! There it is, man."

I could see the East Gate at the end of the lane; it was all that was left of the fortress where the rising had taken place. We maneuvered through a sprawl of brick hutments until we could go no farther. The gate was square and built of gray brick. There was a stairway inside that led to the top, but the entrance to it was locked. It was obvious that there were not many visitors; it was a shrine to what the Chinese had been taught to think was a second-rate revolution.

For forty years it had been treated as a false start, that first groping attempt at democracy that would eventually peter out in the corruption and hypocrisy of the Kuomintang. But now, with communism in disarray, I wondered if it had not been the truer revolution after all, and whether the 1949 revolution had not been the dead end, the wrong turning in the confusing bazaar of twentieth-century ideologies.

The Toyota spun around in a swirl of dust. Chuck leaned out the window, waving his diamond-freighted hand and beaming his big sunny southern California smile.

"You take care now," he shouted. "I gotta make tracks!"

What an awful man, I thought. I liked him immensely.

CHAPTER
SIX

*The First Family
Under Heaven*

TWO HOURS west of Kaifeng the bus broke down. The driver spent an hour turning the wheel joint into greasy rubble. Then he got onto an eastbound bus and disappeared. I knew it was going to be a long afternoon when two men climbed onto the engine bonnet, unfolded a board, and began a game of chess. They played with great gravity, expelling a steady stream of spittle onto the floor and meditatively working it into a lake with their slippers. The woman behind me opened her lunch and began sucking at gummy blobs of boiled dough. The odds of reaching Qufu that day were rapidly lengthening, and the prospects were steadily increasing that I would have to spend the night in Yanzhou. My guidebook described Yanzhou's only hotel: "Not even the mirrors work here—bare bulbs dangle from the ceiling, towels are all over the furniture, there's washing up and down the corridors, and no curtains. Follow your nose to the washroom."

Few foreigners traveled this route. When I climbed out of the bus I was instantly surrounded by wide-eyed peasants with coxcombs of dusty hair who amiably dribbled spittle and mucus onto my feet as they crowded around. Grave mounds bulged everywhere from the flat sepia fields; it was an interesting sign that the peasants had once again begun to think of the land as their own since the dissolution of the communes. Here and there, half a dozen men and girls were harnessed together, leaning hard on ropes slung over their shoulders, pulling wooden plows.

I trotted down the road in an effort to escape from the staring squads. A shepherd was tending a few sheep a little distance ahead. I took him for feebleminded at first. His front teeth were gone and his gums protruded, and gouts of stuffing hung out of his cotton jacket. Then as I passed him he barked, "Hello!" It was stunning.

He had a mile-wide accent that was hard to follow, but he was obviously rediscovering words he had once known, excavating them from his memory. "Yes" . . . "okay" . . . "good" . . . "good-bye" . . . "thank you." He was fairly boiling over with excitement. "America, number one!" He had done something with Americans long ago, but I couldn't quite get it. Possibly he was being vague for a reason. He said he was fifty-eight. Had he served, perhaps, with missionaries before the revolution? If he had, he must have paid dearly for it under the Maoists.

I asked how it was that he had known Americans. But the staring squads had closed in on us, and suddenly the shepherd seemed feeble again. He mumbled in Chinese, "Don't know," and then, "Don't understand," and it was clear he wouldn't say anything more.

The crowd was dribbling spit onto me and fingering my foreign jacket and jeans, and staring at me with the devouring cloddishness of people who were incapable of imagining that a creature so unlike themselves could be sensate, much less angry. I tried to shake them. But my behavior only seemed all the more bizarre, and they trotted after me, first one way and then the other. I tried, and failed, to fight down my loathing for them and for the power of a past that even now could make a man go stupid with fear.

Finally the driver reappeared, leaping from a westbound bus and waving a gasket like a battle trophy. At Yanzhou, miraculously, there was a minibus bound for Qufu at the door of the depot, and by ten o'clock I was walking through a moon gate into the hotel that is tucked into a wing of the mansion that once belonged to the oldest family on earth.

A girl padding ahead of me in soft shoes led me through court-yards that unfolded from each other like Chinese boxes, past low latticed chambers that seemed mysterious and ancient in the cascading moonlight, to a room in a small cobbled court behind the Hall of

Loyalty and Forbearance. There were old, soothing scrolls on the walls, and paintings of cranes and sages, and a vast bed whose canopied eave swarmed with carved phoenixes and wrens. I fell asleep gazing at a vase that was a dreamscape of the old world, watching hermits trek eternally through porcelain peaks bathed in a celestial mist. Outside, bamboo soughed in the chilly breeze.

IF THERE was a true center of China, or at least of the Chinese past, it was here. Confucius was born here, and with him the philosophy that molded the Chinese character and state for most of the last 2,500 years. Showered with titles and land, sheltered for twenty centuries by imperial fiat from the unhappy vicissitudes of Chinese history, the sage's descendants ramified beyond belief; today more than one hundred thousand of the half-million inhabitants of the surrounding county bear his name. (Jesuit missionaries latinized *Kong Fuzi,* "Revered Master Kong," to *Confucius* in the sixteenth century.) Kongs are everywhere in Qufu; they drive its taxis, change money in its back alleys, till the dusty fields outside town, and serve as apparatchiks in the local Communist administration.

When George Kates visited Qufu in the 1930s (he hired a donkey to carry him there from Yanzhou), he found it a "tender" place, a welcome change from "the gaudy formalities of the capital," and pervaded by "a silence stimulating to the mind, charging it with humane reflection." A prolonged thunderstorm kept him confined to the humble Chinese inn where he was staying. "For a night and a part of the next day I was shut up, given the company of grooms and ostlers for diversion, much talked to, constantly questioned and questioning, at ease and very well fed. Everyone in the town, I soon discovered, was apparently named Kung.* It was carefully explained to me, as various people came in to pay visits, how my interlocutor of the moment might actually be older than the one of half an hour before, although

---

* The system of transliterating Chinese into the Western languages was changed after the 1949 revolution; "Kung" in the old system becomes "Kong" in the new.

121

the former was of the 75th generation, let us say, while the latter was of the 73rd. Everyone was aware of these relationships; everyone knew his place and took pride in it."

In this proletarian age it was out of fashion to boast of one's connection to the sage, but a quality of specialness still remained. Nowhere else in China did the forty years of Communist rule seem so brief, and so fragile. There had been Kongs in Qufu for more than sixty times forty years. A dozen dynasties, hundreds of emperors, scores of conquerors had all come and gone. But the Kongs had endured.

Thanks mainly to the superstitiousness of the Yancheng dukes, as the sage's direct descendants were known, Qufu was spared the ham-fisted industrialization that has spoiled the ancient symmetries of most of urban China. When the seventy-fifth Yancheng duke learned in 1904 that a railway was to enter the city, he protested to the emperor that its tracks would interfere with the sacred and benevolent energies that flowed around Confucius's tomb. It might "stop the sage's very pulse," he protested. The mandarins who in those days passed judgment on such things obligingly rerouted the main Beijing-to-Shanghai line, and with it the twentieth century, several miles to the west. An instinctive dignity that has virtually disappeared elsewhere in China still suffuses even the most trivial bargaining of the blue-tunicked peasants who hawk fleshy slabs of bean curd, racks of noodles, pears, apples, and the weird obscurata of Chinese medicine in the town's gray-brick lanes. Qufu's citizens know there is something different about themselves. I asked a vendor of skewered hawthorne fruit what he thought Confucius had given Qufu. He readily replied, "He made us more civilized."

THINGS WERE said about Kong Fanyin; that he had sacrificed himself for the clan, that he had collaborated with the Communists, that he had somehow saved the mansion during the chaos of the Cultural Revolution. Later it seemed to me that Kong Fanyin had one remarkable stroke of good luck in his life, and one remarkable stroke of bad luck, which occurred almost simultaneously. In 1947, the seventy-sixth duke paused in his flight to Taiwan to appoint him overseer of the clan's ancestral home. Then, less than two years later, the Communist revolution overthrew everything the clan had represented since it was founded in the sixth century B.C. and transformed Kong Fanyin into a virtual prisoner in the labyrinth of secluded courtyards, ornate halls, and serpentine passageways he had been left to guard.

Kong Fanyin first entered the mansion in the 1930s as a playmate for the last duke, Kong Decheng. Kong Fanyin was allowed to remain as the mansion's vice-director when the Communists confiscated it in the 1950s. He was now a stout sixty-two, with silvery hairs sprinkling lip and chin, and he bore himself with the stately wariness of a patrician who only barely survived the trauma of revolutionary politics, trundling along gamely despite the autumn heat in a Krushchevian overcoat squeezed over the sort of high-buttoned suit that is de rigueur among provincial Chinese officials.

We passed behind the high white wall that enclosed the once-forbidden realm of the Kongs, past the Gate of Reenlightenment with its sculpted cargo of dragons and billowing clouds, into the lofty hall from which the Yancheng dukes had ruled as lords over the surrounding countryside. All around us wooden staves bore the arcane emblems of bygone power: stylized dragons, carved melons and stirrups, symbolic halberds, pikes, and clubs. I thought, what a sight it must have been when the dukes traveled out into the world of lesser mortals! Trembling townsmen melted into the alleys, or froze with their faces to the ground, as runners hurtled by with vermilion boards on which gilded calligraphy proclaimed the privileges of another age: "Wearer of the Two-eyed Peacock Feather," "Possessor of the Yellow Ribbon of the First Grade," "Duke of the Continuing Line." The duke swung magisterially along in their wake, suspended from porters' shoulders in his silver sedan chair amid brigades of retainers dressed in parrot-bright silks, whose sole purpose was to awe.

"You have been to Taiwan?" Kong Fanyin asked.

I sensed what he wanted to talk about, and that he couldn't bring himself to be blunt. But it was hard to make the connection between these graceful, decaying halls and the traffic, smog, and twentieth-century chaos of Taipei, the boring fundamentalist interpreter from the Ministry of Information chattering at me all the way out through the steamy Formosan hills, and the vague old man that I knew Kong Fanyin wanted to talk about.

"I have been there," I said.

I waited. But the silence lengthened politely, as I knew it would. Kong Fanyin trundled along, letting the exchange hover pregnantly as we went on.

The mansion spread through scores of colonnaded courtyards that opened out geometrically from each other, eventually to embrace more than four hundred rooms. Each one of them represented another cell in what was once a vast human mosaic of minuscule responsibilities and endlessly subdivided power. A "human lock" posted at each gate and threshold used to bar the way to unauthorized visitors and see to it that no mansion underling ventured beyond the few square meters he was allotted for his work.

Kong Fanyin showed me the drafty alcove where, years ago, he decided what messages from the outer world would be sent on into the mansion's sanctum. It was a heady and perhaps lucrative power in the days before telephones and fax machines. A yellowed scroll on the wall somewhat ambiguously proclaimed: "When I serve society, I serve myself."

The ink-stones and brushes that Kong Fanyin had used were set out on his work table, artifacts now. He climbed lumpily into the sleeping alcove, pulled out a brass censer, and set it on a table close to the door.

"Each thing where it belongs," he said.

At the peak of its power, the Kong clan was the biggest landowner in China, with 160,000 acres of land worked by hundreds of thousands of tenant farmers. At the turn of the century, the mansion maintained five hundred servants, including two opera companies and an entire family whose sole, hereditary duty was to trim the ducal dinners with beansprouts. Almost every room had its own ghosts and spirits. A snake that lived above the door of one hall was believed to have practiced Buddhism and become a deity. Books had their own souls; several volumes periodically transformed themselves into a young woman and inhabited the library. Tutors schooled Kong Decheng and Kong Fanyin exclusively in the Confucian classics. They were required to memorize them not only in the correct sentence order but backwards as well; two generations later, the Maoists taught the Red Guards to learn the Chairman's *Little Red Book* the same way.

The Yancheng duke's imperial stipend was cut off after the revolution of 1911, and Confucianism was discredited as the ideology of the ancien régime. Gifts no longer flowed into the Kong mansion, and the system of selling official posts was abolished, leaving the family with no cash income. Vast properties slipped from their control through neglect and poor management. Kong Demao, Kong Decheng's elder sister, recalls in her poignant memoir of life in the mansion that by the time the seventy-fifth duke died in 1919, the clan was so impoverished that it was reduced to borrowing money even "for an oil lamp cover or a glass of wine."

The clan was effectively ruled after the seventy-fifth duke's death by his chief consort, Madam Tao. She was an almost tragically ugly woman, with a peculiar peanut-shaped face. She was also one of those extraordinarily ruthless women who recur throughout Chinese history, whose innate intelligence was warped into cruelty by a society that feared female power. She had the added misfortune of barrenness. Although Madam Tao claimed the duke's three children, including Decheng, as her own by virtue of her seniority, they were in fact all born to a concubine of lowly origins.

Kong Fanyin showed me a photograph of the concubine Wang that was hanging on the wall of the women's apartments. It was old and blurred, but the fleshy cheeks and blank gaze still conveyed an impression of appealing mildness, of fatal passivity. As a concubine, she owed Madam Tao absolute obedience; Confucian tradition demanded it. Madam Tao hated Wang for her fertility. Every evening after dinner she ordered the concubine to strip and kneel naked on the floor, and then flogged her with a whip. When she was finished, she made the concubine kowtow to her to "express her gratitude."

Madam Tao knew that Wang's status would instantly rise if she delivered a male heir, and that her own would correspondingly decline. On the seventeenth day after Kong Decheng's birth, Madam Tao forced the concubine to drink poison. According to Kong Demao, "Mother knelt on her bed, imploring Madam Tao not to make her take the medicine, as she was not ill. Madam Tao was of course unmoved and insisted that she drink it. Madam Wang said, 'I'd love to see the children.' But even this humble request was not to be satisfied, for mother saw none of us again."

The mansion's inmates were only dimly aware of the tide of anti-Confucian sentiment that was sweeping China. When word reached them that local students intended to stage a play about Confucius in the street outside the mansion, "We all clamored to see it, particularly since we'd heard that there were girl students taking part, a real novelty," Kong Demao recalled. Since tradition forbade Kong ladies to venture into the streets, Madam Tao led Kong Demao and the other children to an earthen pile at a corner of the wall where, hidden by silken curtains, they could watch the activities of the commoners in the street beyond. Kong Demao was terror-stricken when Confucius appeared on stage.

"The image was entirely different from his statue in the Hall of Great Achievements. His face was coarse and vulgar and smeared all over with kettle-black. I still remember him pointing to Heaven and bellowing, 'If I had wrong ideas, Heaven would detest me!' "

Below the stage, clapping mingled with shouts of "Down with Madam Tao!"

Kong Demao was sitting at Madam Tao's side.

"Although she remained silent, I could feel her whole body shaking. Turning to look at her I found her face ashen, clouded by an unforgettable expression of gloom."

Later that night, Madam Tao collapsed on her bed. She remained insane until her death in 1930.

We probed through narrow passageways into courtyards plumed with lilacs and punctuated with ornamental rocks that boiled and foamed like frozen surf. The largest—a monster ten feet or more in height—seemed less to be stone at all than a raw slab of the Tao itself set on a pedestal, as evanescent as mist or steam. Kong Fanyin told me it had been put there to contain the earth's benevolent energies, to prevent them from seeping out and trickling away; it was the linchpin of the entire mansion, a mystical fulcrum on which the Kongs believed the safety of all their elegant halls and their own lives turned.

"Did you make many friends in Taiwan?" Kong Fanyin asked.
"One or two."

Again I sensed the unasked question. Kong Fanyin's formality enforced a distance between us. I wanted to tell him what I had felt in Taipei, but I knew the emotion would embarrass him.

In hall after hall, vestiges of the vanished world hung in musty suspension, like fruit in aspic. Confucian austerity blended with patrician opulence to produce compositions of extraordinary power and grace. Slim rosewood chairs confronted each other beneath scrolls that exploded with monochromatic bursts of calligraphy. Marble tables teemed with cloisonné elephants, grave ivory sages, porcelain vases, rococo clocks, ornamental trees carved of medicinal fungus, and life-sized chrysanthemums made of coral, jade, and lapis lazuli. On the walls hung paintings of butterflies, wrens, peach blossoms, strange rocks, and plums; I disliked one of a peony in a vase, and I remarked on its coarseness. "It was a personal gift from the Empress Dowager to the seventy-fifth duke," Kong Fanyin said. "For an empress it's perhaps not so bad."

Chinese tourists, spitting a hail of melon seeds and gobbling slabs of poppy-seed candy, clambered on each other's backs to press against the windows of a suite that had been left untouched since Kong Decheng's 1936 wedding. Dusty red silk swathed every table and chair, and the walls still spoke with faded felicitations from forgotten or executed Kuomintang dignitaries. Here were their gifts, now mesmerizing a generation for whom handwrought beauty was just a historical memory: scepters of sandalwood and jade, bundles of never-opened silk, cut glass, goblets, silverware, and, incongruously, pink-porcelain hurricane lamps. The wedding had been the Kongs' final extravagance before the twentieth-century's politics at last brought an end to their power.

"So you have met Kong Decheng," Kong Fanyin finally said.

At last Kong Fanyin was ready.

"Can you tell us news of him? He hasn't written in forty years."

I remembered. The offices of the Examination Yuan lay in a low, nondescript office building in the hills east of the Taiwanese capital. Plush white armchairs and green jade ashtrays were spaced with geometric precision around the walls of the reception room beneath icons of Sun Yatsen and Chiang Kaishek. A uniformed servant produced cups of aromatic tea and dumplings filled with meat.

The round-shouldered, sixty-nine-year-old man might have been any midranking bureaucrat. But I couldn't resist the impression of history itself shuffling toward me on frail old-man's legs. This was the last Yancheng duke, heir to the blood of Confucius, whose line was already unimaginably ancient in the time of Genghis Khan and Marco Polo, already old when the Roman Empire was born, and stretched back still further past the first imperial stirrings of Qinshihuangdi, beyond the age of Pericles and Aristotle.

History wore a blue-gray business suit, and smiled blandly, and greeted me with a feathery handshake. As a child, he had been the polestar around which the universe of the vast Kong clan revolved. His toys were pearls and kingfisher feathers, agate and gold. Clan elders addressed him as "grandfather" out of respect for his rank. Scores of servants ministered to his whims. As a teenager, he presided over 130-course banquets for Chiang Kaishek and the now-forgotten warlords of Shandong.

I wanted too much. I longed to know how it felt to possess twenty-five centuries of documented history as one's own, as if it bestowed some ultimate key to time itself. But History shied deftly away. When I asked him how he felt about his connection with Confucius, he said, "I don't want to feel noble. I want to feel the same as the common people."

Kong Decheng* reached with small, supple, aristocratic fingers into an inner pocket, found a cigar, and after lighting it began to puff with incongruous gusto. The ordinariness was studied and self-conscious, and it was ultimately defeated by the vaporous, old-fashioned reticence that clung to him like a mist.

The Nationalists had put Kong Decheng in charge of the Examination Yuan, which was responsible for all school and civil service tests given in Taiwan. When I asked him what relevance he thought Confucianism had for the modern world, his reply had the ring of official ideology.

* Taiwan retains the old form of romanization; "Kong Decheng" in Qufu thus becomes "Kung Te-cheng" in Taipei. For the sake of clarity I have used a single form throughout.

"Why have Hong Kong, Singapore, South Korea, and Taiwan made such great economic progress in recent years? Because in a Confucian society, bosses and workers don't see themselves as antagonists, but as brothers who have a duty to cooperate with one another."

I tried to get him to talk about the home in Qufu that he had not seen for forty-two years, but he eluded me again. "I thought things would be the way they had always been," he said. "I never imagined that they could change." When China's civil war began, however, Communist troops rapidly advanced on Qufu. Kong Decheng was in immediate danger of falling into their hands, and he fled. Despite the easing of travel between the two Chinas, as a government official he was still barred by the Taiwanese regime from visiting the People's Republic. "But I can never forget the place of my ancestors' graves," he said with the faintest wisp of emotion.

The line of Yancheng dukes had already ended. The title had been retired long ago, even before the revolution. Kong Decheng's children had never seen China. His son worked in an American bank in Taipei; his daughter, who was married to an American, lived in the United States.

"Will he ever return to us?" Kong Fanyin asked me.

I had asked Kong Decheng the same question.

"He told me," I said, " 'I shall see my home again when the Republic of China reclaims the mainland.' "

It was a way of saying never.

I asked Kong Fanyin how it felt to belong to the "First Family Under Heaven," as the Kongs used to be called.

"One was honored to belong to the line of the most important Chinese who ever lived," he replied distantly. "But one was expected to behave perfectly in accordance with the sage's teachings. Anything less was considered a sin."

I wanted more. I wanted what I had failed to get from Kong Decheng, some kind of proof of connection with Confucius across that stupendous span of time.

"It's difficult to say," he said, with the familiar formula that Chinese use to deflect unwelcome questions.

We sparred for a while longer. I knew my curiosity intruded on that hidden courtyard of the self where every Chinese lives his real life.

"Confucius lived a long time ago," Kong Fanyin at last said, expressionlessly, leaving me to make of it what I would. "But I can see him very close to me, intimately. He has not gone away."

Before he left me, Kong Fanyin said, "If you see Kong Decheng again, tell him that we miss him. Tell him, 'Please come home.' "

CONFUCIUS DID feel startlingly close. But then the prairies and alps and seas of Chinese history seemed to have taken on a strange intimacy in Qufu, to have become as concrete and immediate as foliage in a landscape, or furniture in a room. The sage's home had been memorialized for so long that the monuments had become indistinguishable from the things they honored. A gray-brick cottage of antique design marked the site of Confucius's house and opened on a patch of the cobbled lane he had walked; nearby, a red-columned hall stood where the sage had taught his son rites and poetry, and beyond it lay the family well, and a bit of old wall to commemorate the place where his writings were hidden during China's first book-burning cultural revolution in the third century B.C. As late as the beginning of this century, the Kongs possessed a carriage that they believed Confucius himself had driven through the streets of Lu, as Qufu was known in ancient times.

Confucius was born to a family of impoverished aristocrats in 551 B.C., a generation before the Buddha, and he died in 479 B.C., a decade before the birth of Socrates. Traditional pictures (there is no reason to think that any of them are authentic) portray Confucius as a whiskery old chap with fat cheeks and an opaque gaze. All that is reliably known about him is contained in the small book known as the *Analects,* which was compiled after his death from his disciples' recollections. Nevertheless, it is revealing. The great sage was clearly not a very happy man. He wandered for years among the feudal states of eastern China in search of a prince who would allow him to put his theories of government into practice, complaining that he felt "like a gourd that is fit only to be hung on the wall and is never put to use."

He longed for an ideal past when, he imagined, sons perfectly obeyed their fathers, and commoners their kings. He was impatient with pretension, and more than a little cranky. "If the mat is not straight he does not sit on it," the *Analects* reported. And when he ran into an acquaintance who had wasted his life, he knocked him with his cane and snapped, "Growing old and not dying is just being a pest!" Confucius eventually returned to his house in Qufu, where he became the first professional teacher in Chinese history, holding forth beneath a backyard apricot tree to aspiring young politicians in what was a sort of *Ecole Nationale d'Administration* of its day. The Revered Master espoused the novel idea that the purpose of government was to make people happy, and that those who ruled should do so by moral example rather than force; when a local satrap asked him how to deal with widespread thievery, he replied, "If only you were not so avaricious yourself, they would not steal even if you paid them to." But he was also a realist in a ruthless age. "See much, but ignore what it is dangerous to have seen, and be cautious in acting upon the rest."

Confucianism provided a comprehensive dogma of public ethics, private morality, and family values that was less a religion than a variety of atheism. Confucius had no interest at all in the mystical, insisting instead that man's chief purpose was to act virtuously on the earth: "To see when he looks, to hear when he listens, to be gentle in his looks, to be respectful in his manners, to be faithful in words, to be earnest in service, to inquire when in doubt, to think of consequences when in anger, to think of justice when he sees an advantage."

Convinced that truth lay in the past, and wisdom in imitation of the honored dead, he taught men to fear the unfamiliar. He warned, "It is indeed harmful to come under the sway of utterly new and strange doctrines." His ideal world was one of perfectly ritualized order. He declared, "Speak nothing contrary to the rites; do nothing contrary to the rites"; there were, he no doubt dauntingly added, three hundred rules of major ritual and three thousand minor observances that had to be mastered before a man could even hope to govern. But above all else he valued loyalty and obedience. "The ruler is like the wind and the common people are like the grass," he told his disciples. "When the wind blows, the grass bends."

Confucianism served as the official state cult from the Han

Dynasty (210 B.C. to A.D. 206) until the abdiction of the last emperor in 1912. Candidates for government office were selected through national examinations that measured their knowledge of the Confucian classics. The system produced a professional administration that was, at least in theory, open to any man in the empire. Reports of what was then the world's only impartially selected civil service eventually reached Europe and influenced the philosophes of the Enlightenment, inspiring Voltaire to write *The Orphan of China,* in which he extolled the Confucian bureaucracy as the quintessence of rationalism. The Chinese examiners considered deviant interpretations of the classics heretical, however, and allowed so little scope for originality that by the end of the empire they were grading the essays on the basis of the candidates' calligraphy.

According to tradition, Confucius was born on the slopes of a small mountain twenty miles east of Qufu. I hired a car one afternoon and drove there along a road carpeted with slices of sweet potatoes that peasants had spread over the pavement to dry, through fields where farmers harnessed like oxen to wooden plows were turning stubble for the planting of winter wheat. Eventually a line of dry hills emerged from the haze and became a landscape of scree and terraces, and unexpected aqueducts that marched toward the lowlands with a Mediterranean grace.

An old temple marked the site. Its gray and yellow roofs swept up from a copse of splintered junipers that rose as majestically as the Confucian virtue they used to symbolize. But the brick paths were overgrown and the courtyards empty except for clumps of stelae crowned with dragons frozen in a wild, cloud-riddled embrace. Shreds of oiled paper flapped from the latticed windows.

An old man was wandering among the junipers, passing time with his infant grandson. He wore a cotton skullcap and padded trousers tied like puttees at the calves.

"Confucius?" he repeated, tilting his head. "I heard things about him when I was a boy, but whatever it was I've forgotten."

Probably he was afraid of talking to a foreigner. But it was also possible that he really knew nothing of the sage. Confucius had always been the exclusive property of the literati. "Great imbeciles," the Sacred Edict of the Kangxi emperor had called the peasants. "The rituals are exceedingly numerous. If we were to mention them, you people would necessarily be unable to learn them."

The old man directed me to a village just over the hill. "Somebody might know something there." Some boys pointed me toward a rustic compound of roughhewn stone.

"She's the one you should talk to. She owns a TV set."

A flat-faced woman with a soup-bowl haircut peered smilingly over the wall.

"No, I don't know much about him. I was in school during the Cultural Revolution time, and we didn't even mention his name except to curse it."

I climbed back over the hill to the cave where Confucius was supposed to have been born. A boy in a cut-down army jacket stopped to gawk. There were some stories, he said.

"Baby Kong was so ugly that his parents abandoned him on the hillside to die. A tiger found him and carried him to her lair, where she fed him from her own tit. She knew right away that he was chosen by Heaven. She saved his life, you see."

There was another story about an eagle who fanned the infant with its wing, and another about a well that bent over of its own accord to pour him water.

"Do you believe those stories?"

"Of course. Otherwise the tiger would have eaten him, wouldn't she?"

I supposed he had studied something of Confucius in school.

"Nothing, sir. I can't read."

The boy turned to wave from some distance down the trail. I shouted at him to tell me his name.

"Kong, sir. Kong."

I WAS SITTING in my courtyard, behind the Hall of Loyalty and Forbearance. I felt at peace in the musty silence, folded away from the world. I was reading a part of the *Analects* that concerns Confucius's favorite disciple, Yan Hui. I read: "With a handful of rice and a gourdful of water he dwelt in an alley. Yan Hui was a man of the highest calibre!" Qufu's symmetries were unnerving. Kong Fanyin had told me that Yan's descendants were still numerous around the town. "But they are all very poor. They do nothing but study all the time." Time seemed to turn peculiarly back on itself like a Möbius strip.

Suddenly a camera crew boiled from the arcade in a welter of floodlights and cables, and into the suite next to mine. Tad and Tina explained that Richard Nixon had stayed in it on his last trip to China.

Tad was lean and buoyant and full of effervescent enthusiam. Tina had a chest of seismic dimensions, a freeze-dried bouffant, and the North American lust for unresolved similes. She hosted a midwestern cable TV show and he produced it.

They were gathering material for programs on Chinese religion. "Like Buddhism, Taoism, and Confucianism," Tina said. They had previously done shows on Barbados, Jamaica, and the Yucatán. They liked the Yucatán best.

"Like all those pyramids, with those really weird alignments," Tina explained. "Like the Mayans. Like they just disappeared. We didn't want to be too intellectual about it, but we felt we had a responsibility to let people know about all those connections with the ETs and outer space."

"We dig into something and get the whole cultural dimension, what people really think and believe," said Tad. "It's like 'Lifestyles of the Rich and Famous' except it focuses on travel."

Their best interview so far had been with a pair of China Travel Service guides who said they could move objects and influence people through the manipulation of psychic energy.

"Beautiful guys," said Tad.

"Tad's going to be the next Steven Spielberg," Tina said. He was developing a children's show about robots that flew over the earth and zoomed down to explore things that interested them.

"It was supposed to be a sort of *Star Wars* for a half-hour each week, but we had to scale it down."

Tina had started out as a magazine-show hostess. After that she tried to break into films.

"My best one was about a rock band that comes to a small town where the people think there's something satanic about them, and like they really are satanic. Eventually somebody sets fire to the concert hall and they like vaporize."

"I'm not sure Confucianism was a religion," I said.

"It doesn't matter." said Tina. "It's TV."

THE SYMBOLIC heart of Confucianism was the great temple at Qufu. You enter it today as every temple has been entered since the dawn of Chinese time, from the south, stepping through a tunneled gate in a rose-madder wall onto a marble causeway that progresses through solemn courtyard after courtyard like the eerie and majestic music of ancient China. Tablets over every gate shout the sage's epithets: "Innately Wise," and then "Moral Source for Ten Thousand Generations." You pass through a forest of eight-hundred-year-old cypresses, across a camelback bridge whose balustrades fly on sculpted clouds, and into a courtyard filled with age-splintered junipers, to a wall still scarred with the slogans of the Cultural Revolution; beneath a halfhearted coat of red wash they shriek, "Long Live Chairman Mao!"

You pass through a theatrical gate into a forest of stelae (one says, "Confucius is like food and clothes; without him China never can prosper") mounted upon snarling tortoises, to step at last, in grand crescendo, into the very navel of Confucian China, where the great frigate of the sage's sanctum cruises upon an elevated sea of marble, its upswept eaves billowing like wind-filled sails against the cerulean sky of East China. Over the altar, a tablet proclaims: "Source of Civilization."

In imperial times, few people were permitted to enter its precincts, and those who did came tense and atremble. Even Confucian rationalism succumbed to the impulses of an epoch when panoply was power. Twice a year the gates were flung open and the sage's spirit was invited in, as if it hovered, palpable as the smoke of the city's cook fires, in the air outside. Great drums boomed into the night. Torches threw flickering shadows across the opulent robes of the officiants; in the half-light, the gilded dragons seemed to writhe and leap from the temple's colonnade, while boys brandishing pheasants' feathers danced with infinite gravity to the stony echo of jade chimes. A chorus chanted: "Oh, great Kongzi! Prior in perception! Prior in knowledge! Co-equal with Heaven and Earth! The sun and moon are sustained by thee. Heaven and earth are kept pure by thee. Thou art what never else was since men were generated!"

The sanctum now shelters a new, rather garishly painted plaster image of Confucius; a museum of Han stone carvings occupies the galleries that formerly contained the gilt name-tablets of the seventy-two Confucian sages. Today's celebrants are Chinese tourists, garbed in the blue jeans, Eisenhower jackets, and ill-fitting Western suits that have become the unofficial uniform of post-Maoist China, and who surge with an ear-cracking roar through the lofty halls.

I asked a buck-toothed miner who was there with a busload of his mates why they had come. "Because we don't have to condemn Master Kong anymore," he slyly replied. "Because he is permitted."

I sat down next to an old man who was seated in the kiosk that marks the site of the sage's apricot tree. His face was moon-cool, his eyes heavy-lidded. He wore a rumpled black Mao suit and a cap pulled tightly down on a large bony skull.

"When people came here in the old days, their minds were empty of everything but the Master's presence," he said. "They were afraid even to breathe. In those days we always looked back to what the last generation did. Things were always in order."

I could understand how angry young Chinese must have been in the days when Confucianism was an orthodoxy to be overthrown, how impatient with the mindless imitation of the past, the empty ritual, the moralizing double-talk. But there had been more than that. You could still feel it here in Qufu. I remembered the remark the hawthorne-fruit vendor had made to me: "We are more civilized." It was said without pretension, as a simple matter of fact. People in Qufu had a self-possession that I had met nowhere else in China, that quality that George Kates had called "rubbed," the sense of a people immensely old and sure of itself, without edges.

I was watching the Chinese tourists shoving their way toward the sanctum and kneeling in phalanxes to snap each other's photos on the sacred terrace. They were much better dressed than I remembered from five years before, in well-cut jeans, running shoes, and sporty jackets and frocks. Their complexions were ruddier, better nourished. There was more body language. The difference was striking to me. I wondered whether the old man thought people were much better off now.

"People don't follow the set procedures."

His hands lay limply in his lap; his voice was gentle. But beneath the moon-cool gaze I could see that he was livid with rage.

"These days, anything can happen," he said. "Things are a mess."

Did he mean since the abandonment of Confucian orthodoxy, or since the easing of Communist control? I couldn't tell. I tried to ask him, but he didn't want to talk to me anymore.

ONE DAY I went to Qufu Normal University to meet Li Jinshan, who is the director of the Confucius Foundation of China. He was in his fifties, and flat-bodied and compact, like a well-shaped tool. It was immediately clear that he was a Party official, whose main job was probably to ride herd on the genuine academics, who sat in silence through the entire conversation. I wondered how the official attitude toward Confucius had changed since 1949.

"There has never been an official line," Li declared.

He was lying, of course. As he spoke, his right knee began to jog up and down. It was a tic that recurred every time I touched a sensitive political nerve.

After the 1949 revolution, Confucius was regarded simply as a more-or-less contemptible mouthpiece for feudalism. During the Cultural Revolution, his works were banned completely, and the mere accusation that a person had been influenced by Confucianism was sufficient to ruin a career.

"What happened in Qufu during the Cultural Revolution?" I asked.

"Things were abnormal," Li replied. His knee was now pumping violently. "There were complications."

What exactly did that mean?

I waited for an answer. The silence lengthened painfully. Li's whole leg was bouncing wildly, almost out of control. Everyone in the room was staring at it.

The truth is, the Red Guards invaded the Temple of Confucius. They scoured the tablets of Confucius, of the sage's parents, of the four great disciples, and of the seventy-two sages from their crimson altars and, like so much kindling, burned them to cinders. Then they hitched a truck to the bronze images of Confucius and his disciples, pulled them out like tree stumps, and dragged them in a procession through the streets of Qufu, shouting, "Down with the Confucian curiosity shop!" Then they smashed the statues to pieces with sledgehammers. Kong Fanyin saved the mansion and the clan archives by arguing that they should be preserved as "evidence" of the "criminal atrocities" the Kongs had committed. The Red Guards publicly tortured him anyway on the Drum Tower at the center of town. Later, they marched to the clan cemetery, where every Kong for the last twenty-five centuries has been buried. There they looted the tombs and threw the shriveled corpses of the sage's descendents on the ground amid their jades and ivories, and yellowed and crumbling silks.

"As time goes on, we find that more and more people are interested in Confucius," Li said disingenuously. "Nowadays, we must study Confucius in order to further the country's modernization. We must carry on our traditions so that we can realize both our material and spiritual civilization."

Li's knee stopped jogging. He was back on the safe ground of official policy. Nevertheless, it struck me as an extraordinary admission.

"We take a pragmatic view now," he said. "We should take what we can from Confucius. We mustn't throw the baby out with the bath water."

LATER I ran into Tad and Tina in the restaurant of the Queli Hotel. The menu advertised "Confucian" dishes from the Kong Mansion kitchens. I wanted one that was intriguingly named "Golden Hooks with Silver Bars." I asked the waitress what it was but she looked uncertain.

"Is it meat?"

"No."

"Fish?"

"Not fish."

"Vegetable then."

"No."

"What is it then?"

"It's hard to say."

"Bring it anyway."

Tad and Tina seemed frustrated. They had come from an interview with Li Jinshan.

"He didn't say very much," Tina said, perplexed. "I even read part of the *Analects* before we went."

"Nobody could beat Dr. Wu," said Tad.

"Dr. Wu?"

"You don't know him?" Tina asked in astonishment. "He was Mao's doctor. He's like one of the most famous people in China."

"Beautiful guy," said Tad. "We did him in Beijing."

I asked how he had fared during the Cultural Revolution.

"He said the revolution was still continuing."

"The Cultural Revolution?"

Tina looked a little uncertain.

"Which one was that? Was that the same as the other one?"

"Which one?"

"You know, the revolution. You know?"

Tad and Tina were leaving the next day for the coast.

"We only scheduled two days for Confucianism."

"Anyway," she said, "our *qigong* master is going to send us a psychic letter back home on Saturday. We've got to be there to get it."

Qigong is an ancient discipline, both physical and spiritual, whose adepts believe they have the power to manipulate the cosmic breath, the *qi* that vitalizes all things.

Tina was peeved. I assumed it was because they had too little time in Qufu. But I was wrong. She was annoyed at Confucius.

"I don't see what's the big deal. You ought to know all that stuff by the time you're seven."

"Confucius said, 'Do unto others,' " Tad ventured. "Something like that. It's almost Christian. I kind of like it."

Tina wasn't going to be placated.

Tad looked hurt. He clearly didn't like conflict. Tina saw that she had wounded him. She smiled.

"I guess maybe two thousand years ago people had to study that stuff because it was new to them," she said.

"You have to take people on their own terms," Tad said.

"Tad's really sensitive," said Tina.

They beamed at each other. They were in love.

"There just doesn't seem to be anything really profound in it," said Tina. "You keep looking for the mystery, but it just isn't there."

"You're right, it isn't there," said Tad.

But there were mysteries in Qufu.

The waitress said, " 'Golden Hooks and Silver Bars' all finished."

THE NEXT morning I walked the two or three miles to the Kong clan's burial ground down a road that was Qufu's main street in Confucius's day but now stretched arrow-straight between empty autumn fields. When the Yancheng duke visited his ancestors' graves he was accompanied, according to Kong Demao, by "four men with gongs, two men carrying censers, two personal servants from the Inner Apartments, three grooms, four coachmen, eight sedan-chair bearers, one relief-sedan-bearer, two sedan-chair assistants, four major footmen and five minor footmen, one regular attendant, fifteen family servants, numerous ceremonial guardsmen, two men from the Worship the Shadows Hall, minor servants from the Temple of Confucius, a cushion bearer, a man carrying sacrificial offerings, two men with tea, two with silver, one kitchen boy, four tall-hatted officials, and one firecracker handler." When a duke died, an "Earth-Purging Official" led two platoons of cavalry armed with rifles in an assault on the cemetery, where they battled in shadow play with its ghosts until they forced them to flee.

It was the day upon which offerings were traditionally made to the dead. Men and women, most of them dressed in peasants' blues, were streaming lumpily toward the vast walled enclosure to pay their respects to their more illustrious ancestors. In the past, they would have made offerings of rice liquor and food, and burned quantities of printed "spirit money" so the dead might buy everything they wanted in the netherworld. But that had all been banned by the Communists as superstition. Police with bullhorns were stopping everyone at the gate and searching them for wads of concealed toilet paper that were intended to serve as makeshift spirit money; whatever they found, they confiscated and threw into an oven at the side of the road.

The gate debouched into a forest of cypresses and pistachio trees. It was a very strange place, intensely grave and beautiful, dense with the spirits of the wisest and noblest men who had ever walked the Chinese earth, and populated by heraldic ranks of mandarins and soldiers, lions, hounds, and camels carved in stone and poised in weathered pairs before hundreds of stone altars. Confucius's tomb was a simple mound marked by a slender stele, a place utterly free of pomposity and emphasizing instead the modesty and humility that the sage insisted were the deepest virtues of truly good men. Empty over-grown graves still gaped where the Red Guards had done their work.

Somehow, some of the Kongs had smuggled their wadded paper through the cordon. Telltale gusts of smoke rose from little fires in front of the graves, while ghostly figures in blue boiler suits wandered amid a rain of yellow leaves, searching for relatives' tombs. Police in sidecars were patrolling the forest roads, on the prowl for worshipers, and even as I watched, a pair of them snatched away a heap of smoldering paper from a shamefaced man as he knelt before an ancestor's tomb.

As I wandered through the forest, I wondered what the new Confucianism might turn out to be. I doubted that even amid a ruined communism Confucius could ever be venerated with the superhuman awe that he enjoyed through more than two thousand years of Chinese history. It seemed safe to say, however, that he was destined to play a role of some kind in the Chinese future. Before my eyes, Kongs were climbing over the cemetery wall, passing their bicycles over from hand to hand along with great bales of paper, surging in twos and threes and groups of half a dozen through the perfumed trees toward the ancestors' graves, smiling and unstoppable.

CHAPTER
SEVEN

The Mountain God

HE CITY of Taian had traded on its mountain for three thousand years. Now it was trying to convert pilgrimage into tourism. The waitresses in the hotel restaurant wore English names on plastic tags: "Mindy," "Denise," "Angela." There were mirrored walls in the coffee shop and color televisions in the rooms; one night I watched a variety show in which a man in a jump suit drilled elderly men and women in disco dancing under a strobe, and after that a People's Liberation Army chorus sang a song entitled "Communism Is Good." Across the alley, pet birds twittered amid hoarded lumber, bottles, and coal on the balconies of disintegrating apartments.

Beyond them was the mountain that was a god: Taishan. Chinese of the old world worshiped it as the greatest of the sacred peaks, birthplace of the sun, source of the primal breath that gave rise to the sap in plants and men, root of all life. Taishan was not the home of the gods, an Olympus; it was the deity, its clefts and earth a sacred flesh. Taishan stones were carried all over China, and when a house was built with an unlucky aspect that invited misfortune a rock would be built into the wall and inscribed, "Taishan accepts the responsibility."

The Chinese visualized Taishan as a sort of supreme bureaucrat with drooping moustaches and tufted chin, attended by the mandarins of the celestial bureaucracy that managed all earthly affairs. The great sinologist Eduard Chavannes wrote at the turn of the century, "The emperor and the Taishan god seem like two high-ranking dignitaries, more or less equal, whom the Sky has appointed to ensure the people's happiness; one through his wise government created harmony and virtue among men, the other used his controlling influence to maintain order in the physical world." Taishan stabilized the earth by its sheer weight, prevented earthquakes and floods, gave birth to the life-giving clouds, which at a command made the harvest grow and enriched the world.

From the earliest times, pilgrims came to pay the mountain obeisance. The most pious climbed on their knees; coolies known as "mountain-climbing tigers" muscled the less staunch over the crags in low-slung sedan chairs. Emperors ascended in sumptuous processions that wound up the mountain from its piny foot to the cloud-cradled summit eight thousand feet above.

There is a mural in the old temple at the foot of the mountain that depicts the Zhen Zong emperor's pilgrimage in 1008. Horsemen in bamboo armor, wing-hatted mandarins, legions of attendants travel out from the capital in a welter of fans and banners. Slaves beat gongs and drums. Dragoons gallop on paisley chimeras, flailing at invisible spirits. Guards in red-tufted helmets tug dragonets on leashes as if they were spaniels. There are elephants and camels, chargers with their chests puffed like partridges, and nightmare creatures with tails that stream behind them like green flame. The emperor travels amidst them in a thronelike canopied carriage, impassive and hieratic, swollen with power. As the procession rises into the god's domain the landscape becomes peculiar. Rocks seem to breathe and pulsate with life. Blue mountains swirl and churn like ocean waves. Inky trees loom like atomic clouds. Finally the Son of Heaven arrives at a fairy temple suspended weightlessly in the clouds, a god meeting a god in conclave.

It is disturbing to the Western eye, this blending of the real and the not-real. But the pilgrimage was a metaphysical event, a transformation; to ascend Taishan was to rise from the human to the celestial, to enter temporarily into the sacred chaos of primal energy.

I planned to spend the night on the peak, to await the dawn; the Taishan dawn was embedded almost mythically in the Chinese psyche, a root image of genesis and rebirth. The revolution had colonized the ancient idea with new associations. Communism was called the "red sun rising in the east." Sometimes Mao himself was referred to as the "Great Sun." The intended image was always the dawn at Taishan. It was endlessly repeated in vast paintings that still hang in hotels and public buildings all over China.

I set off along a trail that wound gently upward at first, through a forest of pines and cedars. Stalls alongside the path sold spirit money smuggled from Hong Kong ("currency for the other world," it said), fat plaster babies, narrow-waisted gourds from which the mystics believed all creation issued, fungus like frozen yang—Taoist paraphernalia reincarnated as tourist trinkets, persistent relics of the ancient unconscious. A stone arch proclaimed: "Stairway to the Sky." Then I passed through a tunneled gate and into the realm of the god.

The Shandong Plain disappeared into an ugly sepia smog that plumed hundreds of feet into the air. For the first time since I entered China I felt free of the encroaching present. There was an immense silence except for a breeze that ruffled through the dry leaves. Naked trees on distant slopes were a pale gray haze, like mother-of-pearl. The dilapidated shrines along the trail were almost beside the point, mere punctuation of the vaulting emptiness.

Coolies jogged past me with live chickens in baskets, plastic jugs of oil, bales of cabbage, spinach, Coca Cola, and slabs of squid in panniers slung from each end of a flexible pole, the most ancient mode of Chinese haulage. They were short-legged, sinewy men, and they smoked and swigged from bottles of rice wine as they danced up with an odd sidling rhythm that enabled them to keep their loads half-suspended in the air with each step.

When Chavannes climbed Taishan in 1907, you could still see the plaintive stelae that had been erected by generations of emperors. "When rain is scarce, when the corn wilts in the fields and the peasants begin to fear famine," an emperor of the Ming dynasty proclaimed, "the sovereign of men appeals to the majestic Peak who can and should put an end to misfortune. In times of earthquake or flood appropriate prayers are made to remind Taishan of his duties as the lord of the region, inviting him to restore it to order." The language suggested the latent terror of a world where even the earth and the gods could not be wholly trusted; the nudging reminders were revealing too, as was the barely veiled note of warning. In China one could always invent new gods if the old ones didn't do their job. Even in 1976, the terrible Tangshan earthquake was widely perceived as a dooming portent for the Gang of Four.

Not many climbers bother with the lower slopes since the government built a motor road to the midpoint a few years ago. I passed a few elderly women in velveteen pantaloons, and young people got up in fantasies of foreign tourists' garb. For a while a gay party kept pace with me. There was a girl in a scarlet bridal jacket, a proud father, a bowlegged granny hobbling sturdily on bound feet, a chattering muddle of sisters and brothers togged in red sneakers, checked pants and tams, and dark glasses. The father almost fell over with astonishment when I wished them good luck.

"You speak very good Chinese!"

He said it as Chinese habitually do to strangers who make even a feeble effort to express themselves in Chinese, rather the way a parent speaks to a child who has made a mess that is supposed to be a painting.

"Impossible," I said. "I'm physically incapable."

It was the proper reply, making clear that I understood perfectly well, as all Chinese did, that foreigners were hopelessly unable to speak their language.

"Possible! Capable!" they shouted back politely.

The path accordioned into flagstone steps, straightened, and then rose again among aqueous orange and green rocks. Goats poured over them in streams and down through the pines. Sounds took on a strange clarity. A rooster's cry, a dog's bark, the ring of a quarrier's hammer resonated and lingered in the shimmering air.

Before the revolution, Taishan existed in an eternal midsummer's eve, where a wisp of cloud might be an immortal in flight, a butterfly a sage's dream. For centuries Taoists fled to its woody clefts as spiritual renegades from Confucian constraint. The mountain was a place of infinite possibility, the life of other men the World of Dust. The credulous imagined the hermits as immortals riding on light and wandering the peaks to collect cosmic breath in pouches. They were said to live to know how to manipulate the earth's wild energies and to be able, at will, to transform themselves into any form.

The Taoist perceived existence as a sort of cosmic cauldron in which dark and light, male yang and female yin, the real and the unreal flowed endlessly and unpredictably from one form to another. Its motion could be seen in the drift of mist, the surge of water, in marbled rock. The Tao was unknowable, vast, aimless, perfect. Sanity was aquiescence to its movement. Chuang Tze said: "He who practices The Way does less every day, does less and goes on doing less until he reaches the point where he does nothing and yet there is nothing that is not done."

The Taoists loved the paradox that paralyzed logic. "The Way that can be spoken of is not the constant Way; the name that can be named is not the constant name. The nameless was the beginning of heaven and earth." Such stuff lent itself equally to fraud and poetry, and it made the Confucians fume. Taoist priests concocted "pills of immortality" that murdered their clients, wrote spells that they burned and fed to the gullible as medicine. But a tenth-century poet could also write:

> You ask me why I dwell amidst these jade-green hills?
> I smile. No words can tell
> The stillness in my heart.
> The peach-bloom on the water,
> How enchantingly it drifts!
> I live in another realm here
> Beyond the world of men.

A little further along the trail the entire Lotus Sutra was carved into a vast, flat, bare rock over a stream. Before a dam diverted it, the water must have fanned over the long columns of ideographs, veiling them with a film of water, the retort of the Tao. That the sutra should appear at all on this Taoist mountain was a sign of how Buddhism and the older religion had blurred. Or had the Buddhists attempted to colonize the mountain as their own in some distant, forgotten century? A Taoist would have said that silence was the answer to every question, that questions themselves were illusions.

The wedding party rollicked by and I tagged after them to a temple that lay astride the trail. The presiding goddess was a burnished, smoke-stained creature, majestic and slit-eyed, her slender

149

bronze hands pressed together in enigmatic prayer. There was a memory of incense in the air, and on the altar tidy pyramids of plastic apples. Sparrows swooped and spiraled through the door.

The bride blushed as the mob levered her giggling and shrinking to the floor, and made her kowtow. The mountain, it was said, was a never-failing source of births, and she was praying for sons, as pilgrims had since time immemorial. A boy in wraparound sunglasses snapped her picture from the side.

"Finished!" she said.

"Pray more!" the mob shouted, and she wriggled and blushed and prayed.

I stood away in the shadow, but the bride's father dragged me bodily out and pushed me at her. She cringed behind me with embarrassment and fright.

"Take pictures!" he shouted to the boy.

The mob roared with good-natured laughter.

She would remember me as an exotic curiosity, an artifact of her wedding, unnamed and unknown. I could hear her forever after when they took out the family album: "This is what they look like." There I would be in my worn-out jeans and dusty track shoes, sunburned and baggy-eyed, pack slung over my shoulder, a private icon of the foreign.

"Their noses are so big!" someone would exclaim.

"They really do look like white ghosts!"

"Such round eyes!"

"Do they all wear blue trousers?"

"It is their national costume," she would say condescendingly, remembering secretly that I had scared her and that she had hidden behind my back.

A feeble nun in a black tunic and cap tapped an iron gong. It reverberated with unexpected force and only faded long afterward in the perfumed air.

The trail rose through cedar-shaded ravines and tunneled gates, then wandered through the temple of He-Who-Heightens-Happiness, a down-at-heel deity with a head of electric-shock hair. Gargoyles poised like sentinels of the supernatural on the tips of upturned eaves. I climbed past a pine tree that an emperor had named a mandarin of the fifth grade in thanks for its shade. Somewhere else there was a stone that was said to have flown from afar. Splintered yellow crags loomed overhead. Pines clung to them, aged, still, and benign, immortals in disguise; in the distance, naked silvery branches were a mist, a cloud.

There was more traffic on the trail now. An aerial tramway had recently been built from the midpoint to the peak. But it was expensive, and some lingering tradition still seemed to demand that even holiday makers arrive on the summit by foot. There were more coolies too. A hotel was being erected on the summit, and porters were humping it up piece by piece on their backs from the road. They carried bricks, lumber, plumbing, porcelain toilets and sinks, window frames, and an entire generator lashed to a pair of crossed poles. Men's muscles were still cheaper than a mule.

From the Arch-from-Which-One-Rises-to-Immortality stairs rose almost perpendicularly between two walls of rock. My consciousness drained into my calves. We panted and gasped one and all and hauled ourselves up hand over hand by the iron railings. Wheezing cadres, peasant women, students in ill-fitting Western suits, grunting factory stiffs on holiday all abandoned reserve and urged each other giddily upward.

Descent was hair-raising in the days of sedan chairs. A certain Miss Kemp, who had worked as a governess in Beijing and visited Taishan in 1905, left a description; the prospect of being helpless in a chair terrified her, but she understood that both she and her porters would lose face if she walked. She "resolved to do the correct thing."

"The men carry the chairs sideways, because of the narrowness of the steps, and run down, pitter-patter, as hard as they can go. I had my watch in hand and timed them—a thousand steps in six minutes. The most horrible moment was when they flung the chair, with a dextrous turn of the wrist, from one shoulder to the other. One false step and we should all have been killed together; but the 'tigers' never make a false step. Really the only danger is that the carrying poles may snap."

The Cave-from-Which-Clouds-Were-Born gaped from a cliff. The *Spring and Autumn Chronicles* of the sixth century B.C. described their birth: "They come out, bumping against the stones; they gather in less time than it takes to turn the hand or stretch the finger; in less than two mornings, they cover the whole empire with rain." Below me I could see the dragon veins now, channels of supernatural power, the serpentine ridge lines, valleys, and chasms that swept downward in great rugged arcs, bearing the mountain's primal energies, like blood or semen, down into the land of man.

I flung myself down on the uppermost step. The slopes below had become slabs of shadow, and the stairs dropped away into them like a silver thread. The generator looked like a great black insect as it switched back and forth, creeping almost imperceptibly upward. It possessed a wonderful improbability, this sight of an engine scaling a mountain, seemingly all by itself amid the upward trickle of climbers, for the coolies beneath it were at first invisible. There was at the same time something anciently beautiful in the inexorable ascent of this monstrous contraption by the sheer force of human muscle. As it came nearer I watched each man as he placed one foot in front of the other, gained balance, then levered himself up another step, raising another piece of this Hilton- or Sheraton-to-be exactly as his ancestors had erected the Great Wall and dug the Grand Canal, and done every other monumental job since the beginning of Chinese time. Then I began to make out their faces. Their mouths were contorted with exhaustion, their eyes bloodshot and stupefied with pain. I watched them until I couldn't stand it anymore and fled up onto the stony tableland that was the peak.

Dusk came quickly. The slopes that I had toiled over since morning suddenly turned pale blue and vaporous, and in an instant rushed away into the gathering night.

The inn occupied an old temple that had been less renovated than devastated by its transformation. Frenetic Hongkongese waved money at the manager and struggled to make themselves understood in broken Mandarin. A laconic boy led me through a broken glass door and down a corridor stained with sputum and crushed insects. Four frame beds were shoved against the sides of the room. A grimy bulb dangled from the ceiling.

"The door has no lock," I said.

"Yes, no lock."

"The door doesn't close."

"Yes."

"It will be very cold."

"Very cold."

The boy pointed to a pile of dubious quilts and greatcoats that lay on one of the beds. When I pointed out that the electric light didn't work, he said, "Tomorrow." Then he led me to another broken door that opened onto a muddy yard two or three feet below.

"Toilet," he said.

"I want another room."

"No."

For dinner I ate a tureen of bean curd in a tin shed down the hill from the inn. It had frost on it by the time I got it to the table. Later I packed into long underwear and sweaters and a down coat, and felt my way to the edge of the cliff. Wind boiled like something alive over the invisible crags while the distant lights of Taian blended seamlessly into the multitudinous canopy of stars. I felt as if I had stepped off the edge of the earth.

An eighth-century emperor had left a monumental inscription carved into the cliff behind me. The ideographs had been limned with gold paint, and they shimmered faintly in the starlight. Chavannes had translated it: "For fourteen years I have occupied the high position of emperor. I am, however, troubled by my lack of virtue; I am ignorant of perfect reason. The duties which I have to fulfill are hard to fulfill; the calm which I should preserve is hard to preserve. Now I know not whether I have committed an offense against the gods or the people and my heart is tossed on the floods as though I were crossing a great river." They were the words of a man who had grown weary from the burden of power, unsure of the future. In despair, he had come here to be alone with the god.

A vast moon loomed over me, so close, it seemed, that I could reach out and bathe my hand in its white glow. The goddess Chang E dwelt there in a palace of ice and moonbeams, the loveliest of all divine beings, with hair blacker than the coat of an imperial steed, eyes that shone like moonlight in mountain pools, and exquisitely bound feet that erotically aroused those privileged to gaze upon them.

I leaned into the wind and dreamed that I could step out like the fortunate Shen, into the void.

A young scholar named Shen, so the tale went, rescued a ragged pedlar from wrongful arrest. The pedlar proved to be a Taoist in disguise, and as a reward he offered to take Shen on a journey anywhere in the universe. Shen whimsically replied that he would like to offer birthday greetings to Chang E. The Taoist told him to draw a circle on a piece of paper. The circle steadily swelled until its light filled the room. The Taoist then took Shen by the hand and they stepped into the glow. Shen soon found himself kneeling before Cheng E's silvery throne. "Your Immortality," she said, graciously addressing the Taoist. "We are pleased to reward this young scholar for his timely aid—though why you should travel about the weary world of mortals masquerading like a fruitmonger is beyond Our understanding." An instant later, Shen found himself back in his studio as if waking from a dream, the Taoist gone and everything apparently as it had been before. But there was a strange box on the desk in front of him, and in it two crystals that gave off rainbow-colored rays. When Shen placed them on his tongue, liquid moon-fire raced through his veins. "Thereafter the young scholar abandoned his sterile study of the Confucian classics," as the storytellers put it, and "betook himself to the solitude of the mountains and became immersed in contemplation of The Way." Shen remained ever-youthful until his one hundred sixty-third year when he bade his disciples farewell "and departed for the celestial regions."

The temperature must have dropped from sixty to twenty since the sun had gone down, and I was numb with cold. I made a tent of the rank quilts, crawled into it with my shoes and down coat on, and tried to read in the light of a fast-dwindling candle. Finally I slept, frozen to the bone, struggling in my dreams to reach a vast silver orb that hung just beyond my grasp.

It was the electric light. It had come on at 4:00 A.M. A cacophony of nose blowing and spitting resonated through the corridors. Scores of Chinese milled querulously in the courtyard until someone discovered how to unlock the gate, and then in the pitch-black starry darkness we straggled in a mob over the rocks to an outcrop to wait for the sunrise.

154

The crags seethed in the murk. Chinese tourists had arrived by the hundreds in the night. They continued to come, a migration of troglodytes, lumbering hulks in swarming blue greatcoats, hunkered against the wind until they filled the mountaintop like an audience of dark spectral forms. We were like new souls poised on the brink of creation, lightless, mindless, unformed.

I was geared up for epiphany. In earlier times, rapturous pilgrims hurled themselves into the newborn day from here, convinced they were becoming one with the boiling void of the Tao. But the sunrise was anticlimactic. When the light finally came it was without drama, oozing lethargically through a gray soup of smog and haze. There was no sea of clouds, no red sun, no apocalyptic vision. But the holiday makers yelped and howled anyway and erupted in a frenzy of picture taking. Someone turned on a radio and a pinging Cantonese voice shrilled, "Why don't you fall in love with me? If you love me, tell me now, now, now!"

AT THE highest point of the peak there was a temple dedicated to the Jade Emperor, Creator of the Heavens. The caretaker saw me in the courtyard and called to me to drink with him. There was something beaten down and unappealing about him, and I said no. He asked again feebly, as if he never expected me to stay, and I said yes.

His room was minuscule, really just a corner of a shed. There was a tin cabinet, a bunk, a hot plate, smeared walls.

He made space for me on the bunk and offered me a cup of hot boiled water, the way it is drunk by peasants, and in labor camps. He wiped the cup with a dirty rag and then extended it with a sort of caved-in grace with the tips of the fingers of both hands.

He came originally from Nanjing. "But I haven't lived there for many years." The government had assigned him to Taishan nine years ago. That was about the time, I knew, when the political prisoners of the 1950s had been released.

I waited for him to say more. Instead he rummaged in the cabinet and showed me an American $100 bill, and then a Taiwanese one. He handled them as if they were old jades or ivory, cradling them gently in his hands and smiling, and then passing them to me to hold, as if to share the pleasure.

He had relatives in Taipei. "They got away in 1949," he said, with irony and envy, and with a sweeping un-Chinese gesture. They had come back recently for the first time and had given him the money.

"Of course I want to go to Taiwan. But it is too expensive. You need papers. You have to bribe."

He asked me the conventional questions: Where had I been in China? What had I liked? He had a gloomy intensity that made me nervous, like someone who is accustomed to talking to himself and for whom other people are merely figments of inner voices. We had run out of things to say and I wanted to go, but he made me sit down again and insisted on giving me another cup of water.

Something was supposed to happen, but it never did. There had been some kind of failure. Had he wanted to tell me about an arrest, a wrecked family, wasted decades, and then become afraid? Had he wanted to beg for money but changed his mind? Did he just want to be near a foreigner, an emissary from the outer world?

He showed me across a dusty courtyard to the Jade Emperor's shrine. The place was neglected and depressing. The once-famous effigy of the Incarnation of the Tao was gone and had been replaced by a coarse plaster replica that was crowned, awfully, with the bangled headgear of a Peking Opera princess. Yet lumpy men and women in the solemn clothes of the countryside dropped to their knees and bent face to the floor, honoring something that still survived for them in the pathetic sanctum. Where I saw ruin, they saw limitless power, the god, as alive as ever.

I asked the caretaker if he liked living on Taishan.

"For someone who wishes to be alone it is a good place."

"And for yourself?"

"So silent," he said. "So cold."

THE PRINCESS of the Colored Clouds lived a little way down the slope in a temple of her own, surrounded by an assortment of ladies-in-waiting who included the Princess Who Mysteriously

Nourishes and Strengthens the Shape of the Embryo, the Lady of Suckling, and the Princess Who Guarantees Tranquility and Kindness to Childhood. Her regal effigy gleamed in the morning light amid the biscuits, bananas, and silk streamers offered in prayer by the childless.

The young monk in front of the shrine was tall and muscular, and he wore a blue smock and white leggings; his long hair was tied in a topknot that bulged through a hole in the top of a pillbox cap. Signs in English and Chinese said No Photography. Perhaps it was a subtle urge to capture and possess; unobtrusively, I thought, I looked away and shot twice from the waist.

"You took a picture."

"No," I lied.

"Give it to me!" the monk demanded.

I began to walk away. The monk spun me backward and grabbed for the camera. We tugged at it like a pair of children.

"Just the one picture," he barked. "Keep the rest. Now take it out!"

He had his hands on me, and with the help of another monk was pushing me backward into the temple where, I feared, he would break the camera to get at the film. Chinese tourists watched noncommitally. While the monk shook me and shouted, a boy in a boiler suit asked in painstaking schoolroom English where I was from, and how I liked China, and what was my father's name, and did I have children, and then smilingly said, "I won't help you."

Later I wondered why I wouldn't give up the film. There were pictures on it of a dawn that never happened, of agonized coolies, of rock-cut ideographs that I couldn't read, of nothing that, perhaps, the subjectivity of memory wouldn't have served better. But my pride was at stake, and I held on.

We seesawed back and forth across the courtyard. The monk lunged and I dodged, but he managed to pull loose the flash attachment, and it skittered across the stone flags. I said it would cost the monastery fifty dollars to replace. Translated into Chinese currency the sum stunned, and in the confusion I ran for the gate. But the monk sprang ahead and leaped into a martial-arts stance and barred the way.

A policeman appeared at a dogtrot. He was thin-lipped and unbreachable, and with abrupt contempt he ordered the monk to stand down. Then he ordered us both to an inner room where an elderly, anxious man whom I took to be the abbot told the young monk to get me tea.

The monk's flushed face fairly quivered as he served the tea, pouring it into shallow bowls with an unexpected delicacy. But when I pushed the shutter to show the constable how the camera worked, the monk flew at me and held back only at a curt shout from the abbot.

I had half-convinced myself that the monk didn't really know what had happened. But when I developed the film months later in New York I could see that he was looking straight at the camera, and what I saw in his eyes was sheer terror.

Then I understood. For an instant in front of the shrine, the human and the magical had intersected. The breath of life, the everlasting *qi* that flowed from the mountain through his body and soul, had poured away through the camera into the spirit-shadow of the film.

But the truth of the event hardly mattered now. It was on the brink of becoming a political issue. The temple had only recently been allowed to reopen, and both abbot and constable knew that the monks were there at all only by sufferance of the state. A monk had destroyed a foreigner's property. It was clear to everyone except the young monk that a face-saving solution had to be found.

"Explain," the policeman said.

I opened the camera and said that the batteries were weak, and that I had pushed the shutter to hear whether they were too slow. It was a lie, but plausible.

"You don't understand machines," the abbot told the young monk.

"I do understand," he retorted furiously.

Tremblingly, the old man again told the monk that he didn't understand. This time the monk did understand.

The policeman fitted the flash back on the camera.

"Now fine," he declared.

It wasn't, but I said that it was.

"I offer our apologies," said the abbot. "Profuse apologies."

He gave me a feather-light hand, smiled vaguely with an insincerity that matched my own, and wished me a safe descent.

The police could pretend that no damage was done, the monastery could pretend that its sanctity had not been breached, and I saved my film. The young monk was the only loser. I got away with his soul.

And so I descended into the World of Dust, past the lowland pilgrims, and the coolies with their bricks and Coke and distended faces, past the low-sweeping pines, tumbling two and three steps at a time out of the land of the immortals and the realm of poetry, until the mountain was almost completely lost to sight in the sepia smog, a mere figment of the imagination. My eyes burned and my lungs ached with the pollution, and I began to cough.

At the foot of the mountain, I fought onto a packed bus that arrived belching exhaust. I rode with my face to the window for air, pressed among passengers who clawed silently and ineffectually toward the doors. Over their heads, the conductor shrieked rhythmically for fares.

HELL LAY somewhere near. Chinese of the old world used to believe that since Taishan was the source of life, souls must return there after death. Beneath the mountain, it was said, there was a duplicate China of the dead administered by a bureaucracy as intricate as the imperial court's, where the deceased went on acting as they did during their lifetimes, official posts were much sought after, and recommendations from the influential most useful. To reach it, the dead had to pass through the courts of Yen Lo, who meted out punishment to the doomed.

Each court had its own magistrates and torturers, and punishments were designed with a convincing particularity. Thieves and seducers, according to a popular old tract called the "Divine Panorama," were "stretched to regulation length" and given rivers of lime to drink. Suicides were sent to the Hunger and Thirst Section to be tortured every day "from 7:00 A.M. to 11:00 A.M. sharp." Priests who skipped prayers were condemned to pick out the passages they omitted "by the uncertain light of an infinitesimal wick." Those who "enjoy the light of day without reflecting on the Imperial bounty" were split at the shoulder bones. Those who were late with their rent were "perpetually dosed with nasty medicines." The unfilial were shut up in huge saucepans, where "their marrow is cauterized, and their bowels are scratched." Liars and lax tutors and those "who break up dead men's bones for medicine" were dressed in fiery clothes. "Those who wantonly discharge arrows and bolts, throw potsherds over a wall, who do not bury dead cats, or who alter their walls and stoves at wrong seasons" were to be "crushed by iron dogs" and then tied hand and foot and "have their hearts torn out, minced up, and given to snakes." Those who let their tears fall to the north or who scrape the gilding from images were condemned to "a vast, noisy Gehenna," where sinners were nipped by locusts, crushed to a jelly, and then "flayed and rolled up." Writers of bad books, along with arsonists and poisoners, had their brains taken out and their skulls filled with hedgehogs.

Like the courts of the upper world, those of Yen Lo exercised a certain degree of "flexibility." The dead could haggle, demonic palms could be greased with spirit money, exceptions could be made. A woman seduced by a young scholar, the "Divine Panorama" reasonably informed its readers, "is allowed to send a spirit to the Examination Hall to hinder and confuse him in the preparation of his paper, or to change the names on the published list of successful candidates."

Just where hell was located, however, was not quite clear. "It was traditionally believed that the souls of the dead gathered on a little hill, called Hao-li chan, about a mile southwest of the town of T'ai ngan fou," Chavannes had written. Chavannes had been there in 1907. He saw forests of mournful stelae flanking two avenues that climbed to a succession of magnificent halls where the sculpted judges of the ten hells presided over life-size depictions of every torment known to the prolific Chinese imagination. Beyond them, Yen Lo loomed colossally from the sanctum, shrouded in "an awful air of majesty" and attended by demon mandarins bearing the registers of birth and death.

But Taian had grown since Chavannes's time from a walled citadel to a swollen industrial metropolis. My sketch map showed nothing anywhere that fit the description of the hill, and no one at the hotel recognized the name.

The China Travel Service office was a concrete cubicle where two young men were hunched over their desks, napping in shadowy gloom. They reluctantly switched on the electricity when I made it clear that I intended to stay.

One was lank and vulpine and wadded against the cold with fuschia long johns that kept slipping from the cuffs of a rumpled Western suit. The other, Mr. Fan, was clearly the boss and had the familiar well-fed cheeks and menacing manner of a certain class of officials. Cop, I thought.

There was a detailed street map of Taian on the wall, and it showed a green oval near the railway station. I asked if it might be Haolishan (as Chavannes's "Hao-li chan" is written today). Long-johns bent over and read out the name.

"Yes," he said, carefully pronouncing each syllable. It was obvious that he had never noticed it before.

"The entrance to hell," I said.

He looked blank.

"Where the dead souls went to the underworld."

"Really?"

"What's there now?" I asked.

"There's nothing for you there," said Fan.

"But the temples?"

"Go to the mountain," Fan said. "There are temples on the mountain. That's where foreigners go."

"Go to Taishan," said Longjohns.

"I have been to Taishan."

"There is nothing on Haolishan," Longjohns said.

"You are not interested in it," said Fan.

"I want to see the entrance to hell," I said.

"I was born in Taian and there have never been any temples," Fan said.

"How old are you?"

He was born in 1958. I showed him what Chavannes had written. It was a mistake.

"Do you think foreigners can know more about China than Chinese?" he replied truculently.

"I'd like to find someone who can tell me about Haolishan," I said.

"This is CTS, we know everything important," said Longjohns.
"Perhaps I could find an old man, who might know more."
"There are no old men."
They could have been lying about Haolishan, but I doubted it.
They were the heirs of Mao, born without history, disconnected,
blank, and angry. They frightened me.

I took my bearings by my memory of the map on the CTS office
wall and walked southwest. The air was oily and thick, the avenues
dense with cyclists and half-naked carters tugging wagons heaped
with sacks of cement. Men in sunglasses clogged the curb, selling
cucumbers, grinding knives, telling fortunes. Beyond the railway station a low hill, sure enough, rose up behind warehouses and factories.
I circled its foot searching for a way through until I found a break
where workmen were laying pipe and dodged up into the pines.

It was a strange and withered place. The earth was gray with
soot. The trees had turned orange from pollution. A few chimneys and
factory blocks, and the shaft of a new hotel, probed up like rusty
islands through the sheet of smoke that extended across the city;
Taishan, hardly two miles away, was completely invisible. I worked
my way back and forth across the hillside. The ground underfoot was
oddly corrugated, but there was none of the detritus I expected, no
ruined walls, tiles, stelae.

For a while I watched a man practicing tai chi, waving his arms
with liquid grace, but he fled in panic when he saw me. Lonely men in
boiler suits wandered into view, but none responded when I called,
"Hello." Mostly they stared in silence and then sifted away among the
dying pines, like the spirits of the dead arriving for the hideous hour
appointed centuries or millenia ago in the registers of Yen Lo, searching desolately for a hell that could no longer be found.

At last I caught a middle-aged man with cropped gray hair and
hands stuffed in baggy, unspiritlike trousers, and asked him what he
knew about the temple that Chavannes had described.

"*Puodaole,*" he said, edging tensely away. "In the Japanese
war."

I realized that I had been climbing over shell holes and snaking
trenches that rippled in waves down the slopes. In 1938, the man said,
Nationalist troops had drawn themselves up on Haolishan in hope of

stemming the Japanese advance along the railway. It was a foolhardy hope. They had no artillery and no antiaircraft guns. The Japanese bombed them to pulp.

Probably the men I saw were just workers from the factories at the foot of the hill. But I was becoming more and more nervous. The place was sick with death. It oozed from the ground, dripped from the orange trees, hung like a miasma in the air.

My eyes ached from the pollution. I was covered with dust. I felt suddenly lost, and I began to run. I found myself back where I began and spilled with relief out of the sterile forest and onto a broad avenue in the realm of the living, where caravans of carters trudged out of the smog, bent double against their loads of cement.

"THE SECRET is control," Fan said.

I hardly recognized him as the menacing functionary I had encountered in the CTS office. He had metamorphosed into a sort of Chinese Pat Sajak, rigged out in imported slacks and pullover of a type that only the well-connected can afford. Wide smiles played over his fat cheeks.

A convention of provincial officials had boisterously colonized most of the tables in the hotel restaurant, and a Canadian tour group occupied the rest. Because of the tour, a waitress who wore a tag that said her name was "Tamara" told me, there was a special Western menu, and if I wanted I could have "veal cord-and-blue."

"The ancient Chinese sages taught that if you can control breath you can control the mind and everything else," Fan announced jovially. "Now there are very few masters of these mysteries, but we are lucky to bring one to you tonight."

He was introducing on behalf of CTS a certain Master Li, who he said had "decided to exhibit his powers as a contribution to the Socialist modernization of China." Master Li had spent fifteen years in the famous monastery of Shaolin, Fan said, where he had mastered the secret powers of *qigong*. For a fee, Master Li would later be happy to provide personal *qigong* lessons in guests' rooms.

Strange growths had begun to appear amid the rotting wood of communism. One sensed the old superstitions struggling to burst forth. There were fortune tellers on the streets of every city. Even the official press reported that in some remote areas shamans had buried children in the foundations of new houses. A national newspaper reported matter-of-factly that a *qigong* practitioner who claimed he could see through the human body to diagnose diseases had opened a research center at Shenzhen University. "The treatment has become so effective that the university has begun to offer a new three-year program of studies on human body engineering based on his special talents and techniques," the article said.

Master Li was a springy man in his early thirties, and he was dressed in a sweat suit and Reeboks. At a signal from Fan, he flung his hands out like weapons and crooked his left leg in the air like a stork.

Fan said, "Master Li will now show you the ancient art and science."

Master Li called for volunteers. A dumpy Chinese woman was pushed forward.

"Stand here," he told her. "You will experience the force of *qi*!"

Master Li crouched about twenty feet behind her in a prize-fighter's stance. He extended his arms and began to rotate them, first slowly and then with a deep muscular rhythm, as if he were trying to stir the cosmos like a kettle of soup. He went on for ten minutes or more until sweat burst out on his forehead and the woman began, it seemed, to sway.

"What do you feel?" he asked her.

"I feel warm."

Master Li clapped his hands with a sudden report.

"She feels the heat of the *qi*!" he declared.

There was a faint ripple of applause. Master Li looked disappointed.

Fan called for another volunteer. A slim man in a Mao suit stepped forward boldly. Master Li positioned him carefully in the center of the room and resumed his stance.

Almost immediately, the shill began to jiggle and shake like a rag doll. Master Li played him like a marionette. His legs went rubbery. An arm jerked up and went limp. Then the man slipped onto the floor and began to spin lumpily in time with Master Li's arms. The Chinese were popeyed at the sight. Bulbs flashed. Minicams whirred. Master Li beamed.

"Master Li will now demonstrate with our foreign guests," Fan announced.

Master Li walked among the tables. He selected an elderly man in green-checked trousers, a tipsy young man with a beard, and a blond woman in the sort of tailored safari suit that one might buy at Banana Republic. He set them in a row with the safari suit in the middle.

"Yang, yin, yang," said Master Li.

The master's arms began to spin.

"Watch carefully and you will see the power of *qi*," Fan declared.

We watched.

Master Li waved his arms in great liquid arcs. Sweat rolled over his face. Long minutes passed.

"What do you feel?" Fan asked.

"I don't feel anything," said the woman in the safari suit.

"The lights are hot," said the drunk.

The old man was sagging. Master Li was breathing heavily. Gradually his arms slowed and stopped.

"Foreign *qi* is more difficult," Fan explained. "It takes more time."

Master Li walked along the line, massaging shoulders and temples, and yanking people by the arms. He made the Canadians stand closer together.

"I'm still game!" the old man exclaimed weakly.

Master Li began again. His arms spun. His eyes narrowed, and he emitted a high-pitched hum that ebbed and swelled with the liquid play of his hands.

The audience was growing restive, but the master was indefatigable. The Canadians had been on their feet for perhaps a quarter of an hour when at last the drunk began to sway, and then the blond woman next to him. It was obvious that the old man was going to topple over any minute from exhaustion.

"See the power of ancient Chinese art and science!" Fan shouted.

Before the old man collapsed completely, Master Li clapped his hands and sprang into the air with his arms spread wide.

"Beer! Beer!" shouted the drunk.

"Take pictures now!" Fan commanded.

There were reflexive flashes around the room.

"You have seen the power of *qi!*" Fan declared.

Fan asked the blond woman how she felt and then told the room, "She says she felt the power of the *qi.*"

"No, I said my legs were tired," she protested.

"Yes," Fan said. "The power of the *qi.*"

After dinner I walked as far as an old temple that had once been dedicated to Guan Di, a paladin who was always ready to intervene against sorcerers and foreigners. In a land that was plagued by both he was a popular deity; when plays were performed at the temple, his statue was taken out and put on the veranda so that he had the best seat. Chavannes had seen it happen in 1907. Lucky man, I thought. The temple was a school of some kind now, and a caretaker stared unblinking at me from a window until I went away. I walked up a little further until I could see Taishan looming above me, prodigious and impotent in the night.

Walking back to the hotel, I saw Fan and Master Li. They passed me on a motorcycle that, I could see from its markings, belonged to the police.

Later, in Beijing, a woman I knew told me that her office had hired a *qigong* master for an afternoon. "We sat on one side of a locked door and he sat on the other for two hours. Afterward he told us things about ourselves that no one could have known." She was a very brave and patriotic woman, who had walked across China in the midst of World War II in order to attend a university, and who had until a few years ago remained faithful to a revolution that repeatedly persecuted her for what used to be known as a "bad class background."

"You can't believe that stuff," I said.

"Everyone needs something to believe in," she said.

CHAPTER
EIGHT

The Ten Thousand Things

I FIRST NOTICED the nun on the steamer to Guichi. Her face was wrinkled and soft, and her head shaven; she was dressed in a neat gray cotton smock and trousers, and white gaiters. I guessed that she was in her fifties. She was sitting cross-legged in the corridor deep in meditation, oblivious to the peasants blundering past with slabs of pork slung over their shoulders, and to the tipsy louts, and to the families that had camped around her on scraps of burlap. The shaven head and the neat smock made her seem vulnerable and insignificant, even a little ridiculous.

I saw the nun again the next morning at the bus depot in Guichi. A mob of peasants had gathered to stare at me in the yard where I was waiting for the bus to Jiuhuashan. But they were good-natured and friendly, different from the more opaque, more suspicious folk of the north. They became wide-eyed when I said that I had traveled all the way from Xinjiang, a region of which even today, I suspected, they probably had only the foggiest grasp.

Someone asked what I did for a living, and I mentioned that I had once worked in Beijing for the national news agency. A large officious man almost immediately began pushing through the crowd. Shoving and barking in every direction, he quickly imposed a cordon sanitaire around me, declaring that a "foreign guest" affiliated with an important central government agency needed to be properly protected; this proved to be the stationmaster. When the crowd continued to press, he ushered me insistently into a windowless cubicle furnished with a

169

battered desk and a bench. But the crowd packed into the half-open door and continued to gape, rapt and unblinking, through holes in the wall where slats of wood had fallen away.

A female clerk shared the stationmaster's office. When I sat down and crossed my legs, she stared admiringly at the rubber-soled oxfords I was wearing. She stared for a long time.

Finally she said, "Doesn't fall off?"

"Sorry?"

She tugged at the rubber sole.

"Doesn't fall off?"

She flung a thick leg up onto the desk and pointed at her shoes. They looked like barges, a sort of cross between high heels and work boots.

"Chinese soles," she said wearily. "Always fall off."

Gradually warming, the stationmaster told me that he had come originally from Shanghai and been assigned to Guichi thirty-one years ago.

"Shanghai!" he sighed.

The word played almost sensually over his tongue. Guichi was a half-built river port, a mess of cranes and chimneys and brick barracks strung along the muddy bank of the Yangzi. He would probably stay there for the rest of his life, he said. He sighed again.

"Shanghai!"

Somewhere outside the little room, I could hear what sounded like someone methodically rapping a stick on a plank. After a time, I managed to escape the stationmaster's hospitality and went out to the waiting room. Peasants in the ubiquitous blue boiler suits were standing on the wooden benches, staring at something on the floor. I climbed up to take a look; below, in the middle of the crowd, was the nun from the boat, squatting with her eyes closed and rhythmically beating a wand against a hollowed-out piece of wood, in time with a prayer. The open practice of religion was still a rare sight, and the peasants smirked and made jokes while the nun rapped out her mysterious, clattering tattoo.

When the bus arrived she hurtled out of the station and flung herself at the head of the queue, as if she were terrified that she would be left behind. She perched next to me like a small child on the edge of

170

the seat, and every few miles she took a greasy slip of paper from her tunic and showed it to me, or to one of the other passengers, to reassure herself that she was on the right bus, to Jiuhuashan.

We rode through a pretty country. Whitewashed farmsteads clumped in free and easy disorder at the edge of rumpled green fields where farmers were turning the soil with wooden plows hitched to buffalo. Beneath the eaves of each house there were quaint line drawings of rustic fishermen, Taoist immortals, ornamental rocks, and the heroes of classical opera. As the land grew wilder, the nun began to bounce in her seat, as if she could smell the mountains to come. She clambered over me to reach the window, and a broad smile spread over her face as she watched the land twist through a cleft in the hills and then up around hairpin bends through feathery forests of bamboo and pine. Then through a crack in the hills Jiuhuashan appeared, rising up massively like some awesome pile painted by a Song-dynasty master, all pinnacles and cliffs, and craggy bluffs half-suspended in the haze.

The nun leaped out even before the bus came to a stop at the village of Hua Cheng and scuttled up the road through the ceremonial gate that marked the boundary between the sacred and the profane. The last I saw of her, she was running, almost leaping like a child, her small cotton sack of belongings bouncing on her shoulder, away up a hillside and into the pines.

Jiuhuashan was the preserve of Dicang, the orphic Buddhist god who traveled ceaselessly through the netherworld to redeem the dead. He started out long ago in India as the Buddha's youthful disciple Ksitagarbha, who vowed that he would not become a buddha until he had saved all beings sunk in sin and had led them beyond the river of life and death and into the Happy Lands. The Chinese usually imagined him as a placid, youthful figure, holding in his hand a fabulous pearl whose luster illumined the gloomy roads of hell, plea bargaining with the smug subterranean judges for the souls of the damned. But he could appear in almost any form at all: as a dragon, a ghost, a mountain, a forest.

The first temple was built to honor Jin Qiao Jui, an eighth-century Korean prince who lived as a hermit on the then-uninhabited slopes. Perhaps he was carried away by his devotions; he eventually came to regard himself as an incarnation of Dicang, and his fame spread. When he died, he was interred in a cave, with his legs crossed in the posture of meditation. When the cave was reopened years later, "his bones rattled like gold chains" and his flesh was as fresh as it was in life; proof, it was said, of the bodhisattva's determination to remain in the world of men. Although Jin's body has not been seen for centuries, it is still said to exist, hidden in a secret chamber somewhere in the "Flesh Body Hall" that stands on the ridge that overlooks Hua Cheng.

Hua Cheng's name means "Magic City." It comes from the sutras, from an ancient tale in which a necromancer magically erects a city of illusion for his exhausted followers to rest in during a journey. But the tale, like the name, is really a spiritual metaphor: the pious say that just as Hua Cheng serves as a resting place on the pilgrim's ascent of the sacred peak, so the reassuring doctrines of the faith are ultimately just a temporary oasis for the intellect on the way to transcendental enlightenment.

Hua Cheng surrounded the old temple of Dicang like a protective cocoon. The town's whitewashed walls and tile roofs, the balconied houses, the flagstoned plaza curiously suggested an older Spain, the Moorish quarter of Córdoba, perhaps, of a few generations ago. In earlier times, Hua Cheng served only pilgrims and monks, but since the revolution peasants had been sent up to till the basin in which the village lay, and there were now a few shops and eating places, and a theater that was showing a film that lurid posters promised would include a fight to the death atop the Great Wall.

The pilgrimage season had ended and most of the inns were closed. I found a small hotel whose courtyards and open galleries must have made it charming in warm weather. But it was December now, and there was no heat. Mao Zedong had declared that the weather south of the Yangzi was sufficiently mild that no buildings constructed there needed to be equipped with heating; but Hua Cheng lay two thousand feet above sea level, and it remained oblivious to the Chairman's dictates. It was so cold in my room that my breath froze in front of my face. The electricity also kept giving out at dinnertime, so that meals were a blind fumbling with chopsticks at frosty platters of pork and fish. But the air was crisp and the sun so bright that, during the day at least, the cold didn't seem to matter.

For a thousand years, most pilgrims had terminated their journey at the Hua Cheng temple, where they offered up prayers for their family dead. But the temple had now been turned into a museum. A hunchbacked nun sat in the door, collecting tickets. I bought one, and she pushed me toward the spectacular statues of the thousand-armed Guanyin, and then on toward Dicang, murmuring *"Namo Amitou fou"* as we went. "Homage to the Buddha Amitabha!": the ubiquitous greeting exchanged everywhere on the mountain, usually with a smile and a gentle nod, sometimes with a gust of laughter, or an explosive shout.

I was instantly struck by the statues' state of preservation. I remarked that the Red Guards had failed to find such treasures during their rampage. But the nun told me that the statues had been made in Hong Kong and were a recent gift from pious and pragmatic Hong-kongese who hoped to develop the tourist trade. So the Red Guards had come after all, I said.

"Here too," she replied, shifting into the universal Chinese sign language for the era, hammering her hand down, chopping, whacking her nut-brown head, as if with a stick.

On the walls were copies of the frescoes that had existed before the Cultural Revolution. They showed the courts of hell, where the judges of the underworld sat ensconced like pompous mandarins, blandly directing legions of knobbly-headed demons, who were delightedly burning, sticking, boiling, pricking, and sawing at the hapless souls of the damned.

The mountain's spiritual center of gravity had shifted to the Dicang Temple that stood a thousand feet higher on Tiantai, the highest of the Jiuhuashan peaks. Hua Cheng nestled like an egg at the bottom of a steep basin; it was an easy climb up a flagstone trail to the rim, and I was unprepared for what met my eyes when I reached it. Immediately beneath me, the land dropped away suddenly into a narrow valley; on the other side of it, a range of wildly shaped peaks spread out as if they had been clawed up from the earth's innards.

Nine peaks stretched north and south, the "nine flowers" from which Jiuhuashan took its name; marvelous lotuses that Buddhists believed had bloomed from the body of a dragon who to this day, they said, lay trapped deep in the belly of the earth. Ridges receded in every direction in pinnacled waves, like sea-flung foam suspended blue and vaporous against the sky. An emerald-green cloak of pines hung below them, so richly infused with sunlight that it seemed like an optical illusion.

From where I stood, I could see monasteries perched on crags like the fairy palaces of a painted landscape, and I could see the path that I would follow, winding up among them, through clefts and shadowy vales, like one of the painted roads that in a scroll beckons the eye toward secret glens. The ancient painters were understood to be magicians, and each painting an incantation that invoked another world, like the secret realms that Taoists believed might be hidden inside a stone, or a gourd, or a dream. "It is as if you were actually in those mountains," the eleventh-century master Guo Xi wrote of these mist-wreathed mountainscapes. "The blue haze and the white path arouse a longing to walk there; the sunset on a quiet stream arouses a longing to gaze upon it; the sight of hermits and ascetics arouses a longing to dwell with them." The painter's job, like the shaman's, was to capture the secret spirit that pulsated eternally through everything in existence, seen and unseen. To the painter's eye, rocks and stones were the earth's bones, water its lifeblood— everything was alive.

I felt, as I climbed down into the valley, that I was stepping into the antique scroll that I had seen from above. From the edge of the ridge, the trail dropped dizzyingly through forests of spruce and pine. Shrines were wedged into rock niches, and over them inscriptions read: "The soil gives birth to the ten thousand things." The valley gradually revealed itself like a secret text as I descended. A hamlet of whitewashed cottages lay on the valley floor like a port at the edge of a vast undulating sea of bamboo. Peasants were stacking hay on minuscule terraces, bending and folding, bending and folding in time-polished rhythm. The sounds of woodsmen's saws lingered on the air and then sifted away slowly into the oceanic rustling of the bamboo. A room in almost every home had been turned into a shrine, and as I passed I could see through the windows the homely buddhas gleaming within, shadowy and serene in the candlelight.

I sat for a long time in the shade of a tree on the edge of the hamlet and imagined that I had stumbled onto the secret village of the Peach Blossom Spring, whose inhabitants had been forgotten by the outside world, living out the eternal Chinese fantasy of peace and escape, of that world beyond, that might lie somewhere in the psyche or in a dream, or in a painting or a secluded garden, or be hidden like this in a fold of the mountains. In the tale there was no government or religion, just plain folk living a self-sufficient existence of the greatest simplicity; it was the secret world that the Chinese imagination always craved, beyond the reach of Confucian moralism, recruiting sergeants, and the emperor.

I wished that the motor road would never penetrate the valley, although even as I climbed that morning I could hear the muffled detonations of workmen blasting their way around the mountainside from Hua Cheng. Tiny stalls that sold refreshments to pilgrims already hinted at the other, more powerful, world that must one day devour this secret corner: Along with glasses of tea and skewered chestnuts, they sold Kodachrome and RC Cola, and plaster casts of the Venus de Milo, and porcelain statuettes of children in old Dutch costumes bending to give each other a kiss, resurrected, I supposed, from old molds that had been found somewhere and were now being palmed off on the pilgrim trade.

But the moment was still perfect. I treasured it, held it quivering like a bubble, knowing that it would sooner or later burst. The fisherman was always destined to leave the Peach Blossom Spring and to return to the pedestrian world. He must never find his way back. It was all part of the tale.

Small children came up to me where I sat and stared at me with benign curiosity, until I was the center of a circle all dressed in miniature boiler suits. Finally one of them gathered up the courage to speak.

"Namo Amitou fou!" she piped.

I smiled.

A second, and then a third joined in.

"Namo Amitou fou!"

Then the dozen of them began shouting in unison, shrilling gaily at the tops of their lungs.

"Homage to the Buddha Amitabha!"

BEYOND THE hamlet, the trail climbed sharply through forests of bamboo. I began to see the monasteries and temples more clearly now, where they spanned clefts in the rock and clung to dizzying precipices with fingers of buttressed stone. Man had come unobtrusively to the mountain, and the monasteries' names spoke of a time when human works could aspire to span the gulf between heaven and earth: the Celestial Bridge Temple, the Sun-Greeting Retreat, the Sutra-Homage Altar.

The Maoists had driven the Buddhists off Jiuhuashan and put them to work on communes in the flatlands below. But after the Cultural Revolution the monks and nuns had begun to return, and there were now said to be several hundred of them scattered over the mountain. There was an atmosphere of jolliness and bonhomie everywhere. Monks bowed smilingly from shadowy sanctums, and coveys of nuns whose shaved heads lent them a cocky, gamin look fluttered down the trail, murmuring a prayer and a blessing as they passed. I had the sense of a gratefully rediscovered solitude and of ancient institutions coming back to life. Once I climbed straight through the middle of a small temple that straddled a cleft in the rock; an elderly monk was tending the altar, and when he saw me suddenly pop up like a jack-in-the-box through the floor he giddily shoved a log that was suspended from ropes against a monstrous iron bell, so that it rang with a clap that must have addled the brains of every demon down to the tenth court of hell. *"Namo Amitou fou!"* he roared.

I stopped to rest on a ledge and looked out over the valley. Far below me, the sea of bamboo spread away in an electric green tide. It was midafternoon, and the angle of the sun had suffused the bamboo with a luminous green light that seemed to glow mysteriously beneath the ephemeral dazzle. I thought suddenly of Du Fu's magnificent line: "In dark rooms, ghost-green fires burn." It was the most haunting image he ever wrote, and it had tantalized me for years. Du Fu was describing a ruined mansion in the ravaged Tang capital of Changan; the image of "green fire" was powerful and lurid, but it had always seemed to me an implausible touch. I realized now that the poet must once, 1,200 years ago, have stood on exactly such a mountainside, in just such afternoon light, and seen in the same play of sunlight a metaphor for the disintegration of his whole world.

The silence was luxuriant. I watched a distant climber toiling upward past the rustic cottages and the monasteries. He was wearing a flowing garment of some kind, and it was easy to imagine him as the tiny figure that you always found somewhere at the bottom of a classical landscape painting, the woodsman or the rambling scholar whose diminutive size marked the scale of man in nature's immensity. He would disappear at a bend in the trail, then I would see him a little higher up, climbing with a slow but determined stride. He paused at the Celestial Bridge Monastery, where he spoke to a monk in a brown robe; I watched the monk bob up and down, pointing upward and murmuring, I knew, "*Namo Amitou fou!*"

I imagined the climber as the painter Guo Xi, whose mysterious mountainscapes I deeply admired. Somewhere behind him there would be a boy toting a lute, as there always was in a painting of a scholar enjoying an outing in the mountains. When he reached the ledge he would greet me like an old friend. We would settle ourselves beneath a crooked pine. The boy would build a fire and prepare tea. Later the boy would unwrap the lute, and the painter would pluck its solemn strings as we gazed out over the mist-wreathed peaks. I would beg him to teach me how to see the mountains through his own eyes.

" 'Winter mountains are covered by dark storm clouds; the people are silent and lonely,' " he would graciously say, quoting his own charmingly named *Great Message of Forests and Streams.* " 'Mist and clouds of spring mountains are downy and diffused; the people are happy. Luxuriant trees of summer mountains are abundant and shady; the people are contented.' "

"So man and the landscape are fused," I would say. "You see man in the land, and the land in man."

The painter would smile blandly, and say, " 'Autumn mountains are clear and pure, while leaves fall; the people are quiet.' "

Chastened, perhaps I would quote Li Bo: " 'I dare not speak aloud in the silence / For fear of disturbing the dwellers of Heaven.' "

"Precisely," he would say.

The climber at last reached the ledge where I sat; the flowing garment, I realized, was just an olive-drab greatcoat. He was in his late twenties and well built, and fairly bounced up the last few steps with a springy stride. When he saw that I was a foreigner he stopped abruptly. For a good half-minute his jaw pumped frantically in silence, until he finally blurted, "I can't speak English! Please teach me a lesson!"

His English was difficult to piece out, and it was some time before I could make sense of what he was saying.

His name was Hong; it meant "Red." It was a polemical name, the sort that Communist parents gave children born in the 1950s. Others might be named things like "Greatness of Labor," or "New Dawn," or "Love of Mao."

He said vaguely that his family lived somewhere near the foot of the mountain, but his neatly pressed khaki slacks and well-barbered hair betrayed, I thought, an urban connection of some kind. The monasteries meant nothing to him. He was climbing for the exercise, he said, as he always did when he came home.

He had been studying English for eight years, he said. But I was the first native English speaker he had ever met. The sheer release of using words that he knew only from textbooks gradually nudged him in directions that I suspected he hadn't intended.

He asked me how I liked China. I told him that I was happy to see people so much better dressed and better fed than I remembered from five years before. I thought of the tourists on Taishan and said that it was good, too, to see Chinese traveling freely and seeing their country. But the thing I noticed most of all was the explosion of small businesses.

"I hate businessmen," Hong said. "They don't do anything! They don't produce anything! They just make money!"

Contempt for businessmen was an ancient thing; Mao hadn't invented it. As far back as the Han dynasty, Confucians maintained that commerce corroded morality and spoiled social harmony, while the Legalists maintained that it drained into private hands wealth that

178

the state ought to control. There were periods when merchants were forbidden to wear silk clothing or to ride in carriages, while their descendants to the third generation were disqualified from official appointments.

"Businessmen can earn 1,000 yuan a month!" Hong said fiercely. "My father is a teacher and he earns only 150 yuan a month. Intellectuals are suffering worse than during the Cultural Revolution! Then they attacked you because of ideology. Now people think you are stupid to be educated because you don't make a lot of money."

Hong came from a family of teachers. His great-grandfather on his father's side was a peasant who had migrated from the north, in the aftermath of the Taiping rebellion of the 1850s. The rebellion had depopulated the land, and the great-grandfather had done well. Hong's grandfather had aspired to the mandarinate and spent much of his life studying for the imperial examinations; but the 1911 revolution intervened, and he wound up a village teacher. Hong's father had become a teacher too, and an ardent Communist, as so many idealistic young people did in those days.

Hong's maternal grandfather was a rich landlord who had been stripped of his property after the 1949 revolution. Because of her bad class background, Hong's mother had had a very difficult time during the Cultural Revolution. Although her grades were high, she was refused admittance to the first teachers' college she wanted to attend. A second college accepted her, but then at the end of four years told her that it could not grant a diploma to a landlord's daughter.

"She was cut," Hong said, making a chopping motion with his hand.

Her marriage to Hong's father was a clever stroke. By marrying into a "red" family she raised her political status, and the college came around. She was allowed to collect her teaching certificate in 1973.

The spacious house that Hong's maternal family had owned was also taken away and given to a succession of local party leaders to use as a residence. Although such confiscations were declared invalid after the Cultural Revolution, it took twenty years for his father to recover the house. In the course of the last twenty years, Hong's father had paid out a total of six thousand yuan in bribes to what Hong referred to as the "responsible officials."

Hong related all this quite matter-of-factly. It was a history that he took for granted.

"Your family must be very angry," I said.

"Sometimes China is a difficult country," Hong said mildly.

I wondered if he was studying to be a teacher too, but his answers were vague. For a while, I thought it was a problem of language, that he couldn't find quite the right way to put it in English.

"You would like to be a teacher," I ventured helpfully.

"Not exactly," Hong replied.

"What would you like to do?"

Hong looked uncomfortable. Finally he said, "It's a state secret."

I thought that I had failed to hear him correctly.

"What are you studying?" I asked.

Hong took on an opaque look.

"Where is your school?"

"I don't know," he said. "I haven't been there."

I was sure that I hadn't understood.

"What city is your school near?"

"Wuhan is a large and beautiful city," he said. "Guangzhou is also a large and beautiful city."

The school's location was another state secret.

Suddenly it dawned on me that Hong was a soldier; the military greatcoat, the khaki trousers, the crew cut at last made sense. Soldiers were forbidden to talk to foreigners about anything. The fact that we were having a conversation at all was an extraordinary event.

Uneasily, Hong admitted that he was a lieutenant and that he was attending a staff college, somewhere north of the Yangzi. He liked military technology; he was the sort of young officer who, if he were American, would have been chattering about throw-weights and megatons. But he found the academy dull. Most of the other students were peasants and much less well educated than Hong.

"It is very difficult to get books to read. There are no interesting people to talk to. It is very lonely. I would like to go abroad, but . . ."

Hong let the sentence drop off. He sat quietly for a while, opaque and thoughtful, staring out across the incredible panorama of peaks. Monasteries nestled in the rock like great white mountain birds, serene and majestic in their aeries of stone.

After a while he asked, "Are there many secrets in America?"
"Not so many as in China," I said.
"In America, could I tell you where I live?"
"You could."
"And what I do?"
"You could."
He pondered this intently.
"Can American soldiers travel?"
"Of course," I said.
"Even to a foreign country?"
"Certainly."
He looked doubtful.
"But won't people steal their secrets?"

W E HAD come to the top of the mountain. The Dicang Temple lay up a last flight of steps, battened onto the summit like an eagle huddled against the wind. An inscription over the entrance read: "The One-Cavern Heaven," a poetic euphemism for a spiritual way station on the route to salvation. Hong held back at the door. Perhaps the monks and the mysticism repelled him. Or perhaps military officers were banned as a matter of policy from entering religious institutions.

"I don't want to go in," he said bluntly.

Inside, a smiling monk with a mouthful of silver teeth swept me onto a wooden bench and pressed on me a tin mug of aromatic mountain tea. The great gilded idol of Dicang radiated a faint ruddy glow in the oblique late-afternoon light. In the sanctum beyond, the fat-cheeked Buddhas of Past, Present, and Future were afloat on gilded lotuses, encircled by aureoles of golden clouds; how reassuringly well fed they must always have seemed, I thought, in a land where almost everyone had known hunger. A crimson altar stood before them, freighted with blue porcelain vessels whose shapes repeated the earliest ritual objects of Chinese history. Hundreds of tiny lacquered buddhas beamed down on me from the rafters.

A middle-aged woman in a black overcoat approached me,

mumbling, but I found it impossible to understand what she was trying to say. Finally she said, "I'll give you a look."

She took a red cloth from inside her coat, slowly undid it, mumbling plaintively all the while, and finally removed a small vial. Inside the vial was another scrap of red cloth, and inside that a minuscule brass image of a baby, hardly bigger than a pin, dressed in swaddling clothes of the Qing dynasty. Perhaps the tiny effigy represented a dead child lost in the courts of Yen Lo; or perhaps it was a votive offering, representing a prayer that a daughter or sister might bear a child of her own. But why was she showing it to me? What did she want? I tensed involuntarily. Then I understood that she wanted nothing from me, except perhaps a moment of shared hope, for the damned or for the not yet born. After a while, gravely and mysteriously, she wrapped up the figurine again and slipped away into the shadows.

Outside the window, rock pinnacles split the sky, and beneath them strange liquiform promontories dripped away toward the fiery sea of bamboo far below. It was a secretive landscape, infinitely suggestive, so ethereal that it might have been a figment of my imagination. An exultant thrill surged through me. So much of Old China had been destroyed, or had simply collapsed from old age, or had succumbed to the impatient imperatives of twentieth-century man. But the landscape was indomitable; it had survived the collapse of empires, communism, the Red Guards, and, so far, even the entrepreneurs of tourism. What I saw before me might have come an hour before from the brush of Guo Xi, or any of the other painters who had glimpsed these peaks a thousand years ago, and who had shaped for all time the world's perception of the Chinese landscape.

Some said that the ascent of Jiuhuashan was a mirror-reflection of Dicang's descent into hell, that Dicang's power could be felt in the forbidding cliffs and his compassion in the caress of the pure air, that dharma could be learned from the birdsong, and other, better worlds sensed in the sweet incense that billowed from the temple altars. This moment then, suspended beneath the buddhas' eyes before the vast pinnacled landscape that spread away below, was the moment of climax, the moment of the soul's final release.

Behind me, the woman in the black coat had pressed her hands together and knelt before the idol of Dicang. The monk began to chant. At every word he struck a wooden block, and at the beginning of each verse he rang a bronze bell. It was, I guessed, the ancient prayer for succor and rebirth:

Thou whose Pearl illumines the ways of the Celestial Palaces,
Whose Wand opens the doors of the underworld,
Deign to guide the soul of this departed one.
That upon the Lotus-Flower Terrace it may adore the Most
    Compassionate.

I found Hong where I had left him. He was squatting on the naked rock outside the temple, staring into the misty empyrean.

"There are so many secrets in China," he said, slowly. He thought for a while longer. "Maybe we don't need so many secrets."

I FELT AT ease on Jiuhuashan, more than I had anywhere else in China. But it was becoming more and more difficult to cope with the cold in my hotel. I went to bed every night wearing a thermal shirt, two sweaters, and a down coat, and sometimes it was still too cold to sleep. Meals had become a trial. It was hard to manipulate chopsticks with gloves on, especially in the dark, when the electricity went off. Sometimes even the tea water came cold; then a mouse ate the cellophane package in which I kept my tea. It had been days since I had seen hot water; baths were out of the question. I began to think obsessively about clean socks. It was time to leave.

On my last morning I climbed up to the Baisui Temple, which lay almost directly above Hua Cheng, on the rim of the escarpment. Its name meant "centenarian" and was derived from a peculiar artifact that was a popular attraction for pilgrims, the mummified body of a monk.

The monks were a merry crowd. An elderly monk in gray cotton robes and a brown skullcap waved his chopsticks and called to me to sit down and share his bowl of rice. A young monk practicing kung fu in the courtyard shouted "Bruce Lee!" and grinned, but I gave him a wide berth. A novice gaily skittered ahead of me, identifying the great gilded idols that presided over the Buddhist universe. He pointed to Dicang and gave me the thumbs-up sign.

"The best!" he said.

I found the mummy inside a glass cabinet, in a chamber behind the main altar. The famous saint was shrunken to the size of an eight-year-old and swathed in orange and red silk. The arms were folded, and the legs crossed, forever locked in the meditative posture in which the monk was said to have died. The mouth and eyes had disappeared completely beneath layers of golden lacquer, and in the crisp morning light the mummy gleamed like a gilded idol. I had heard rumors that this was not a real mummy at all but a copy made in Hong Kong, that the original had been destroyed during the Cultural Revolution. But the monks continued to insist that the body was that of a hermit named Wu Xia who had come to Jiuhuashan from Shanxi during the Ming dynasty and had died serenely at the age of one hundred twenty-six.

This was not Jin, the Korean anchorite prince, whose mummified body had lain hidden for centuries somewhere in the Flesh Body Hall across the valley. But it was hardly possible to separate the two. Like Jin's, this body too had been discovered only years after his death, perfectly intact, with a copy of the Huayan Sutra written in his own blood by his side. In some mysterious way, in this faith of endless reincarnations, this was also the Korean prince, as well as Dicang himself, and the Indian Ksitagarbha, and countless others who had lived incalculable kalpas ago in the Buddhist past.

The monks seemed unfazed by the morbid thing in the middle of their temple. But for them, of course, it suggested nothing of death at all, but only eternal life. It was proof in the flesh that the bodhisattva had rejected nirvana for mankind and that mercy and salvation did after all exist in a world of unending damnation.

There was a small buddha snugly enshrined in the gatehouse at the top of the steps. On my way back down to Hua Cheng, I paused for a while in front of it and suddenly heard shouting behind me.

"Foreign guest! Foreign guest!"

I turned to see a nun scampering down the stairs toward me, waving her hands as she came. She scrambled beneath the altar and surfaced with a handful of incense, and then stuck it in a bucket of sand and lit it, so that in a few moments sweet musky clouds filled the tiny room.

"Get down, get down," she said, giving me a grandmotherly shove toward the floor in front of the squat idol and motioning me to bow with my hands pressed together in the Buddhist fashion. I bowed three times.

I ventured a prayer, wondering idly whether Dicang could find his way to New York, where my ancestors were buried. I pictured them in some dour Irish Catholic hell and thought how astonished they would be by the sudden appearance of Dicang in his Chinese robes, telling them to pack their bags and make tracks for limbo. Probably they'd tell him to get proper clothes on and to mind his own business.

When I rose and finally looked her full in the face, I suddenly realized that it was the same nun who had ridden next to me on the bus up from Guichi. She was grinning at me from ear to ear, almost giggling with evident joy.

"*Namo Amitou fou!*" she exclaimed. "*Namo Amitou fou! Namo Amitou fou!*"

With a wooden wand, she whacked an iron bowl which responded with a deep-throated clang.

"*Namo Amitou fou!*"

She whacked the bowl again, and then a third time.

"*Namo Amitou fou!*"

When I had risen, the nun scrambled again beneath the altar and pulled out something wrapped in cloth. I expected a treasured relic of some kind, or perhaps an expensive votive that she hoped I would match. Instead, she extracted two shiny new photographs. The first showed a young couple dressed in Western-style clothes, seated on a sofa in a modern concrete-block apartment. The nun clucked fussily for a few moments over the television and the refrigerator that I saw in the corner of the picture.

"My niece," the nun said. "Isn't she pretty?"

The second picture showed the nun and the niece standing in front of Tiananmen Gate.

"That's me in Beijing!"

I said that I had lived in Beijing once.

"You've been there too?" the nun exclaimed. She fairly hopped with happiness, whether for me, or in memory of her journey to the distant capital, or for having discovered this slender bond of coincidence, I couldn't tell.

"Namo Amitou fou!" she cried.

"Namo Amitou fou," I replied politely.

"Namo Amitou fou!" she cried again, more vigorously still.

"Namo Amitou fou!"

CHAPTER
NINE

Gardens of the Mind

*M*ARCO POLO knew Suzhou as a "large and very splendid city" possessed of "vast quantities of raw silk," inhabited by "capable merchants, distinguished professors of learning, as well as others who may be called magicians or enchanters." *Suzhou,* Polo asserted, meant "City of the Earth," while another city, whose name meant "City of Heaven," lay not far away; the other city was Hangzhou, to the south. The names actually meant nothing of the sort. Surely what Polo had heard and then garbled was the old proverb, "In heaven there is paradise; on earth, Hangzhou and Suzhou," which tour guides tirelessly continue to repeat to foreign tourists even today. Until the twentieth century, Suzhou ruled Chinese taste in matters of fashion; it was home to the subtlest artists, the most brilliant scholars, the richest merchants, the best actors, the nimblest acrobats, and the handsomest women with the tiniest feet. Suzhou symbolized to Chinese all that was best in Old China.

The city had become ordinary. Since the revolution many factories had been built, the air made gritty with smog. Canals still laced the city; they were really commercial highways, crowded with stumpy gray barges in long motionless jams. What was left of the old grandeur was submerged beneath soot and neglect. Still, there were things that charmed: the old plastered houses with shops on the ground floor and wooden bays sagging above, the humpy bridges that spanned the canals, puncturing the dreariness like ironically raised eyebrows. Mottled plane trees lent softness to the dowdy lanes, but they had nothing to do with Old China; civic improvers had imported them from France earlier in the twentieth century.

Then there were the walled gardens. Hardly anything like them survived anywhere else in China; they were museums not just of a half-forgotten art but of a sensibility, a whole way of seeing the world. They were scattered around the city, down alleys, behind high sooty walls, alongside the canals. They had been built as urban retreats by the men who ruled China, but they were not simply that; they were bolt-holes from Confucian reality, where the retired official or reclusive scholar could dream himself the fisherman of the Peach Blossom Spring or among the immortals of the Eastern Sea. "Cultivating one's garden" became a byword for renunciation of the public world, for flight into the psychic interior.

History had decided to call these men "literati," a clumsy coinage that tends to suggest July in East Hampton and binges at the Algonquin. Nearly all served in the imperial bureaucracy, but they were also painters, calligraphers, scholars, and connoisseurs. The rarified life that they lived was difficult to imagine, or to respect entirely, in the democratic twentieth century. In New York I had come across fragments of a memoir by a literatus named Li Rihua, who lived not far from Suzhou at the turn of the seventeenth century. He wrote: "All I want is that I have white rice to eat, fish for soup, good wine and fine tea to drink, and in my home ten thousand volumes of books and a thousand stone rubbings. After I have lived like this seventy or eighty years, I shall be a citizen of the Kingdom of Eternal Happiness." This kind of genteel simplicity was partly a pose; imperial service bred disdain for the less favored. When peasants in the surrounding countryside agitated for food, Li wrote, "Rioters today do not become so because they are hungry, but because they want to plunder. One or two must be executed and their heads displayed in the open as a warning to those agitators in order to stop them. If they are merely beaten to death, it is only child's play."

I WENT OFTEN to a small garden that lay off an alley not far from the hotel. It was like stepping into a potted landscape.

You wound through a maze of tiny courtyards and galleries, finally to arrive at a small deep pool surrounded by rockeries and pavilions. Winter-bare plum trees formed a calligraphic scrimshaw against milk-white walls. Oddly shaped windows opened onto mere fragments of space, tiny alcoves occupied by a single rock, a spray of bamboo. A round door in a white wall led to the inner courtyard, where foamy-looking boulders had been built up into an artificial mountain. The courtyard's focal point was a small open kiosk that enshrined a majestic rock like a sacred icon, or a slab of wind.

It was an awesome thing, twice the size of a man. Connoisseurs collected grotesque stones the way others did fine jade and calligraphy; rare specimens fetched such enormous prices that buyers had to be warned against forgeries. Petromaniacs valued rocks for their wild hollows and craggy outlines that suggested clouds, mist, or the primal surge of the Tao, and they read handbooks that told them how to mount fine specimens so that they seemed to "fly and dance." Beneath all this lay the profounder belief that wildly shaped rocks were a sort of spiritual shorthand for all the mysterious powers of the earth.

The garden was just an acre and a half in size, but it was a masterpiece of understatement, a cursive of the gardener's art, like a bold ideograph that with a few strokes suggested volumes of meanings. It took many visits before I began to grasp the text. Yet in it I began to feel a sense of culmination, that I was nearing the frontier of the old Chinese psyche.

Tiny as the garden was, the first time I went there I somehow lost my way in a cul-de-sac near the entrance. I heard someone urgently calling to me in antique English.

"Halloo! Halloo!"

I turned to see a lank, elderly man in a rumpled boiler suit motioning me back the way I had come.

He asked, "Will you allow me the kindness of showing you the art department?"

"I was on my way out," I said.

"Please," he said, coaxing.

The old man was tall for a southern Chinese; his eyes were lively, and a few bristles of an ambivalent beard wandered over his chin. Asking where I had come from, he eagerly led me back through the

191

maze to the Pavilion of the Accumulated Void, where a collection of paintings was on display.

"They are the works of noted and respected local professors," he declared with a flourish.

There were coy pandas, generic clumps of bamboo, laughing buddhas, lurid flowers, and an assortment of Suzhou views that resembled the "Parisian" streetscapes that are the stock-in-trade of five-and-dime art counters.

"This one has been selected for a calendar," he said encouragingly.

He indicated a pair of cranes on a riverbank. I supposed that I was meant to be impressed, but it didn't seem to bother the old man that I wasn't.

I couldn't quite make him out. I suspected that he was one of the "local professors" and that his own works were somewhere in the display. I tried to guess which, in order to compliment them, but they were all so awful that I couldn't bring myself to do it.

"You must be a painter," I said.

He giggled boyishly and pointed his finger at his nose in embarrassment.

Then he showed me a caricatured tiger in the jungle.

"This artist's work has been accepted by President Reagan," he announced.

Sure enough, stuck in the frame was a photocopy of a note from the president, thanking the artist in form-letter prose for "this symbol of friendship and international understanding."

"It must be yours," I said brightly.

"No, no, no, no, no," he protested.

He giggled to himself, and said slyly, "And this one is a rose, your state flower. New York. State flower, the rose. State bird, the bluebird."

He ignored the paintings now.

He recited: "California. State flower, the golden poppy. State bird, the valley quail.

"South Carolina. State flower, the Carolina jessamine. State bird, the Carolina wren."

Astonishment must have shown on my face. Smiling, the old

man explained that in the 1930s he had studied at a missionary school run by American Baptists.

"My teachers were the McMillans, from Spartanburg, South Carolina!" he piped merrily.

The good McMillans had probably taught him plenty of other things that had proved less than useful in the China of Mao Zedong, I supposed. He obviously remembered the missionaries with fondness.

He said he was sixty-nine. When I asked his name he wrote it out for me in my notebook in an elegant, spidery hand: Tung. It was revealing. For a generation, a new system of transliteration had been in effect; virtually everyone would now spell the name Deng.

"Sometimes I prefer things the old way," he said.

He was vague about his life. He had worked in a bank, and then in a government import-export firm, until his retirement.

"Now I am paid a little to introduce people to the paintings," he said. "It is not a bad job for a useless old man."

His eyes twinkled.

"I watch the garden," he said. "I read the poets. The silence pleases me."

CHINESE ROCKERIES made a terrific impression on the first Europeans who saw them. "There is not any one thing wherein the Chinese shew their Ingenuity more, than in these Rocks or Artificial Hills, which are so curiously wrought, that Art seems to exceed Nature," wrote Jan Nieuhof, who traveled to China for the Dutch East India Company in 1655. "These artificial Mountains or Cliffs are commonly contrived with Chambers and Anti-chambers, for a defense against the scorching heat in Summer, and to refresh and delight the Spirits; for they commonly make their great entertainments in these Grots, and the learned seek to study in them rather than any other place."

Nieuhof's book, entitled *An Embassy from the East India Company of the United Provinces to the Grand Tartar Cham Emperor of China*, was a best seller; it was translated into almost every major European language. When the engravers attempted to convert

Nieuhof's reports into comprehensible images, they showed colossal piles of rock waving bizarrely like flames in the wind, dwarfing tiny human figures who scaled them on imperial staircases. Some of the book's other engravings showed peasants harvesting pineapples bigger than a man and Christian angels fluttering around a figure who might have been Confucius, as well as quite authentic pagodas and walled towns. The same precise Flemish hand mingled myth and fact with equally vigorous conviction. For more than a century the Nieuhof engravings provided almost the only images that Westerners had of China. Their effect lingered subliminally long after Nieuhof's book was forgotten: They helped define the look of Cathay, land of the grotesque and improbable, of the baroque made real.

In the northern part of Suzhou there was a famous garden of stone where the painter Ni Zan lived for a time in the 1350s. I made my way through a maze of galleries to an interior courtyard; at the center of it there was a small, deep pond, and around it some pines and bamboo, and a pavilion or two. But the rest of the garden, the true garden, was a phantasmagoric tumult of huge perforated boulders that curled and twisted like smoke or mist, or ocean foam. They boiled out between the pavilions, prodded up from the water, brooded like living creatures through windows and doors, loomed at every bend in the path, swarmed everywhere into hectic ranges of peaks and valleys.

The garden was, like all those in Suzhou, a three-dimensional *trompe l'oeil*, encapsulating both the real earth with all its subtle power and the interior landscape of myth and fantasy. "The aim is to see the small in the large, to see the large in the small, to see the real in the illusory and to see the illusory in the real," an eighteenth-century gardeners' handbook advised. I tried to experience the garden as a Chinese of the old world might have; as I followed serpentine paths over diminutive cliffs, then down into tot-sized glens, I imagined Jiuhuashan's hazy crags and the sea of bamboo, and Taishan and the Jade Emperor's court, and Qingchengshan and the snowy peaks of Tibet receding hazily in the west.

I crossed stone bridges that like alpine spans leaped miniature gorges, and crept through artificial caverns so cramped and tortuous that I had to bend double in order to pass. Processions of lumpy men in identical boiler suits pushed and shoved their way through the tunnels, poking their heads up from crevices and chattering gaily to friends who had popped up in other holes; more Chinese tourists perched everywhere on the rocks, posturing like calendar girls for snapshots.

The crowds made me tense, and I switched uneasily back and forth over paths that I knew I had crossed before, stumbling into claustrophobic nooks shadowed by grotesque crags, and then back into tunnels that unexpectedly opened out from blank rocky walls. It was a nerve-racking experience in the end, and I was grateful when I found myself on a quiet terrace surrounded by the slim green-speckled monoliths that used to be called "stone bamboo"; Chinese in earlier times believed they were so filled with cosmic breath that they actually grew, like plants.

Ni Zan was a determined Taoist, in permanent revolt against society and power, the follies of his age, the tug of possessions. He allowed no one into the garden who he felt lacked a sensibility as refined as his own; he washed himself constantly throughout the day and scrubbed down the garden seats after visitors left. His paintings were as spare and austere as his life; it was said that he hoarded his ink like gold. But Ni's fussiness represented neither weakness nor effeminacy; contemporaries regarded his bleak brushwork as the product of superhuman self-discipline. Nor did he lack humor. Criticized for his lack of realism, he replied, "Ah, but total lack of resemblance is hard to achieve; not everyone can manage it."

It was said that Ni had designed the garden. But as I thought about it now, among the stone bamboo, I couldn't believe it. The garden was too agitated in spirit, almost overdone in a way that was at odds with Ni's ostentatious austerity. Ni left several paintings of the garden, and they bore no resemblance at all to what I saw. They were strange paintings; cold and charmless, usually just a few slim bare trees, a bit of rock, a glimpse of a lake. They were landscapes distilled to the absolute minimum.

Ni's coldness was ultimately a facade, like the wall that hid each exquisite garden from the outer world. Ni believed that mass appreciation would contaminate his art, so he invented a repellent style to confound the untutored. It was such a Chinese solution: simplicity as deception, brilliance left buried within, like a shameful secret. In the end, Ni abandoned everything and sailed off with his wife, to spend the rest of his life in a houseboat, wandering among the lakes and rivers of Jiangsu, giving away his paintings to anyone who asked for them.

ALL THE gardens were now owned by the government, which had coerced them from their last private owners after the revolution. The government also operated a nursery where potted landscapes were cultivated. One afternoon I received a call saying that my application to visit the nursery had been approved by the Bureau of Gardens and that a student from the gardening school would come to the hotel the next morning to escort me.

Wu arrived on a wobbly bicycle, peering like a mole from a cocoon of sweaters and mufflers, beneath a huge furry Manchurian hat. But he seemed brisk and efficient, and on the way to the nursery, he told me that the first garden in Suzhou was built in the tenth century and the last at the turn of the twentieth. More than three hundred existed during the Ming dynasty, he said. Half that number still survived at the start of the Cultural Revolution, in 1966.

"How many are left today?" I asked.

"Fifty-eight."

Wu said that of the fifty-eight, only seventeen were still actual gardens. The rest were occupied by factories, offices, and schools that had moved in during the Cultural Revolution.

I gave up asking Wu about himself, because I could see that he didn't know how much he was allowed to say to a foreigner. But he peppered me with unanswerable questions. What did I think of the "gardening department" at the University of Arkansas? How much did Chinese garden architects earn in America?

At the nursery, Wu introduced me to a sallow man in a woolen sport jacket who he said was the youngest master gardener in Suzhou; Chen Longwei, who was twenty-eight, had recently been appointed the nursery's vice-director. He wasn't used to it yet, and he kept slipping into a friendly smile and then catching himself and straightening out his face again into the opaque official mask.

We walked through a doll-sized forest of pines, cypresses, plum trees, and boxwood. They were all stumps and boles and twisted little limbs, tufted with flurries of minuscule blossoms and needles. It was an art of suggestion, Chen said. Three trees together implied a forest, a single stone a mountain, a certain configuration of branches a felicitous ideograph.

Dwarfing was an ancient craft that went back at least to the Han dynasty. In the beginning, it was probably an incantatory art that was meant to invoke the powerful spirits of the earth. But there was something else at work, too, the ingrained impulse to cramp and constrain that surfaced so often in Chinese character. Until well into the twentieth century, women's feet were dwarfed in much the same way. At a very early age the foot, below the instep, was forced into a line with the leg; the toes were then doubled down under the sole of the foot and wrapped with tight bandages to force the foot to conform to the desired shape. Men called them "lilies," and the mere sight of one unbound was sometimes enough to provoke orgasm.

But the tortured little trees were undeniably beautiful. I asked Chen where he found inspiration.

"Sometimes from classical paintings, sometimes from the land, as I see it."

There were many styles of dwarfing. Suzhou gardeners preferred a triangular look and specialized in extremely old trees. Some of those we were looking at were centuries old.

Chen said, "If you put a beautiful tree next to an old one that is less beautiful, I would choose the old one. It's like appreciating an antique, a Ming jade."

We looked at a tiny plum tree and an evergreen that were growing together inside a dead cypress trunk.

"I call it the 'The Old Man and the Strong' or 'Death Meets the Spring,'" Chen said.

Then he showed me a splintered plum stump. It had looked dead when Chen found it; he had teased it back to life, and a few small branches now sprouted from the top.

"It shows the polarity between life and death, youth and old age; it implies that even the oldest tree can still put forth new shoots."

So could man, it suggested. It was an idea rooted in the old Taoist dream of immortality.

"Most people pay more attention to the outer shape," Chen said. "But there is also an inner spirit in every composition."

"It was made by man, but it should look as if it was made by nature," Wu interjected stuffily.

It struck me that all this seemed to be irritating Wu for some reason. But I was more interested in what Chen had to say.

"Capturing the spirit of the tree is the highest purpose of the art," Chen went on. "When you find an old stump on the mountain-side it's ugly. It's just a tree, not art. You try to find its essence, the beauty that is inside the ugliness, and then to draw it out. When he does that, the gardener puts his own special spirit into the tree. Of course, every gardener's vision is different. Each viewer's idea of beauty is different, too."

Chen sounded more like a young Ruskin than a budding com-missar; he was rediscovering the beautiful. What he was saying im-plied that not only did man need beauty, but that everyone had a right to perceive it in his own way. Anywhere else in the world these would have been platitudes. But here in China they poked at the whole foundation of Marxist aesthetics. Just a few years ago people had gone to jail for saying what Chen was telling me so casually now.

The Maoists had rejected the beautiful as bourgeois. As recently as the early 1980s, official critics were still insisting that all art had to "serve socialism and serve the people." No one could pretend that potted landscapes served socialism. During the Cultural Revolution, the Red Guards had systematically destroyed thousands of the little trees. Even more were destroyed by private owners who were desper-ate to demonstrate their loyalty to the revolution.

By now we had moved on to the greenhouse. I asked Chen to show me how the dwarfing was done. He ran a palm thread through the split root of a tiny pine sapling and lashed it to one of the branches so that it formed an abrupt angle. Then he deftly trussed up half a dozen more branches in the same way until the pine took on the shape of a tree wildly blown in a mountain wind. The thread would remain in place for six months, he said. By that time, the trunk would be set permanently. If trees could speak, I thought, these would scream.

Wu, my guide, had also studied classical gardening at the bureau's school. On the way out of the nursery I asked him what he wanted to do with himself. To design gardens, he said.

"What will they be like?"

"There will be big meadows with no buildings and no walls, just big open spaces everywhere, and really big trees all far apart, where people can run, and run, and run!"

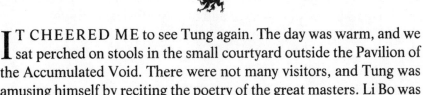

I T CHEERED ME to see Tung again. The day was warm, and we sat perched on stools in the small courtyard outside the Pavilion of the Accumulated Void. There were not many visitors, and Tung was amusing himself by reciting the poetry of the great masters. Li Bo was his favorite. Like the gardens, the old vagabond's poems had for more than a thousand years been an escape hatch for the imagination from the solemnities of the Confucian life. Tung recited, first in the sibilant Suzhou dialect, and then in the stolid English of the McMillans of Spartanburg, South Carolina:

In the morning, I left Baidi amidst the colored clouds;
I journeyed a thousand li to Jianling, yet returned in a day.
Monkeys cried from the shores without cease;
How many mountains the late boat has passed!

Tung exclaimed, "It was all in his imagination, you see, but how he enjoyed the trip!"

It was as if he were reading a postcard from an old friend.

We sat for a time in silence. I noticed that tiny buds had appeared on the plum trees, promising spring.

I felt an immense ease. The somber colors caressed and sedated; the strange stones had become familiar presences, unearthly and benign. The garden seemed somehow larger the better I came to know it. The effect was created partly by the walls, whose ivory surfaces recorded the passage of time like a screen. As the sun arched overhead the shapes of banana leaves, rocks, and branches played across them in ever-changing combinations; then in bright sunlight they seemed to disappear completely, leaving just their roofing of gray tiles floating above the ground, Chinese of the old world used to say, like dragons writhing in the air.

The pond increased the effect. It was deliberately sited so that it reflected the upturned eaves, and plum trees and pines, and the walls with their cargo of shadows, creating a double world scarcely more evanescent than the one it mimicked. A large mirror hung in a small open pavilion across the pond, producing, as it mirrored the water, a reflection of a reflection, an illusion of an illusion. I remembered the ancient parable of Chuang Tze and his paradoxical butterfly:

"Once I, Chuang Tze, dreamt of being a butterfly; a butterfly that flitted hither and thither, enjoying itself as it wished. Nor did it know that it was Chuang Tze. Now know I not: is it really Chuang Tze who was dreaming he was a butterfly? Or is the butterfly dreaming it is Chuang Tze?"

Beyond the intellectual refinement and the puns there was something immensely comforting about these gardens. It had something to do with the smallness of things, and the secrecy, and the enclosing walls. The gardens recollected the private haunts that children create, the little nests they build in an attic or thicket, beyond sight and reach of adults. They recalled childhood's innocence and secret play, and safety; all those illusions, too.

"Listen," said Tung.

He began to recite a poem by the Song poet, Lin Sun:

Hills beyond hills, pavilions beyond pavilions
Will the singing and dancing never cease?
Drunk in the warm breeze,
They take Hangzhou as Bizhou

Tung explained (a little pedantically) that Bizhou was another name for the old Song-dynasty capital of Kaifeng. The poem was nostalgic and tinged with bitterness. It carried the implication that when the Song officials fled south in 1127, they shamefully forgot in their revelry the abandonment of their capital to the Mongol barbarians.

He wrote the poem out for me in what he pointedly emphasized were the old-style characters, before their simplification in the 1950s. It distressed him that few people could read them anymore.

Each Chinese ideograph was a complex architecture of strokes and implicit ideas that had, like a historical sediment, accumulated over the centuries. By reducing the number of strokes needed to write thousands of ideographs, simplification had made Chinese much easier to learn; but in the process allusiveness had been lost, multiple layers of meaning removed.

"In English, 'culture' implies a citizen, a man of the city," Tung said. "But for us the word 'culture' means language, the ideograph itself. Five thousand years of language is slipping away!"

People had begun to gather in front of the doorway where we sat: a middle-aged couple, a pair of teenagers, a visiting peasant or two. I was so used to being stared at by now that I hardly noticed them. But Tung became increasingly skittish.

"We can't go on!" he said. "We mustn't say anything more."

THE IMPERIAL censor Wang Xianchen who laid out the "Humble Administrator's Garden" in the sixteenth century took its name from an adage: "To cultivate one's garden to meet one's daily needs, that is what is known as the politics of a plain man." Read thus, the garden's name implied conventional Confucian humility. But it was really a masterful pun that could equally be translated as a sly retort to the bureaucrats who had hampered his career: "The Garden of the Stupid Officials."

The garden was conceived as a series of cells, like the panels of a painting, and like a scroll it was meant to unroll before the eye as you wandered through it. There had originally been three of these cells, but the outermost one was empty now. Probably a factory had been installed there during the Cultural Revolution and had now been removed; only a brook remained, and a few crumbled hillocks. But a handsome new teahouse had been built, and early each morning I saw elderly men and women there practicing tai chi, fat as dumplings in their winter padding.

Secluded within the garden's next cell was the most delicate landscape I had ever seen. A slender green lake meandered among craggy islets, ranges of artificial hills, and airy pavilions that suggested some riverine city of fantasy. The colors were the solemn ones of the painter's palette: green trees, gray roofs and rock, and white walls that separated the garden's cells like the clouds that divided a painting's panels. Often damp mist lent dreamy uncertainty to the scene. Then the upturned roofs hovered weightlessly above the water, and the hewn-stone bridges seemed to link only islands of white mist. A pagoda rose in the distance, sited so that it suggested an antique world beyond the garden. The pond ended at a circular moon gate in another white wall. Windows in the shape of flowers, cracked ice, and felicitous ideographs leaked glimpses of new vistas further on; an inscription above the gate promised "Another Universe."

The garden was a labyrinth, and it drew me inexorably in. Pebbled paths wandered over the diminutive peaks and the plum-forested islets, into hidden vales and out again through tortuous caverns, playing tirelessly at concealment and discovery, hinting always at some ultimate sanctum or final truth that was never quite revealed. The garden was a deliberate intimation of paradise, the search for the Peach Blossom Spring made real.

Everything was dense with multiple meanings. Any Chinese of the old world knew that the serpentine ponds simultaneously suggested the earth's blood, Confucian purity, and the Tao, and that the wild stones were nodes of cosmic energy, and that together the rocks and water spoke of the eternal polarity of yin and yang, the female yielding and male strength that infused all life. They knew, too, that the gnarled pines symbolized enduring virtue, the lotus flower the Confucian gentleman because it emerged unstained from the mire, and peonies wealth and rank; when they bloomed, fêtes were held in their honor.

The islets were intended to represent Penglai, the disappearing isles of the immortals that hovered in the mists of the sea off the coast of Shandong. It was said that the specially favored could sometimes see the immortals themselves moving about, disporting themselves with their wives and children and working diligently in their fields, a mirror image of the world of men.

There was a curious story connected with the islands of Penglai. In the third century B.C., the First Emperor Qinshihuangdi sent boatloads of handsome young men and women in search of them, to bring the secret of eternal life back to his court at Changan. But none of the young voyagers returned, and for two thousand years Chinese saw their journey as the poignant archetype of man's dream of immortality.

It was the quest for Penglai that inspired the first gardens. Two hundred years after Qinshihuangdi, the Emperor Han Wudi built miniature mountains planted with mystic herbs and exotic flowers in an effort to lure the immortal spirits to the imperial court; he erected statues of the immortals atop high columns, holding up bowls to catch the dew, "reaching out beyond the defilement of the world's dust to gain the limpid elixir of pure transparent *qi*." The immortals never came, but gardens remained magical places, saturated with intimations of immortality.

The odd thing is, there really are islands off the coast of Shandong that, because of a quirk in the atmosphere, can occasionally be seen from the mainland, suspended in the sky; people who have seen them in recent years report that the inhabitants have now been blessed with trucks, power stations, and all the other accoutrements of modern Chinese life. I often wondered whether Qinshihuangi's young folk had found Penglai after all and had decided that life on the disappearing isles was preferable to the opulence and danger of the imperial court.

The garden was a popular one with Chinese tourists. I had come early one day, in the hope of having it to myself for a few hours. But as soon as the gate was opened, streams of Shanghainese day-trippers flowed in with an exuberant roar. There were hundreds, then thousands of them, swelling as the day went on into a vast, chattering crescendo.

I retreated to the third cell, the innermost courtyard, beyond the mysterious moon gate. I stepped through the gate, as if into the scroll's next panel, and the garden transformed itself yet again. The pond passed through a sluice beneath the gate, to emerge into craggy gorges that wound beneath tiny cliffs; the rockeries were more abrupt here, the garden even more intricate. A fan-shaped kiosk punctuated the rocky islet that separated the channels. It was called the Whom-to-Sit-With pavilion and took its name from an old poem:

With whom can I sit?
The bright moon, a light breeze and myself.

Inside it, two nervous Chinese lovers were grappling with quiet desperation in their layers of heavy winter clothes.

I followed the path on around the rim of the tarn, searching for a silent spot. But privacy was impossible. Wherever I went, the mobs followed in a squall of laughter and high spirits. At the end of a small bridge I came to a mahogany pavilion whose name was Stay-and-Listen.

Later I found that the pavilion had briefly been the home of the insurgent emperor of the Taipings, who in the 1850s nearly overthrew the crumbling dynasty of the Manchus. I pictured him surrounded by his fanatic courtiers, an increasingly mad monarch who had been convinced by a smattering of Christianity that he was the son of God. This garden of illusion was an apt place for him, I thought, with his dream vision of the Kingdom of Heavenly Grace on Earth.

Thinking of the pavilion's name, I remembered Chuang Tze's advice: "Listen not with the ears, but with the mind. Listen not with the mind, but with the spirit." Gradually I let the garden fold in upon me, and time melted. Chimneys reminded me that the twentieth century was still out there somewhere beyond the garden's walls. But for the moment it seemed as ephemeral as the mist.

I found myself thinking of George Kates. This was the world that he had discovered and had carried inside himself ever since. I remembered the hard New England light slanting into his hospital room, the brass seal, the box with the jade dragon on top, the ring with the bats, all smooth from years of handling, talismans of the life he had left behind in Beijing. Fifty years ago, he had found his own Peach Blossom Spring and re-created the magical garden in his courtyard home, with his soft-footed servants and the solemn routines of a life that was even then on the cusp of extinction.

I supposed that Stay-and-Listen had originally been a studio, decorated with scrolls and calligraphy, and jades and ivories to soothe the eye and stimulate the imagination. Here men like Li Rihua swapped poetry with friends, refracted the miniature pond and rockeries back into painted landscapes, invited fellow connoisseurs to "watch the moon bathe itself" in the pond. At its best, I thought, their life was a vocation of appreciation, in which even the smallest experience might be transformed into art. "It has been clear and warm for ten days," Li wrote in his memoir. "The narcissus and the plum in the small pot were in full bloom, their fragrance spreading all around. I was totally drowned in this aroma all day. Someone came in to ask me to go somewhere. I declined, for I did not want to miss this pure delight."

So thoroughly had all trace of these men been removed from the daily life of China that it was difficult to believe they had ever existed at all. Just enough of them remained half a century ago that George Kates could fall in love with their rarified life. He described them beautifully to me as "rubbed people"; he admired them as men whose surfaces had been smoothed and polished by immemorial convention and made impervious to the heat of human friction.

I valued spontaneity and bluntness more than I suspected Kates did, and I had far less patience with artifice than a man bred in the Victorian shadow. It was also impossible now to ignore the brutality that existed side by side with the literati's life; the concubines who shared their gardens were bought slaves, and their feet were dwarfed like Chen Longwei's dainty plums. But all the same, I felt deeply seduced by the same things that Kates had: the grace of manner, the incredible delicacy of feeling, the constant presence of an immense and accessible past.

I remembered Kates saying to me, in that paper-thin, lighter-than-air voice, "There is an inestimable benefit in having a past that stretches back so many centuries, Mr. Bordewich. It gives such insight into the human dilemma. China made me more mature, and I am grateful for it."

If the garden had an ultimate secret to yield, I thought, perhaps it was the past itself. Something of that past still survived in suspended animation here, vivid and intact, waiting, like the secret valley of the Peach Blossom Spring, to be rediscovered and made use of by a people who for forty years had been starved of the beautiful, the whimsical, and the absurd. Then I thought of Chen Longwei, teetering between the two worlds of art and officialdom like the literati before him, uncomfortable with the mask of convention, yet afraid to drop it. I visualized him for a moment as the fisherman of the Peach Blossom

Spring, struggling to find his way back to the lost domain. I hoped he would make it.

The tourists continued to surge around me, leaving behind them their spoor of melon seeds, cigarettes, and spent flash bulbs. I wondered whether they were so very different from Chen and George Kates, or whether they sensed, like a tropism, that they too needed something more from history than what had been bequeathed to them by the commissars.

The garden seemed alive and atremble with possibility. I wanted never to go. But it was already evening, and the stark white walls had become mere shadows; impatient guards began blowing tin whistles, barking at everyone to leave. As I went out, the lovers were still working at each other in the Whom-to-Sit-With Pavilion, struggling with increasing desperation or passion (it was hard to say which) to enfold themselves in each other's wadded arms.

I WENT TO say good-bye to Tung. I walked one last time through the garden. Since my last visit, a few days ago, the plum buds had burst open, and the air was filled with a dense narcotic sweetness. In a world so small and self-contained, even the most minute change seemed momentous.

Since my first visit, I had wondered what happened to the McMillans, the Baptist missionaries who had thought it so important for Chinese boys to memorize the state flowers of California, New York, and South Carolina. I asked Tung about them.

The Communists had ordered them out of China in the 1950s with the rest of the Americans who still remained, he said. He thought they were close to one hundred years old at the time. The ironic thing was, they had lived in China so long that they had no home left in the United States.

"It wasn't fair. They were just thrown away." Tung's placid face abruptly twisted in contempt. "Communists . . ."

He left the rest of the thought judiciously unexpressed. Then he grew suddenly vehement.

"You couldn't speak the truth, couldn't say anything at all! It was all a big fraud. Lies, lies!"

By now he was shifting nervously back and forth from one foot to the other, craning to peer back over his shoulder through the elegantly screened window. The bamboo, the rockeries had suddenly become ominous; they could shelter unseen listeners.

"If they hear you, you're finished!" he whispered. "That's the way it is. They'd send me to the far West . . ."

That was what Xinjiang meant to Chinese of Tung's generation; not Marco Polo, or nomads, or the picturesque legends of the Taklamakan, but concentration camps.

The memory of something terrifying and unsaid was palpable in the air between us. I sensed that many years ago a threat had been made or that friends had disappeared and never returned.

"You have the garden," I said, in a poor attempt at reassurance. "And Li Bo and Du Fu."

"Yes, I tend my own garden," he said.

It was the ancient phrase, the byword of generations of literati as they retreated into the inner courtyards of the self.

It struck me that Tung was as near to a literatus of the old world as the China of the 1980s would allow. He had subtly made the garden his own, and in it re-created what he could of the old life, alone with the strange stones, and the knobbly pines, and the endlessly mirroring water, and the ubiquitous hinting at better, secret worlds.

"Let's stick to poetry," I said.

"Yes," Tung replied. "It is always better to stick to poetry."

Before I left, Tung handed me an envelope. Inside, in handsome old-style ideographs (and in English), was the following poem:

> Though I was old, I never lost the wish to travel,
> To enjoy the cherry blossoms on the slopes of Yushan.
> We were well-met, my friend
> And we drank tea in the Huan Tsai Pavilion.

It was one o'clock, time for Tung's siesta, and in a long gentle flurry of handshaking we parted. I asked if I might see him again the next time I was in Suzhou. "With the greatest of pleasure," he said, as if I were a fellow scholar visiting from some town a few stages away on the Grand Canal.

CHAPTER
TEN

Twilight
at the Rhythm Café

I T WAS unexpectedly difficult to find good food in Suzhou. The big state-run restaurants in the center of town
were expensive and bad, and the street stalls were a disappointment. Finally a clerk at the hotel pointed me toward
an inauspicious-looking cottage wedged against the canal. Strings of
gaudy lights were draped across the front; a hand-lettered sign said
"Rhythm Café." There were just four or five tables jammed into a
single dim room, but the food was simple and good, and eventually I
ate there every night.

George could have been anywhere between forty and sixty; he
was slim and vigorous, and he took your order with a flourish of old-
fashioned formality that seemed exaggerated because it was so out of
scale in the tiny café. George's shy wife managed the accounts. There
was also a strapping, good-natured son and a svelte daughter who
slithered around in snug jeans, but they worked mostly in the kitchen
and I rarely saw them.

George? The name puzzled me a little. But Western names were
coming back into fashion. An acquaintance named Dagong liked to be
called Doug; Xiaorong became Sharon; Peita, Peter; and so on. I
didn't think much about it.

George had worked as a tailor since his release from the mines;
his wife had been a teacher. Last summer they had pooled their life
savings to open the restaurant. It was doing well, so well, in fact, that
some of the son's unemployed friends were asking him to give them a

211

piece of the business, George said. The son was technically the owner; George had put the restaurant in the son's name so they could get a government loan intended to help "job-waiting youth," as the unemployed were called, to set up small businesses. The son's friends were jealous of his success.

I saw the friends a couple of times. They were in their early twenties, and bullying; five or six of them would sprawl in the café so that paying customers couldn't sit, drinking beer and expecting to be fed. They worried George.

"Loafers, 'teddy boys' you would call them," he said.

The turn of phrase was part of his old-fashioned style. He meant hoodlums.

George's home was in Shanghai, an hour and a half away by train. But it had proven too expensive to get a business started there, George explained. So the family crammed together in a cheap hotel room in Suzhou and took turns visiting Shanghai. George's ambition was to buy the family's way out of China.

"It doesn't matter where," George said with a shrug. "My own life is over. But I want my kids out."

He knew it was difficult to get into the United States. Australia was a little easier. Taiwan was also a possibility; his wife had relatives there.

George spoke remarkably good English. When I asked where he had learned it, he said, "I'm a foreigner just like you."

I thought he was joking.

"You think I'm Chinese?" he asked humorously. "The Chinese, they don't think so."

I looked at George more closely. I hadn't noticed before, but his eyes were rounder, his nose more aquiline, his bone structure sharper than the average Chinese. He handed me a name card; it said "George Battista."

There were layers and layers of his story, and he peeled them only slowly and ambiguously, over time. He was born in Manila, he said; his mother was Chinese, his father Filipino. His father was an accountant by profession, who had come to China to work for the revolution and had eventually risen to an important post in some kind of development agency.

"He never did anything wrong," George said. "But they said he was a foreign spy, and they attacked him and attacked him. He went crazy from it. He wanted to go back to the Philippines, but they wouldn't let him leave China. They tore his passport up right in front of his eyes. Finally he gave up. The last three years, he wouldn't get out of bed. He stayed there until he died."

George had been educated as an engineer. Before the Cultural Revolution, he worked at planning new railway lines. Then, because of the allegations against his father, George also came under attack.

"Nobody would talk to me. When they passed me in the street they closed one eye so they could pretend they didn't see me."

The fact that George and his father were Catholic made it worse. In the 1950s the Communists forced the Chinese church to sever its connection with Rome. They jailed hundreds of priests and amalgamated the church with the Protestant sects in a single organization administered by the government. Believers who remained loyal to Rome were regarded as spies for the Vatican.

George was sentenced to "reform through labor" in a coal mine in Shandong. He worked ten hours a day, six days a week. Sometimes he worked the seventh day too. "They called that 'self-work.' Maybe you would say 'volunteer.' But of course you didn't volunteer. They told you to do it." He was allowed to write occasional letters home. "I could write that I was just fine and very happy to be 'serving China,' and 'learning from the workers,' and how much I hated my father for filling me up with 'capitalist' ideas, and how happy I was to be having my brain trained." He spent twelve years in the mine.

Through all this he remained devout. The political commissars kept nagging at him about that. "They said, 'How can you believe in God? You can't see him, can you?' So I told them, 'You can't see Communism, can you? But you believe in it, don't you?' They said, 'Of course.' So I said, 'What's the difference?' " When George finished he asked if I was a Catholic.

"I was baptized Catholic," I said.

It pleased him. It was a connection.

I liked George. He was at ease with himself in a way that Chinese almost never were. Chinese were always walled-in and on guard,

213

always ready to bolt. When I asked George how he had survived the years in the mine, he said, "I just took it easy." It was such a hilarious answer that we both laughed. But he meant it.

All the same, something didn't fit. George had said that his father came to China after the revolution. But another time he told me that he was fifty years old and that his father had brought him to Shanghai at the age of three. If that was true, it meant that he had arrived in China in 1941.

One evening I said, "Your father came to help the revolution."

"That's right."

"To Shanghai?"

"To Shanghai."

"But in 1941 the Communists were still holed up in Yenan."

I had caught him out. He waited to see what I would say. I was sorry I had embarrassed him, and decided to let the moment pass. We sat for a while in an awkward silence. Then a big smile broke over George's face.

He said, "Where are you spending your Christmas?"

The holiday was just a few days off. I had been planning to go to Hangzhou. I wanted to see the West Lake in the rain, but the weather was unexpectedly bright and balmy.

If I had in my mind's eye a single vision of medieval Cathay, it was Song-dynasty Hangzhou. The imperial court fled there in 1138, to escape the barbarians who had overrun the north, and for the next century and a half it was a city of incredible wealth and sophistication. Its population reached 1 million at a time when Venice was home to a few tens of thousands. Posh restaurants decorated their walls with the scrolls of celebrated painters; there were fashionable inns that served everything iced or lured customers with delicacies like plum-flower wine and silkworm pie. There were shops that sold eyebrow-black and false hair, and pet cats and fish to feed them with, and crickets in cages. Jugglers and acrobats performed on the street corners, and men who exhibited circuses of trained ants. There were teahouses where you could take singing lessons, and others where you could hear storytellers who specialized in obscene tales, or accounts of baffling crimes, or comedians who burlesqued the rustic speech of Shandong and Hebei. Even prosaic trades were invested with a kind of poetry: The keepers of bathing establishments were known as "the companions of fragrant water," and shoemakers as "companions of the double thread." But disintegration was in the air. The capital was packed with refugees who were so impoverished that they would sell their family members in order to survive. Certain restaurants specialized in the famine-bred cuisine of the war-torn north. In them, you ordered human flesh prepared for gourmets; it was advertised as "two-legged mutton."

I knew medieval Hangzhou was gone. Hangzhou was better known now for the manufacture of chopsticks and silk than for courtesans or jugglers. But the West Lake remained. I knew the lake mostly from paintings; it was famous for its mists and the delicacy of its atmosphere. When the court moved south the imperial academy fled with it, and as time went on, the lake's ambience shaped an entire school of art. The court painters gradually abandoned the huge scrolls and awesome mountainscapes, and turned moody and intimate. In their new paintings, a wren stood mesmerized by a plum, infant princes played in a mysterious garden, a sage drifted along a moonlit stream or poised on a precipice, listening to the silence of the universe. It was an evasive art, of course. The omnipresent mists masked unspeakable horrors; there was no hint in these paintings of the barbarians at the gate, or of those awful restaurants. But they were mesmerizing images, like snapshots of the dream-world of Cathay.

I began to explain this to George, but I could see that I was losing him.

"Come to Shanghai," he said.

There would be a midnight mass on Christmas Eve at the old French cathedral. George was closing the Rhythm Café for the evening and taking the family back to Shanghai for it.

"Come with us," George urged.

"I'll try," I said.

"You'll come," George declared.

"I will," I said, in the end.

But I wondered about that lost decade.

215

SHANGHAI SEEMED strangely familiar. The city bore an eerie resemblance to New York, but it was the New York that I remembered from my childhood, when the ornate skyscrapers of the 1920s and 1930s still defined the look of the modern. It was a through-the-looking-glass vision of a future that had already become the past and run to seed, as if the South Bronx had taken over everything from Madison Avenue to Wall Street.

Shanghai was not an old city. It was founded only in 1843, as a concession to the British, after their victory in the First Opium War. It began as a clutter of warehouses and merchants' homes on the pestilential mud flats alongside the Huangpu River. In less than a century it became the richest city in Asia, reaching its shimmering apogee in the 1920s and 1930s, when it achieved a critical mass of sophistication and depravity that has seldom been equaled anywhere.

In 1933 forty-eight different nationalities were listed in the city's census. There were British, Americans, and Japanese; there were French and Greeks, and Parsees and Annamese; there were Jews in flight from Hitler's Germany, and White Russians fleeing the Reds. There were boulevards named for Edward VII and for Marshal Joffre, and across Suzhou Creek in the American Settlement an avenue called Broadway after its namesake in New York. Aldous Huxley called Shanghai, "Life itself. Nothing more intensely living can be imagined." In no other city in the world had he ever seen such "dense, rank, richly clotted life." It was a city of incredible extremes. Financiers made fortunes over drinks at the long bar of the exclusive Shanghai Club, while a few miles away waterfront gangs battled openly over barges of opium. Mobsters housed their concubines in Tudor mansions, while European ladies of unsurpassed elegance gathered for tea in the roof garden of the *Cercle Sportif Francais*.

I found a guidebook written in 1934. The chapter on entertainment began this way:

Whoopee!

What odds whether Shanghai is the Paris of the East or Paris the Shanghai of the Occident?

Shanghai has its own distinctive night life, and what a life!

Dog races and cabarets, hai-alai and cabarets, formal tea and dinner dances and cabarets, the sophisticated and cosmopolitan French Club and cabarets, prize fights and cabarets, amateur dramatics and cabarets, theaters and cabarets, movies and cabarets, and cabarets—everywhere, in both extremities of Frenchtown, uptown and downtown in the International Settlement, in Hongkew, and out of bounds in Chinese territory, are cabarets.

Hundreds of 'em!

High hats and low necks; long tails and short knickers; inebriates and slumming puritans.

Wine, women and song.

Whoopee!

My hotel had been the most fashionable in Shanghai before the revolution; Noel Coward had written *Private Lives* there in a mere four days while he was laid up with the flu. When I checked in, I could hear a piano somewhere playing "White Christmas," and in the lobby there was a tree decked with colored lights and tufts of cotton to simulate snow. There were still frosted-glass sconces in the dining room and polished woodwork in the dim halls, and the waiters in the coffee shop wore black silk dinner jackets and starched shirts.

I walked down the riverfront boulevard called the Bund, which still curved with a certain dowdy majesty alongside the oily Huangpu. The crowds were dense and dressed mostly with the same tacky monotony that you saw everywhere in China. But something of the old energy remained. Like New Yorkers, people moved more briskly and purposefully than they did elsewhere; other Chinese even said the same things about Shanghainese that Americans said about New Yorkers: that they were brash and pushy and loud, too foreign in their ways.

The palatial towers that once were home to imperial satrapies like the Banque de l'Indo-Chine, the Asiatic Petroleum Company, and the Hongkong & Shanghai Bank still stood along the Bund. But they had been replaced, the brass nameplates informed me, with tongue-twisters like the "China National Cereals, Oils and Foodstuffs Corporation" and the "China National Native Products and Animal

By-Products Import and Export Corporation." Jerry-built stalls had been shoehorned between the marbled columns, selling disco tapes, dumplings, bootlegged cigarettes. The marbled lobbies were chock-a-block with spare lumber and wiring and obscure hunks of metal, and with guard boxes for the extrawatchful eyes that the Communists had added to every workplace and dwelling. The only hint of an underworld came from seedy Uighurs at the curbside who furiously whispered at me to buy black-market renminbi.

At the lower end of the Bund, I found what used to be the Shanghai Club. Its long bar was a famous microcosm of Shanghai hierarchy. There was a tacit rule that the end facing the river was reserved for the taipans of the great trading houses; next to them were the bullion brokers, then the assistant managers of the big firms, and so on down to the end of the bar, which was inhabited by the lowlier forms of expatriate life, such as journalists and the unemployed.

The building was now a hostel for seamen. I sat for a while in the lobby, struggling to imagine the taipans sweeping in from their limousines of an afternoon for their chota pegs of scotch. But the neo-classical atrium worked like an echo chamber and resonated with hawking, racketing crockery, and high-decibel disco from a badly tuned radio. Broken light fixtures dangled from the ceiling, and the slim Doric columns were submerged in heaps of bicycles that were for sale on the cracked checkerboard marble floor.

The bankers, the brokers, and the foreigners had all been driven away, almost to a man. George Battista was one of the last, a relic of Shanghai's hybrid past. The political campaigns in the 1950s had systematically wiped out the gangsters and the whores, and the cabarets, and the native entrepreneurs. Life was still dense and rank and clotted, but it was no longer rich.

But China had almost come full circle. Capitalism was now being promoted again. One day I read this headline in the English-language *China Daily*: "Shanghai on Stock Spree." The manager of the Yanzhong Industrial and Commercial Company, a man named Zhou Rongxin, was quoted as saying, "I always bear in mind my responsibility to the sixteen thousand shareholders of my company and work hard so as to live up to their expectations." Jin Delin, who had bought one hundred shares of the company's stock, confidently told the

reporter, "Since I have invested in the company, I expect it to flourish." They were like archaeologists rediscovering a half-remembered
tool whose function was still not quite clear; there was such a quaint
innocence to it all.

The truth was, Shanghai was on the verge of complete collapse.
Half of the city's industrial plant dated from before World War II and
most of the rest from the 1950s. Housing was so overcrowded that
three hundred thousand couples were delaying marriage until they
could find accommodation. An official report blandly remarked that
during peak hours, city buses held twelve riders per square meter. I met
an American diplomat who had taken the trouble to work out the
mathematics involved. He told me, "It is in fact impossible to fit twelve
pairs of shoes into one single meter, so it presumably means that at any
given time some thousands of riders cannot touch the floor."

Every evening a band played jazz in the hotel coffee shop; it was
another déjà vu experience. The musicians were jowly, spectacled
men in their sixties and seventies, who had played with big Shanghai
bands before the revolution. They began to perform again a few years
ago, when the authorities decided that jazz was no longer counterrevolutionary. They played "When the Saints Go Marching In," "My
Heart Belongs to Daddy," "Take the A Train," over and over. When
they played the "Waltz of the Toreadors" a waiter marched across the
floor, clapping his hands like castanets over his head. The jazzmen
were like the old buildings; you thought that you were seeing yourself,
your own culture. But they were really images of a dead world. It was
like looking at old scrolls or jades in a museum, exotic artifacts that
had been brought from far away across the desert on camelback and
then hidden for centuries in a forgotten chamber, like the manuscripts
at Dunhuang. Only the artifact this time was Duke Ellington. In the
end, the jazzmen put on their old men's sweaters, picked up their
lidded mugs of jasmine tea, and went home.

THE NEXT day's weather report promised rain after all; I
bought a train ticket and hurried to Hangzhou. Shanghai's suburbs stretched far into the countryside. Then gradually I began to see

peasants in azure tunics wading through low-lying mist, hoeing fields, and sometimes slim barges filled with produce bellying along narrow canals. Villages in the distance were dense clumps of white, two-story farmhouses, like the solid, *bürgerlich* towns of southern Germany.

Even after its fall to the Mongols, Hangzhou dazzled. Marco Polo marveled at the twelve thousand bridges that spanned its canals, and at its paved streets, and the sophistication of its citizens, who still managed to enjoy "dainty living, to the point of eating fish and meat at one meal." So skilled were the city's courtesans "that foreigners who have once enjoyed their charms remain utterly beside themselves." The West Lake stretched from the city's edge to the shallow hills that lay three miles to the west. What a sight it must have been, its islets studded with lavish pavilions, and the hills with pagodas, temples, and mansions "of such workmanship that nothing better or more splendid could be devised"! Pleasure seekers thronged the water in anything that floated, from contraptions propelled by pedals to richly ornamented barges that carried scores of people. "A voyage on this lake offers more refreshment and delectation than any other experience on earth," Polo sighed.

The present-day city resembled Suzhou, with its whitewashed houses and plane trees; but the canals had all been filled in and made into roads, so that there was more traffic and bustle, and an impression of tawdry modernity. Billboards advertised pop singers, Volkswagens, electric guitars, red sneakers, and billiard balls, and on the corners knots of unemployed young people hawked cheap prints of blond, bare-shouldered couples in a cheek-to-cheek embrace that I supposed seemed risqué to people raised prudishly in the shadow of Mao.

All but a handful of the old temples were gone, but otherwise the lake remained almost unchanged. I walked to the shore and then along a slender dike freighted with plum trees and willows. Mist sifted over the water, making the landscape beyond seem pale and weightless, and pregnant with mystery. The hills to the south and west rose one behind the other, like palimpsests, the furthest ones so faint that when I blinked they disappeared completely and then slowly reformed themselves before my eyes. Closer in, islets lay on the water, a deep, smoky emerald against the white void.

A particular painting hovered in my mind as I walked. It hung in the Metropolitan Museum of Art, in New York. In it, a robed sage peered over a stone balustrade into a chasm where a waterfall arched through a slit in the hills; all the rest was a misty nothingness. I don't know how many times I had stood in the gallery, craning over the shoulder of the painted sage, into that abyss. So real, so intense was the painted scene that I often felt that with a nudge from behind I might have tumbled into it and found myself next to the startled old man in the antique robe. The mist was endlessly tantalizing; I longed to see what lay on the other side of it.

Drizzle had turned into rain, and cyclists glided by like large land-bound birds, swathed in plastic ponchos. A young man in a blue poncho emerged from the mist, watching me as he pedaled past. He rode on for a short distance and then turned his bicycle around on the narrow pavement.

"Are you American?" he asked.

He pulled a roll of much-handled documents from his tunic. He extracted one and handed it to me. It was a letter of admittance from a small college in Michigan.

"They expected me in September," he said forlornly.

Pan was wiry and bowlegged, so that when he approached on his bicycle he looked as if he were about to topple over; his face was intense and flat, and intelligent. He taught physics at the local university. The college in Michigan had accepted him for graduate work, but he couldn't get a United States visa without a sponsor. He spent his afternoons cycling around the lake, looking for Americans.

"Will you be my sponsor?" he asked hopefully.

I said, "But I don't even know you!"

"But I have been admitted!"

Students all over China wanted to go to the United States now. In some cities, I ran into them almost every day. I wanted to help, but I couldn't afford it.

Pan's salary was fifty dollars per month. His tuition would be twelve thousand dollars, never mind living expenses and airfare. He had no grasp at all of what it cost to live in the United States.

"Don't worry," he said encouragingly. "Please just sign. I can get a job, any job. I want to work!"

I tried to explain, but he became agitated.

"I have been admitted!" he cried, more insistently.

The fact seemed like a talismanic thing to him, like an amulet. I had the sense that he knew he would never get away.

Pan stuck with me doggedly, walking his bicycle alongside me in the rain. I didn't have the heart to turn him away.

We walked to a curious shrine that stands on the northern shore of the lake. Formerly it was a temple to the hero Yue Fei, a Song general who was put to death by a treacherous minister in 1141, at the peak of his career. Pairs of stone mandarins, soldiers, horses, rams, and lions flanked the path to the grave, which was a conical mound enclosed by a small battlement. There was a large hall nearby in which the cult statue had stood; the original was destroyed in the Cultural Revolution and had been replaced by a pompous effigy waving a sword and wearing the same expression of belligerent determination that you saw on the poster art of the Maoist era.

"Yue was admired for his unswerving loyalty to the throne," Pan explained. "He did whatever he was told to do. He never questioned orders. Chinese governments have always liked him."

Yue had been drafted by the Red regime as well. Several overbearing murals celebrated Yue's supposed love for the peasants and his defeats of the northern barbarians. Images like these always had a double meaning in China.

"Are the barbarians meant to represent the Russians?" I asked.

"Could be," said Pan.

"Or the Americans?"

"Could be."

"Or just foreigners in general?"

"Could be."

Inside the gate were statues of the minister who ordered Yue's execution, his two sons, and his wife, a sort of Lady Macbeth who urged him to the deed. They were portrayed kneeling, stripped to the waist, with their heads bowed and hands bound behind their backs. The statues embodied the old Chinese belief that the dead remained in the world as spirits, who even after death could be made to suffer humiliation and shame. A sign said: "Honor to those who practice hygiene. Disgrace to those who don't." But I still saw people spitting on the four statues. It was a traditional thing; in the past, people used to beat them with sticks, too.

The shrine was popular with Chinese tourists. Hordes of rambunctious Hongkongese in pastel sweat suits were surging like a tidal bore over the shuffling crowd of mainland bumpkins, chattering in mile-a-minute Cantonese. Pan kept wrinkling his tiny nose. He envied their affluence, but he didn't like them.

I asked him why not.

Pan wriggled.

"They look like foreigners," he finally said.

I said, "They look like Chinese to me."

"They have big noses and round eyes."

Of course it wasn't so; it was a way of saying they were ugly.

"Tell me the truth," I asked Pan. "Do you think foreigners are attractive or ugly?"

"I don't know," he said.

I made him tell me.

"Not so beautiful," he mumbled.

I could see him wriggling inside the blue poncho.

"Some of you have blue eyes, and some have brown eyes, and pink skin, and white skin, and red hair, and yellow hair, and brown hair. You all look so different!"

Oddly enough, even I had unconsciously begun to see Caucasians through Chinese eyes. One evening I watched a European diplomat being interviewed on television by a Chinese journalist. Something seemed strange about the diplomat, and it was a while before I realized what it was. He was white, very white; unpleasantly white, like uncooked pork. His hair was red and eerie, and his eyes preternaturally large and round. His whole body projected an oppressive heaviness. It was a relief when the camera shifted to the Chinese journalist, who was a reassuring ivory color and modestly flat-bodied, with pleasant, brown, petal-shaped eyes.

It was an ancient thing, this loathing for the foreign and barbarous. There was an eighth-century poem that mourned the fate of Chinese who had been held hostage for years by the Western tribes:

I am the most bitterly tormented of all—
Such an injustice cannot have occurred since ancient times
A Chinese heart, a Chinese tongue speaking through the body of a
foreigner!

"But I have heard that the people in America are more beautiful," Pan said reassuringly. "And very generous."

There were launches that would take you around the lake. I hired one and we chuffed out into the mist. Here and there, other launches glided across the water, each like a quick brushstroke on the silky surface, scattering water birds from its path; they rose slowly with an almost theatrical deliberation, like a rehearsal for some greater event that was yet to come. From the other boats, I thought, we too must seem just a hook of ink, a device to add human dimension to the pale infinity of hills and water.

We landed on an island that was another of those visual puns that the Chinese loved. It was, in effect, a mirror of the West Lake itself, a narrow ring of land that encircled another lake, in the middle of which was another minuscule islet. There was an octagonal pavilion furnished comfortably with wicker chairs and tables, where a giggly waitress supplied us with bowls of sweet, warm lotus-root paste and perfumed tea that was grown in the valleys west of the lake. Mynas and parakeets whirred and twittered in cages overhead, while goldfish with bulbous eyes tumbled through a tank in the middle of the floor.

Pan was jittery. Every now and then he pulled the sheaf of documents from his tunic and rolled it in his hands, and then put it back again.

"They said I could come in January, if I had a sponsor."

To the west, I could see the slender dike that crossed the lake from north to south; plum and camphor trees grew along its edge, and palms, and willows with yellow-red fronds that swept over the shore in a feathery haze. The poet Su Dongpo built it when he was governor of Hangzhou in the twelfth century. His plea for money from the crown was famous: "The West Lake is like the eyes and eyebrows of a face. It would be a crime to neglect it." He ultimately raised the funds he needed by selling certificates of ordination for monkhood, which he exchanged for cash and rice to pay his coolies. Su loved Hangzhou so much that he was convinced that he had known it in a former life, and later, when his career was broken, he dreamed of it in exile:

Looking back I see only the lonely city
Buried in gray mist.
I can remember the time of singing,
But of the time of returning I can remember nothing at all.

There was a fine drizzle now, all across the lake. Gradually the mist thickened, sapping the last color from the landscape. It sifted over the emerald islets, crept in waves past the teahouse's glass walls. There were two or three other people in the teahouse, and the giggly waitress, and Pan, but I felt utterly, blissfully adrift in a watery universe. Time and space seemed to disintegrate.

The modern city was a pale gray shadow to the east. In that wonderful mist anything at all seemed possible. For a brief moment (I don't know how long it really lasted) I had an intense sensation that the old city still existed there, a mile from where I sat; it seemed simply self-evident that I could climb into a boat and go there, to the foot of the great whitewashed battlements, to walk among the ladies with their head ornaments in the shape of phoenixes and flowers, and the whores who beckoned from crimson arcades, past shops that sold the best Fujianese jasmine and rhino skins from Bengal, to dine on Mother Sung's choice fish soup outside the Cash Reserve Gate and boiled pork from Wei-the-Big-Knife at Cat Bridge, to listen to the riddlers who demonstrated by means of clever wordplay that the Buddha, Lao Tze, and Confucius were women, and to buy turtles and carp that I would set free for merit in the next world, on the shore of the lake. I finally stood next to my friend the sage, whom I had known for years in his silent painting, staring into the void that contained, like the eternal Tao, all that had been, and everything that was yet to be. I thought, it was as near as I would ever come to Cathay.

A launch took us to Su Dongpo's dike, and we walked back from there toward my hotel. The rain had stopped, and there was a spectacular stillness. I remembered a poem that Su wrote about a painting he admired. He described a wanderer making his way through a fantastic, dreamy landscape of smoky peaks and rivers:

I want to know where this place is,
For I have the greatest desire to go there
And buy two acres of land.

Looking at the mist, and the water, and the fairy islands upon the lake, in that stupendous pregnant stillness, that was how I felt.

I said good-bye to Pan at the gate and wished him luck with his studies.

"I have been admitted!" he said meaninglessly.

I TOOK THE train back to Shanghai on Christmas Eve. I had almost forgotten about George. But he turned up promptly at 9:00 P.M. at my hotel, wishing me a Merry Christmas. He looked haggard and tense. It was obvious that he hadn't slept. It was too early to go to the cathedral, so we went up to my room and I ordered him a Qingdao. We talked about Hangzhou for a while, and then I asked him how business was. He told me an awful story.

"The Rhythm Café doesn't belong to us anymore," he said gloomily. "The teddy boys took it away."

A few nights before they had taken over the restaurant, thrown out the customers, and held George's son hostage until he signed a contract agreeing to sell the place to them. The teddy boys promised to pay ten thousand yuan in cash and twenty-five thousand yuan more later on. George was convinced that he would never see any money at all.

There was no point in going to the police in Suzhou, he thought. "It's hopeless without connections." One or two of the teddy boys had relatives in the security forces.

George's wife had a cousin who was a ranking police official in Beijing. George thought that as a last resort they might ask him to intercede. But George hated him. A few years ago they had gone to him and asked for help in obtaining an exit visa, to leave China.

"He just talked to me a lot of propaganda, about how terrible everything was abroad and about all China had done for me. All it meant was that he was refusing to help us, but he wouldn't come right out and say it. I hated the guy's whole place. I had to sign in and out of his house every time I went across the street to buy cigarettes."

At 10:30 P.M. we went downstairs and hailed a cab. It had begun to drizzle. There were no streetlamps, and the driver honked his way wildly through the glutinous mass of cyclists that clogged the length of Nanjing Road.

Police ordered us to climb out at the cathedral gate. Then we passed through a cordon of laymen who checked the credentials of Chinese trying to enter and turned away anyone who couldn't demonstrate that he was Catholic.

"Catholic cadres," George whispered under his breath.

The church was rapidly filling up. The French who erected the cathedral in 1918 no doubt had Rheims and Chartres in mind. But the red brick that it was built of gave it a homely, more earthly ambience. The next day's newspaper said that five thousand worshipers had attended, but it looked like more. All but a handful were Chinese. As we went in, a choir was chanting the rosary in Latin; the Chinese church was frozen in the rituals of forty years before. George seemed to know all the clergy.

"That priest over there, he's what we call a 'before-liberation father,'" he whispered, indicating a portly priest in a beret. "He had a very hard time. They arrested him the first time in 1954, and they trained his brain for four years. They let him out. Then they picked him up again and trained his brain for another twenty years, but he never gave in."

There were a number of younger priests assisting at the service. George contemptuously called them "after-liberation fathers." He said, "Their brains stayed trained."

"O night divine!" the choir was singing throatily, now in Chinese. "Night of our dear savior's birth!"

I began to think of my grandmother; I often did in churches. She was a hardscrabble Catholic of the old school, and to placate her I was sent to church a good deal more often as a small child than my parents, left to their own native skepticism, really liked. Her faith seemed novel to me as a child, an exotic element in a suburban boyhood. In Shanghai on Christmas Eve, it was the church that now seemed familiar, as plain and comfortable as an old garment unworn for decades.

It was now 11:55 P.M. Bells were rung. Acolytes in white robes approached the altar, carrying crosses and tapers. The bishop strode behind them in majestic progress, crosier in hand, in a cloud of sweet incense.

Not wishing to offend, I knelt like everyone else. I meant it as an act of solidarity. For the Chinese, it was not just an affirmation of faith; it was also a political act for which lives had been lost and careers blighted for decades. Between Gothic pillars, I watched the bishop bend to kiss the Bible. Then he spread his hands wide in a gesture of benediction.

"When he was in prison, he cooperated," George whispered. "He translated military documents for them."

"*Gloria in excelsis!*" the choir sang.

Their voices multiplied over and over, ebbing and surging, echoing through the apse and the transept, where we sat, flooding over us. The organ rose to a crescendo.

"*Gloria in excelsis Deo!*"

George asked if I would take communion with him. He meant it as a comradely thing, and I could see that he was hurt when I declined. But he went on anyway, into the throng.

When he came back, I asked George whom he went to for confession. He smiled.

"This is China. You never know who you are talking to, or where it will go. Communion is enough."

"*Adeste fidelis!*" the choir thundered.

The sense of climax was intense and infectious. There was no mistaking the joy on George's face and on the other faces around me. I wondered, was that what I had felt on the islet in the West Lake, staring out into the surging mist—the same absurd, thrilling certainty that the impossible really existed after all?

"*Laete triumphantis! Venite! Venite!*"

People were starting to leave. I knew that I wouldn't be seeing George again. I was determined to find out about the missing decade. This time, when I asked how he came to Shanghai, George admitted that his father had simply run away from his wife in Manila. In 1941, before Pearl Harbor, Shanghai just seemed like a smart place to hide from domestic trouble.

The Chinese woman he called his "mother" was not his mother at all, he said. He had lied in Suzhou, when he told me that he was half-Chinese. His real mother was Filipino, too.

"Yes, I'm a foreigner just like you," he said. "Only I can't go home to my real country."

That wasn't all. The story about his father's helping the Communists was a red herring, the kind of thing people of George's generation said to cover up an awkward political background. During the war George's father had worked for the Japanese, but only as an accountant, George maintained; but in China it was a lifelong taint. That was the missing link, the reason for the evasions.

"Why didn't you just go back to the Philippines after your father died?" I asked.

"There was no proof anymore that I was Filipino," George said. "When my father came to Shanghai he bribed the officials to issue me a birth certificate saying that I was born in China and that his new Chinese wife was my real mother. It made me a Chinese citizen. He thought he was doing me a favor."

George's entire life was an accident. He should never have been stuck in China at all.

"I tried to apply for a passport at the Philippine Embassy, but they just said, 'Sorry, you're Chinese.' "

I dropped George at a corner near his house.

"What will you do about the restaurant?" I asked.

"Maybe we will go to Germany," he said, brightening a little.

One of his daughter's schoolmates had married a man working in Munich.

"Maybe she can find my daughter a German husband," he said.

"But what will you do now?"

George sighed and shrugged, and smiled.

"We will all try to learn German!"

After my experience with Pan, I had worried that George would ask me for money for the restaurant, and it made me nervous. But he never did. He just needed to talk. In a country where even the confessional couldn't be trusted, an honest ear was a precious thing.

CHAPTER
ELEVEN

An Island

WAS SO frustrated that I almost gave up on Putuo-shan altogether. I was furious at the assistant manager, and I was trying to get him to admit that he had misinformed me.

I said, "Last night you told me there was a boat in the afternoon."

I had tried to make him call the wharf to check, but he wouldn't do it.

"Don't worry," he kept saying. "It is my job to know."

Then in the morning, when he finally did call, it was clear that there was never an afternoon boat and that the morning one had already left.

His face was now at stake.

"There is no afternoon boat," he said blankly.

"But you told me!"

This went on for a while, stupidly.

The assistant manager was one of those reinvented Chinese that you met more and more often now. He sat at a mahogany table in the lobby of the hotel in Ningbo, wearing a swallow-tailed coat and a plastic tag that said "Clifford." He had been trained to smile if you came near and say, "May I help you?" It was a Westerner's reflex that made you say yes.

Beneath the facade I sensed a suppressed loathing, perhaps for the flashy Hong Kong style of the hotel, or for the foreign clientele. I couldn't tell. But he reminded me of the defeated Maoists I knew at the news agency where I worked in Beijing, who quietly hated the new infatuation with the West.

There was another boat to Putuoshan the next day. But I was tired and impatient. It was a bad combination in China.

Finally Clifford said I could go by car.

"To an island?"

Brusquely, he explained that there was a road that connected with a ferry and that I could switch to another ferry at the island of Zhoushan. It would be expensive, but I could reach Putuoshan before evening. He called over a driver from the taxi line.

"Are you certain?" I asked.

"No problem," the driver said.

"Trust me," Clifford said. "I know."

PUTUOSHAN WAS the home of Guanyin, the Goddess of Mercy. She was one of the stranger deities of the old pantheon, having left India as the male bodhisattva Avalokitesvara and blurred over the centuries with some far older Chinese deity associated with childbirth. Scholars said the confusion could be traced to a misinterpretation of Avalokitesvara's eponym "Treasure of the Womb." But the Chinese didn't split such academic hairs, and Guanyin was sometimes represented androgynously, Indian fashion, with a multitude of arms holding the symbolic tools of mystical power, and sometimes as a white, rather mysterious figure that bore a remarkable resemblance to the Christian Madonna.

Before the revolution, Westerners who lived in Shanghai vacationed on Putuoshan. They put up at the monasteries and hiked in dense forests of arborvitae, chestnut, camphor, oak, catalpa, maple, and sophora; kingfishers and ducks haunted the shores, and barking deer could be heard in the woods. In 1931 a traveler counted more than one hundred monasteries, hermitages, and shrines. Sometime in the 1950s the monks had been driven away and the island repopulated with peasants. It had been opened again to foreigners a few years ago, and it was said that the Buddhists were coming back.

But I had something more particular in mind, and I kept thinking about it as I rode out from Ningbo in the rain: an old engraving that I had bought for twenty dollars at a Greenwich Village flea market. In the background there was a rugged coastline, with towered buildings and junks tacking picturesquely out to sea. This part was realistic enough, in the rather dreamy style of early views of China. But the rest of the picture was very peculiar. A giant flower was erupting from the sea like a rocket, while a robed figure knelt on one of its leaves, gazing up into a human face where the flower's blossom would have been.

Much later, I learned that the picture related somehow to Guanyin and that the island was a real place, a nub of rock in the archipelago off Ningbo. By then, the image had already settled into my mind as one of those quintessential and alluring images of Old China, like the rockeries in Nieuhof's book. An air of mystery hung around Putuoshan, along with tales of apparitions and miracles. That fused with the old engraving in my mind, and as we drove through the gritty sprawl of factory compounds and brick yards, I had a feeling that common sense couldn't eradicate that something strange was bound to occur.

The suburbs petered out into sodden fields where, in spite of the driving rain, peasants were stolidly ladling night soil over rows of cabbage and onions. The road was dreadful. Pits and gullies corrugated the pavement for miles, so badly that I worried that the aged Lada might break an axle. There was a gray village, then a range of low scrubby hills, then another shabby village afloat like jetsam on the flooded land.

Finally we arrived at a jetty that stuck out into a muddy bay amid a slum of concrete sheds and work sites. While we were waiting for the ferry a policeman walked over to the car and motioned to the driver to roll down the window. He ignored the driver and stood staring at me, rain pouring off him, for a minute or so. Then he tersely announced that foreigners were not permitted on the island of Zhoushan.

I explained that I was going to Putuoshan but he cut me short. *"Xingde guiding,"* he said. "It isn't permitted."

The driver was losing face. He told the cop that there was no such regulation, then that the regulation had been abolished, and then, miserably, that I would keep my eyes shut and promise not to get off on Zhoushan.

"*Xingde guiding,*" the cop said.

"Does he want money?" I asked.

"He doesn't want money. He just doesn't want you to go on the ferry."

"*Xingde guiding,*" the cop said again.

"Why?" I asked the cop.

"*Xingde guiding.*"

The ferry had arrived by now. It was a flat, rusty contraption, and the cop ordered us out of line so that the trucks that had pulled up behind us could get on. There was nothing for it but to return to Ningbo. The driver climbed in and started up, and made a U-turn. We had a flat tire.

The rain was coming down in torrents now. The driver waved me toward one of the buildings nearby, but when I dodged inside it the men there barked, "*Xingde guiding*" and pushed me back toward the door.

So I stood in the rain while the driver fixed the tire. Louts collected from the construction site, and pressed around me and stared. Then passengers climbed off the bus and joined the crowd, and ran their hands over the Lada as if it were an exotic animal. The cop stared too, presumably to see that I didn't make a break for the ferry.

I bounced back over the corrugated road to Ningbo, sunk in gloom. I spent the evening in the hotel restaurant talking to a Japanese engineer who kept showing me snapshots of his home plant in Nagasaki, and then to a Greek sailor who was between ships and wanted to emigrate to Brazil, and then to an Egyptian seaman who was married to an ex-whore in Mobile, Alabama. Clifford saw me on my way up to my room.

"You're back again!" he said. "You made another mistake!"

THE *LUOSHAN* worried me. Her hull was rusty, and she coughed and shuddered the next morning as she levered herself away from the wharf and into the gray flood of the Yong River. But she plowed along steadily enough against the drizzly wind and out through a welter of barges and freighters and high-pooped junks toward the China Sea. Drydocks and warehouses gradually gave way to scrubby wastes, and then finally there was the sea, muddy and gray, and stretching away into foggy infinity. It smelled of oil and salt, and I had the sudden sense that there was, after all, an end to China.

The passengers were mostly peasants and monks. There were a few young Chinese tourists, and at first I took Chen for one of them, dressed as he was in the stone-washed jeans, down jacket, and running shoes that young Chinese affected in imitation of their stylish cousins in Hong Kong.

He was swarthy in a way that suggested some Mongol or Manchu blood; I wasn't surprised when he said he was from Changchun, in the Northeast. He was twenty-six and an aspiring painter. He liked Matisse especially. "His shapes are like Chinese ideographs." And Van Gogh. "He cut off his ear." His own painting, he shyly suggested, was "something like Miro." In his spare time he read Sartre, Nietzsche, Freud, and Piaget, in Chinese translation. But his favorite book was Lee Iacocca's autobiography.

"He had a lot of problems but he changed them and went on to succeed," Chen said.

I supposed he was going to Putuoshan to paint.

"No, to do this," he replied, pressing his palms together.

Then he was making a pilgrimage?

"Not exactly."

I asked how long he planned to stay on Putuoshan.

"Maybe ten years."

I thought I hadn't heard him correctly and said, didn't he mean ten days? No, he meant ten years.

"I want to change my life," he said.

He was on his way to Putuoshan to become a monk.

Chen had failed to pass the extremely competitive university entrance examinations. He had tried his hand at a small business that manufactured children's toys but had failed at that too. "The toys weren't much fun." He had worked in a foundry, been a stoker in a locomotive, and driven a pedicab to earn enough money to keep painting. But the state of his clothes, which were much torn and patched, and in urgent need of laundering, suggested that it hadn't gone well.

"If you are following a road and run into a wall that is too high to climb, then you must find another road," he said.

He felt a special affinity for Guanyin, although he couldn't explain it very well. It had something to do with the sea and a sense of infinite power, and a craving for solitude. He visualized a life of silence, immersed in the sutras and Guanyin. He thought he would be lonely at first but that he would get used to it after a few months.

"And your painting?" I asked.

"It won't matter anymore. I'll belong to Guanyin."

Islands lay scattered in the sea like lumps of cold metal, and beyond them the inky hills of the mainland hovered in the distance. Now and then fishing boats passed like ghosts in the mist. Putuoshan lay buried in fog until we were almost upon it. Then, five hours out from Ningbo, the murk thinned and a shoreline of emerald hills and orange beach spread out ahead of us.

Chen wanted to be helpful and trotted ahead to find the trail that led into the hills. We climbed up through a small village of gray-brick cottages, and then up further through plantations of tea, and groves of pine and camphor trees whose perfume filled the damp air. Eventually the path led us down into a deep vale, where we found a pond ornamented with belvederes and a yellow pagoda, as neat as a painted silhouette on a porcelain plate. Beyond these soared the yellow roofs of the Monastery of Universal Salvation. Huge red ideographs on its wall proclaimed: "To Save the World, Come and Live in These Hills."

The atmosphere inside was lulling. Incense boiled lazily through the inner courtyards. A deep-throated iron bell chimed somewhere deep in the bowels of the monastery, and from another quarter came the homely clack of an abacus. Elderly monks wandered abstractedly through the shadowy sanctum, fingering rosaries. Small windows high overhead suffused the towering statue of Guanyin in coppery-gold light; in twos and threes, peasant women dropped to their knees and kowtowed with their heads to the floor, begging for a baby, Chen said, or for health, or just luck.

"Her face is so smooth and gleaming, so beautiful," Chen whispered. "It makes you see the ugliness of the world that men live in."

Chen spoke to a little monk who was loitering in the shadows. He was from Hebei, beyond the Yangzi; a "north-of-the-river man," Chen quaintly called him. The north-of-the-river man told us a story about the creation of Putuoshan. The spirit of the Immortal Liu Dongbin was flitting across the sea one day when he spied what he thought was an island of stunning beauty far below. When he alit he was astonished to find beneath his feet, instead of terra firma, an immense fish that was on the brink of devouring him. In the nick of time, Guanyin descended from the heavens on a lotus flower and transformed the fish into the isle of Putuoshan, which would forever remain blessed with her grace.

The monk said that the Monastery of Universal Salvation was built on the site of Guanyin's workshop, where she had created the island and all its temples and shrines. He motioned to us to look around, as if we might see the goddess herself sweating over a forge with her thousand busy arms.

Chen helped me find the hotel up an alley behind the monastery. Not far away there was a lane of shops where tiny open-front eateries displayed the day's catch of prawns, squid, eels, oysters, and an assortment of fish that were unfamiliar even to Chen. We ordered something that looked like sole but proved tougher, and prawns that went into the pan still squirming, and bowls of dumplings to eat on the side.

"I have so many troubles," Chen said.

I waited for him to go on.

"My parents are so typical. They just work, come home and eat dinner, watch television, and go to bed. That's their whole life!"

I said there were worse things in China than that.

"My father is afraid of everything. He tells me to be quiet and not make trouble, and not to try to be different, and just to do what I'm told. But I can't stand it. I begged them to change, but they're not interested. When I told them I needed to change myself, they said, 'What's wrong with you the way you are?' But I think it's important for everyone to live his life his own way. Why shouldn't people be different? Why should everyone be the same?"

Two tourists at the next table had been craning into our conversation in the uninhibited way of less-educated Chinese, and I was aware of them struggling to repeat to themselves the odd English word or two that they thought they understood. The older of the two finally asked where I was from, and then when I told him he broke into a smile.

I guessed he was in his fifties. He was wearing a stylish imported pullover, but along with it so many layers of long johns that his trousers wouldn't stay closed.

"I fought the Americans in Korea," he said, speaking Mandarin with a slushy southern accent that even Chen had a hard time following. "I even volunteered for it. We believed anything in those days! I even believed in the Communist Party."

He made a face. He said he was a salesman for a porcelain plant in Wenzhou, and we shook hands all around. The salesman ordered another platter of prawns, and everyone laughed at my delicacy when I broke the heads off before eating them.

"Marx was a failure," said the salesman's companion, a Shanghainese in his thirties; he had a curious wedge-shaped face that made him unpleasantly resemble a snake. "Everyone knows it. No one believes in it anymore. But everyone's afraid to say so."

He put his hand over his mouth. But in fact he was fairly shouting, and passersby leaned through the window to listen.

"At least things are getting easier," the salesman said. "You can make money now, if you work hard enough."

"Getting better!" the snake-faced man said contemptuously. "You don't know what you're talking about, you old Marxist."

"I'm no Marxist," the salesman retorted. "I just think things will get better, that's all."

"Whenever you try to get something done it's, 'not allowed,' or 'no way,' or 'against the rules,' " said the snake-faced man.

I asked the veteran what he believed in now.

"Now? Nothing. It makes life easier."

"I think we've lost touch with something in our heart, and we need to regain it," Chen ventured, rather tentatively.

There was a third man at the other table who had remained silent. He was also in his thirties, I guessed. Later he said that he traded in fish in Shanghai.

He leaned over and said to Chen, "I saw her."

"Who?" Chen asked.

"Guanyin. This morning."

He said that a year ago he had come to Putuoshan and prayed to Guanyin for the birth of a son. Nine months later his wife had given birth. He had come back now to thank the goddess. He had seen her just that morning at the Cave-of-Guanyin's-Voice, at the far end of the island.

"Tell me!" Chen exclaimed.

"She was wearing a white robe, the way she looks in the statues. She was carrying the lotus flower in her right arm, the way you always see her. Her expression was sweet. I thanked her, and then she disappeared."

Chen closed his eyes and folded his hands in front of him and bent his head, monklike.

"Things like that happen on Putuoshan," the salesman said amiably.

"Only on Putuoshan," the snake-faced man said. "Nowhere else."

It was too late for Chen to go on to the Monastery of Enlightened Salvation, which lay further up in the hills. He said he would find a bed for the night at a pilgrims' hostel in town.

I wished him well, but he hung on and then asked shyly if I would let him keep me company on the island. He could practice his English, translate for me. I sensed that I was his last accidental hold on the world of ordinary men and that he wanted a way of letting go slowly. But I had also begun to feel protective toward Chen. I liked his determination. But I worried that another failure here would leave him more depressed than ever. Of course he could join me, I said.

Then I teased him and told him that he'd better enjoy the pork in the dumplings because it would be his last for the next ten years.

THE NEXT morning Chen met me at the gate and we set off into the hills. The rain had stopped and the landscape had emerged more clearly. The lush forests were gone (and those barking deer), but the island was still beautiful in a starker way that framed naked rock and windswept ridges against the orange beaches and the sea.

There were signs of past violence almost everywhere: gutted monasteries, ruined shrines, looted and overgrown graves. Old inscriptions had been cemented over and replaced with Communist slogans; but now these too were falling away. We found a large rock covered with chipped ideographs, and Chen clambered over them, deciphering the layers like palimpsests. One read, "The great joining of the Dragon of the Sea and the Earth of China." On top of it, half-obliterated ideographs of the Cultural Revolution proclaimed: "A thousand years to Chairman Mao!" Then there was a prayer to Guanyin, signed by a famous prewar gangster; someone had written over his signature, "A thief doesn't deserve to have his name seen." The fractured texts had apparently blurred together in the minds of the pious and illiterate, who had stuck twigs in the rock beneath them all as votive offerings and set incense burning in tin cans in front of the scarred rock.

But other inscriptions had inexplicably been left alone, or perhaps restored. We climbed up through a natural gate in the rock, which red-painted ideographs announced to be the "Portal of the Western Paradise," the passage between the worlds of the living and the dead. Another boulder higher up was engraved "The Most Famous Stone in the World," and contained deep within it, Chen speculated, the entire Buddhist afterworld in miniature. Not far away, still another stone was carved with an enormous ideograph for "heart." Chen climbed up to it and got into a lotus position and began to pray. When he finished, he shouted, "It means that Guanyin's heart is as big as the universe!"

We heard the rhythmic susurrus of prayers somewhere below us. We made our way down the hillside, following the sound until we found a path that led us to a small temple, where an elderly nun with extraordinarily long and aristocratic fingers motioned us toward a hole in the cliff. I peered in and was startled to see something move. Like a slab of darkness come to life, a squinty crone leaned out and handed us water from a spring, in tin cups, saying feebly that it would cure all our pain. People came all the way from Hong Kong just for a drink, she said. Even here, I thought, the Hong Kong cachet had become the measure of value.

The long-fingered nun motioned us deeper into the cave where there was a gilded idol surrounded by offerings of plastic flowers. The figure was unfamiliar, and when I asked who it was she said, obscurely, "The Emperor of the Night." That meant nothing to Chen, but when he asked the nun to tell us more, she refused.

"You have to ask the chief sister," she said, shying away.

We found this august personage dressed in a brown robe and sitting at a desk in the prayer hall in front of a large gilded statue of Guanyin. Except for her, the hall was completely empty. I realized that the prayers we had been hearing were coming from a cassette player on the desk. Taped prayers seemed a little like cheating to me; I wondered ironically what the Buddha might think.

We called politely to the chief sister. She waited long enough to rise to make it plain that we were to treat her as a person of authority. The other thing that struck me about her was that she was fat. There were no fat nuns.

Chen explained that we were curious about the cave.

"I'm not permitted to say," she said. "We are not allowed to talk to foreigners."

Then Chen foolishly told her I was a writer.

"What good is he going to write then?" she barked. "Where is his written permission to talk to me?"

"I'm just curious about this 'Emperor of the Night,'" I said placatingly.

"You can make an application, and we will consider it."

"The story is a state secret?" I said sarcastically.

"What?" she asked, not getting it.

I said, "*Xingde guiding,* eh?"

"Yes, *Xingde guiding.*"

On the way back to the hotel, Chen tried to engage me in a serious discussion about Mickey Mouse and Donald Duck, whom his friends in Changchun had only just discovered.

"We love them because they're just like real people!" he exclaimed. "Like American people, of course, not Chinese people."

243

ANOTHER DAY, we walked a couple of miles along the shore. The land seemed softer that day; haze obscured the bare stone, and clouds poured in steamy rivers through gaps in the hills, making ridges just a mile or two distant seem to stretch away into a milky infinity. Peasants were at work in a crazy quilt of little fields alongside the beach, hoeing winter vegetables. Chen was waving his short arms as we walked, complaining that his father kept badgering him to marry and settle down.

"I don't have a job. I don't have any money. How can I be responsible for a wife and a baby? But he thinks there's something wrong with me because I'm not married."

I said, "Tell me about your father."

Chen said that as a teenager in the 1940s, his father had served in the Nationalist army and was captured by the Communists at Nan-jing; most of his unit had been machine-gunned to death after their surrender. Because of the Nationalist connection, he was sent to a labor camp for three years in the 1950s. When Chen was six years old, during the Cultural Revolution, he watched a neighbor who was a Red Guard invade their home and force his father's head to the floor until he confessed his "crimes." Soon afterward, Chen's entire family was sent to a remote village where they were forced to work as peasants for the next eight years.

The father had a job in a truck plant now. It was easy to imagine him, wracked by the lifetime of political campaigns, thinking that simply to have survived at all was a great deal indeed. But Chen was the child of a different era, for whom, almost incredibly, those horrific experiences were just old men's tales.

"Maybe you're too hard on him," I said.

"He doesn't understand that I have to change my life!"

"You could try changing your life little by little instead of all at once," I suggested. "Maybe you tried to do too much before. You could change what you know you can succeed at and put off the rest until you're ready for it."

"I never thought of that," Chen said, but then resolutely re-joined, "I have made my decision."

After a while we came to a small hermitage that stood on a rocky headland on the southern shore. A genial nun of perhaps seventy set out tea in lidded cups, bowls of saltines, peanuts, candy, and oranges. Without prompting, she began to tell us a story about the place. I couldn't follow her at all, and at first I only got bits and pieces that Chen translated into English. There was something about a Japanese monk who had once lived here and then decided to go home, and something about Guanyin commanding him to stay. Then there was something about the goddess appearing from the sea in the shape of an iron lotus, to prevent the monk's boat from departing.

It was the engraving! The strange flower was of course Guanyin herself, and the figure on the leaf was the monk borne aloft by his devotions. The dreamy coast in the picture was the headland where we now sat.

The nun said that the monk remained until his death many years afterward. The convent nearby was named after him; it was called "Reluctant-to-Go."

"Why an iron lotus?" I asked.

"I am only a beginner," she said mildly. "It hasn't been revealed to me."

The Japanese monk's experience wasn't really unusual, she said. The headland was famous for sightings of Guanyin. The goddess had visited most recently in June.

"She came in from the sea like a star and then went back and forth over the headland, and then back out to the sea," the nun said matter-of-factly.

She led us out to where the sea racketed through a cleft in the rock that ran all the way across the headland. Guanyin was always present there in a different form, the nun said, not exactly in the sea or the rock itself, but in the surge of the water through the cleft and in the sound of the waves against the rock walls. In the past, pilgrims often threw themselves into the sea here and committed suicide, in the hope of becoming one with the goddess. The nun said that no one did that anymore; but at the edge of the cleft there was a freshly painted sign that read: "Don't Jump."

I tried to get the nun to tell me what had happened on the island when the government drove away the Buddhists. But she wouldn't quite say.

"They tried to destroy the walls of the convent, but they couldn't do it," she said smilingly. "It was under the protection of Guanyin!"

But when I looked inside the old convent I saw that it was just a shell. The shrines and altars were gone without a trace. Only the side galleries were left. They were inhabited by peasant families now. Grimy babies scrambled on the flagstones, around listless women and ragged men who were weaving baskets from bits of bamboo.

Chen decided that it was finally time for him to go on to the Enlightenment Salvation Monastery, and his new life. I knew, even if he was too shy to say so, that he would be grateful for company during his last hours in the World of Dust. On the way, we decided, we could pass the most sacred site of all, the Cave-of-Guanyin's-Voice, where the Shanghainese fishmonger had seen the goddess a few days before.

The cave lay on a precipitous headland on the less-populated northern shore. We followed the island's only paved road through a wild, empty landscape. The rain had begun again, and a hard wind beat in from the sea. Foamy waves thrashed at the shore. The pavement petered out, and for a mile or so we walked uncertainly along a rutted track through banks of spiky reeds that stood taller than our heads.

We began to worry that we had gotten on the wrong path when we saw the butter-colored walls of a temple ahead of us. A high-walled passageway funneled us into a stairway that led down a sheer cliff face to an altar of Guanyin-of-the-Thousand-Arms, and then further still to another platform built out over the water, which faced not an idol this time, but an enormous raw crack in the black cliff, through which the sea poured with a deafening roar. It was a dangerous place; if you slipped, you would be crushed to death in minutes in the rocks.

The Guanyin who resided here was a very different one from the ethereal creature of the monasteries; there was nothing here of the subtleties of the sutras, or the eloquent disputation of scholars. The place was dark and primeval, almost sexual in its intensity. Here, finally, was the unvarnished Guanyin, or that now-nameless chthonic

246

predecessor who lay buried like an older text beneath the Buddhist myth, an awesome thing of oceanic feminine power, dark and uncontrolled, and terrifying. My heart began to race and I felt short of breath.

A banner hanging overhead said: "Ask here and Guanyin must grant your wish."

Chen stood for a while with his head bent and hands folded in front of him.

"What did you pray for?" I asked.

"Peace."

But the place made him jumpy too, and we raced each other back up the stairs.

We hiked back around the coast to the staircase that ascended (a thousand steps, it was said) to the Enlightenment Salvation Monastery. The shadows were lengthening and there would be barely enough time for me to get back to the hotel before dark. The China Sea spread out below like a sheet of polished steel, growing vaster with each upward bend of the path. The aroma of camphor was almost narcotic in the wet air, and the silence soothed immensely after the creepy intensity of the cave. Peasants trotted past us from time to time, hauling sand and bricks suspended from carrying poles, murmuring greetings as they went by.

A young monk was climbing slowly ahead of us. Chen struck up a conversation with him as we passed and discovered happily that he not only belonged to the Enlightenment Salvation Monastery but that they hailed from the same part of Manchuria.

"He speaks my language!" Chen exclaimed.

The monk was extremely thin, and shaven bald of course, and dressed in a baggy gray cotton smock and white leggings. He said he was twenty-nine and that he had lived on Putuoshan for the past year. He spoke in a very soft voice that grew steadily less controlled as we neared the monastery.

"You must be happy here," I said politely.

"Of course, quite happy," he replied, politely.

Chen chattered gaily to the monk about his own plans, and then said that he must feel like a buddha himself to live always so close to Guanyin. The monk hesitated and then took Chen by the arm.

"You never get any rest! They're always banging something for prayers in the night. And the food!"

He grimaced and pulled at his stomach.

Chen's swarthy face froze.

The monk said, "When you leave Putuoshan and visit some other place in China, people look at you with awe. They think of you as Guanyin herself. You're so special to them! But it isn't that way."

I asked the monk what had brought him to Putuoshan.

"A very few come here because they are called by Guanyin. But most come because there is nothing left for them in the outside world. I was in the second group."

He explained that he used to be a schoolteacher in Shenyang. He had lent his brother-in-law his life savings of five thousand yuan, but the man gambled it away. Then his wife ran away with someone else and took their three-month-old baby with her. He joined the Air Force in hope of starting a new life, but he was dismissed after a few months because of his health.

The monk sat down on a rock to rest. He was suffering from some kind of chronic liver or kidney problem, and he tired quickly. Chen squatted next to him and peppered him with questions. After they had talked for some time, Chen turned to me.

"What a terrible story!" he said. "He says that the abbot is rich. Lots of pilgrims come here to ask the monks to say prayers for the dead. The abbot charges each of them seven hundred yuan and keeps it all for himself. He gives ordinary monks like this man just twenty or thirty yuan per month. The monks also have to pay for this abbot's 'friendship,' and if you don't you get the worst jobs in the monastery. He says the abbot hates him because he can't pay and that the abbot's friends beat and kick him if they give him orders and he doesn't obey."

"Everything here is *guanxi*," the monk said miserably. "Everything is 'connections.' The abbot is emperor here."

Chen said, "It's just like outside!"

"That's the way it is," said the monk.

I asked, "Why don't you go home?"

"I don't have a home anymore."

His wife was gone. His parents were dead. He had no money. He had no work unit to take care of him anymore.

248

"*Meiyou banfa,*" the monk said. "There is no way for me."

Without much conviction, I tried to remind the monk that he was young and that many things might change for him; it was an American sort of notion.

"This was my last hope," he said. "I am always in pain. There is nothing left for me."

We walked along in silence for a while. The Monastery of Enlightened Salvation lay just a little way ahead now, cupped in a small wooded vale.

"Do you have a gun?" the monk asked me, not very hopefully, as politely as if he were asking for a match.

"What's he going to do?" Chen asked.

I said, "He's going to kill himself, one way or another."

Chen looked petrified.

A passageway led us to the inner courtyard. A rite of some kind was underway in the prayer hall and, peering in, I saw half a dozen monks ringing bells, whacking clappers and sticks, and beating small drums before the beatific effigy of Guanyin. At the end of one row of monks stood the abbot, a tall middle-aged man in a brown robe, serenely pinging a metal wand on a tiny bell.

The unhappy monk invited us to dine in the pilgrims' refectory. This was a small room adjoining the kitchens. Eight or nine pilgrims were already there, slurping at bowls of noodles. The monk graciously seated us on small stools and then went away to find us some food.

I didn't pay much attention at first to the ruckus in the hall. Then after a minute or two a huge, furious monk swarmed through the door, shouting, "Foreigners not allowed! Can't eat here!"

The unhappy monk scrambled behind him, obviously mortified. The pilgrims bent deep into their bowls, slurping deafeningly. The giant shoved Chen and told him to get me out.

I apologized to everyone and said I didn't want to cause trouble. But I surmised that it all had less to do with me than with the poor monk who had invited us, that it was meant to humiliate him still further.

The monk saw me to the gate, blubbering apologies. He wrung my hand as he said good-bye.

He said, "You don't have a gun?"

"No," I said. "I don't have a gun."

I shook hands with Chen. He looked terrified. I said good-bye and wished him good luck. He fumbled desperately for something to say.

He finally said, "What do you think Miro would do?"

I said, "I think he would go home and paint."

"Perhaps I will go with you," Chen said hesitantly.

Then his face fairly exploded with relief. He bounded ahead of me back down the stairs toward the darkening sea, taking the steps two or three at a time.

At the bottom he opened his eyes wide and said, "You saved me!"

WE STOOD at the rail of the *Luoshan,* watching Putuoshan slip back into the drizzly mist of the China Sea.

Chen said, "So many things in China are like that, just not what you dream."

"What are you going to do now?" I asked.

The closer we got to Ningbo, the more worried he looked. I suspected that he didn't even have the train fare to get home to Changchun.

Before we reached Ningbo, I gave him one hundred yuan and told him to buy some paint and canvas and brushes. In spite of his poverty he was offended. But I told him that it wasn't a gift, that he must send me a painting someday in New York. Finally he took the money, and we stood for a while in silence at the rail, watching the junks and sampans slip by, and then the derricks and slums of Ningbo appear from the drizzly haze. Chen was looking at me oddly.

"Maybe you are Guanyin helping me," he said slowly.

I could see in his eyes the glimmer of a thought that I might really be.

CHAPTER TWELVE

The Great Within

Y HOTEL used to be one of the best in Beijing. It lay on a quiet block in the old European Legation Quarter and was built in the sturdy Stalinist style that architects favored in the 1950s. But when I arrived, the first room I was assigned had a brick wall built halfway up the outside of the window. The next room had three spare beds upended against the wall. When I told the clerk to give me another room, she looked at me in that particular way of the Pekingese that is opaque and accusatory at the same time.

"*Meiyou,*" she said grumpily. "Don't have."

I knew she was lying. I also knew that she wouldn't give me another room. I took the room with the beds. Then I noticed that there were ashes and dust all over the carpet. I asked the floor attendant to clean it, and he came back and rubbed the dirt in with a wet mop. It was a homecoming.

I remembered Beijing as a place of erasures and omissions; no other city I knew gave so little of itself away. Things, people, slipped away, out of one's grasp. The gray lanes, the walled-in courtyards, the too-wide boulevards, the blank new apartment towers defied the eye. There was a peculiarly amorphous quality to human encounters, too. Glances went unmet, questions were left unanswered, promising conversations trickled away into platitudes.

It was much colder than it had been in the south. Bitter winds blew in day after day from the Mongolian steppes, churning the dust through the air and leaving the sun a whitish hole in a washed-out sky. Every boulevard was a panorama of cyclists bent double against the wind, pushing with all their might against the invisible wall of air. The atmosphere was gritty with coal smoke, and radiators leaked only a grudging trickle of heat.

THE OLD Manchu's house should have been easy to find. It was only a couple of blocks from Tiananmen Square. But I kept getting turned around in the warren of lanes under the wall of the Forbidden City. They kept leading me into courtyards and dead ends, or spilling me back onto the boulevard where I had begun. I asked directions, but I couldn't get the lane's name quite right, and people stared at me in that uneasy Pekingese way and motioned me ambiguously to move on.

But finally I found the right gate, and then, across a dusty courtyard, Chang himself perched on a hard, old-fashioned armchair. Huge flared eyebrows that were a trait of the Manchus bristled like triremes armed for combat over his eyes. His hands caught my eye too; they were very small and bony, like birds' claws, and so light and slender that I had the illusion they were transparent.

His ancestors had arrived with the conquering Manchu armies in 1644. Later on they "suppressed national minorities in the southwest," he said, chuckling facetiously at the Marxist turn of phrase. The grandfather who raised him was a lofty figure in the old regime, a bannerman of the Sakada clan and a seventh-rank mandarin of the Imperial Treasury.

"We had a garden, bamboos, rocks, all that stuff. It was the cat's pajamas!"

He salted his speech like that with slang he had picked up from American marines he tutored in the 1920s. But that was part of another story.

He got up and began to rummage in a drawer. I became aware of the room. A cast-iron stove vented smoke through a tin pipe that doglegged across the room and out through the front wall. There were a few stools and square tables, and a colossal Ming-dynasty armoire, and a television under a tiger-striped dust cover. A grandson who had just flown back from Shenzhen was asleep against the wall, and his snores resonated from time to time as Chang and I talked.

"There used to be nifty photographs of that garden, but the Communist tore them all up!"

Chang's rummaging was a little theatrical, since the pictures had been gone for years. By "the Communist" he meant his daughter, and there was an edge to his voice. I wondered if he had urged her to join the Party as a kind of insurance, the way families worried about the future were now trying to get a child to Canada or the United States. She had become a zealot, and during the Cultural Revolution she had destroyed everything that belonged to his earlier life.

He remembered the grandfather's old courtyard home as the center of his childhood. Everything that was necessary to life came through the gate. Water arrived on a wheelbarrow, coal on camel-back, groceries on a carrying pole slung over a coolie's shoulders. There were peasants who came with trained bears, and entertainers in women's clothes who sang "romantic ditties" while they swayed like courtesans in boats made of bamboo and paper, and impresarios who set trained mice scampering up aerial stages of pagodas and turrets; a servant would look them over and, if he approved, allow them into the garden to perform for the children's delight.

"We lost everything, even our teacups. After the 1911 revolution, our farmers—that's 'peasants' in Communist lingo, you know— just stopped paying rent. We were in poverty ourselves, but it would have meant a terrible loss of dignity for us, so we didn't dare go out and try to collect from them."

When the dynasty was overthrown, the aristocracy that had ruled China for three hundred years disintegrated overnight. Families that fled back to the Manchu homeland in the northeast survived. Those that stayed in Beijing starved; many Manchu women resorted to what Chang called "their last means" to make a living. One of his uncles sunk to pulling a rickshaw and died on the street. The grand-father lost his home in 1917 or 1918; Chang remembered students marching through the streets as they left, shouting, "Down with the Kaiser!" Chang's memory of his last hour there had remained with him for seventy years.

"My granddad had a wonderful library. Somebody had already

taken away all the books, or stolen them, and there were scraps of poetry and calligraphy and woodcuts blowing all around in the wind. I began picking them up and reading them. Granddad had written a lot of it himself. I was just a little fellow, but I knew it was beautiful stuff. I ran around trying to catch all the scraps, but it wasn't any use. It was too windy, and I was too small. I gave up, in the end, and just watched them blow away over the weird stones and bamboo."

Chang's shy wife shuffled in with a plate of fried peanuts for a snack, and a little later brought some oranges too.

"Oranges, anyway, never used to be so sweet in the old days!" Chang chirped.

A friend who knew Chang's background told me to ask him about the pigeons. Fanciers used to send them whistling in trained flocks over the old city; every foreigner who had lived in Old Beijing remembered them. The descriptions were as tantalizing as the idea of Cathay itself; an "aeolian orchestra," George Kates had called them, "fluting through the air with graceful sound." Fifty years ago, they seemed as immutable a part of the city as the great walls, or the laden camels that padded eternally in long lines against the horizon like a child's picture of the Bible lands.

I used to dream about those aerial orchestras during the claustrophobic year that I worked in Beijing. I would cycle through the gray lanes on my way to work, imagining that they were still there and that any minute they might come hurtling symphonically over the courtyards. They seemed to epitomize the grace that Old China was capable of producing even in the midst of squalor and decay. I thought of them as the voice of the lost world.

Chang remembered them, soaring through the sky over that courtyard of his childhood. He explained matter-of-factly that delicate flutes were attached to the birds' tail feathers; craftsmen carved them from tubes of bamboo, until they were as thin as eggshells and had almost no weight at all. He took my pen and sketched different flutes, thin ones like reeds, and round ones like tiny gourds, and one called the "thirteen princes" that produced as many different tones all at once.

He exclaimed, "See how clever they were, those old Manchus!"

Chang maintained that there were still flocks in the city. One day when I was walking among the lanes behind the old Bell Tower I heard something in the air. It was an indefinable sound, a sort of hum, swelling in the breeze and then receding. I stood still and waited, tensed with anticipation. The sound hovered near for several minutes, faded away, and then came back from another direction. I tried to will birds to appear. For ten or fifteen minutes more I walked up and down the gray lane, pausing to listen. But it was only the sound of a factory carried by the breeze, or the tremor of a power line.

AT THE turn of the century, E. R. Scidmore, who had just arrived from the coast in "the small torture chamber" of a springless cart, found Beijing to be "the most incredible, impossible, anomalous, and surprising place in the world." Beggars clung to his cart wheels, while starving convicts hung suspended over his head in tiny cages. But the cruelty was accompanied by "the bewildering interest and richness of the street life, something of which at every moment catches and dazzles the eye." The shops outside the Front Gate were a *"coup de l'oeil"* of ermine and snow leopard, and cloth-of-gold. Brides passed "like jeweled treasures" in gorgeous red wedding chairs trailed by coolies bearing dowries of silks and satins. Funeral processions were phantasmagoric too, stretching for miles with paper houses and carts, jewels, clocks, and curios of every kind to be burned in extravagant shows so the deceased could enjoy them in the next life.

The city's real glory was its walls. They stood forty feet thick and thirty-six feet high and were punctuated at regular intervals by massive embrasured gates that rose ninety-nine feet over the flat North China Plain. They still stood in the 1930s, producing, George Kates thought, a sense of deep security that enhanced composure and lent dignity to even the simplest of the city's inhabitants. He wrote, "So important are these in Chinese eyes that their demolition would rob Peking of something fundamental."

Imperial Beijing was unlike any other city on earth. It evoked Egyptian Thebes or Mayan Tikal more than Paris or London. It was, in effect, an immense mechanism whose physical orientation aimed at no less than achieving the total harmony of man and nature. Chinese

257

regarded the north-south axis upon which it was centered as the very spine of the kingdom, the mystical core of imperial power. Sacred altars lay at each of the four poles like celestial rivets that linked the world of men to the invisible forces of the universe. At the heart of the grand scheme lay the Forbidden City, the Great Within, and at its center the Son of Heaven, hidden from the world of mortals behind towering madder-rose walls.

The old approaches to the palace have disappeared beneath the gloomy Maoist sprawl of Tiananmen Square. But the great processional lane still leads north from Tiananmen between galleried arcades to the double-bastioned Meridian Gate. Architecture shaped the style of imperial power: Civil mandarins were directed through a tunneled gate to the right, military mandarins to the left, and lesser functionaries to gates further to each side. The lofty central tunnel was reserved for the emperor alone, when he traveled out to the southern altars or on his rare journeys beyond the walls.

You come out of the Meridian Gate into a vast cobbled courtyard. The palace already begins to overwhelm, through harmonies of proportion and color rather than mass or novelty of conception, and through the effect of the low colonnaded galleries and the tiled roofs that rise and fall in great undulating yellow waves, so vivid and light that on clear days it seems as if they might lift off and fly. This goes on for half a mile, gate after gate, wall after wall, until you are so deep in the labyrinth of courtyards that it becomes easy to understand how the emperors could forget that there was a world of ordinary men at all.

Five marble bridges span the stream that flows through that first great courtyard. You cross one of them and approach the gate that looms theatrically at the top of a marble ramp; when you step through it, you stand at the very navel of the old empire. Here, where the Hall of Supreme Harmony rises atop its triple-tiered marble terrace, the ancient texts said, earth and sky met, the four seasons merged, wind and rain were gathered in, yin and yang joined in perfect harmony. Dragons writhe over the hall's nine gilded columns; behind its great crimson doors, they wriggle over the lintels and rafters, curl in the ceiling's deep coffers, slither over the coppery-gold throne from which the Living Dragon gazed southward down the mystical axis, his power pouring out in what was imagined to be an ever-benevolent flood. His duty was explicit: "to stand in the center of the earth and stabilize the people within the four seas."

Here at the plexus of empire power and secrecy blurred until they were indistinguishable. "Hide your tracks, conceal your sources, so that your subordinates cannot trace the springs of your action," the third-century B.C. philosopher Han Fei advised in a work that Chinese rulers read and took to heart until modern times. "Discard wisdom, forswear ability, so that your subordinates cannot guess what you are about. Take hold of the handles of government carefully and grip them tightly. Destroy all hope, smash all intention of wresting them from you; allow no man to covet them." When the emperor traveled out from the palace the entire route was curtained with silk and lined with soldiers, so that no unworthy eye might pollute his sight; commoners were forbidden even to tread upon the path he would take for hours before he passed.

Most of the palace was a museum now; government departments occupied some of the western quarter, while the imperial park of Zhongnanhai that adjoined it had been taken over for the residences of the Communist Party elite. The galleries contained vestigial collections of paintings, jewelery, seals, and the like that the Nationalists had failed to get off to Taiwan. But sometimes in a less-visited courtyard, or some peeling gallery, you can feel the ghosts of the emperors; of Qianlong who, in 1793, could dismiss the first British embassy to Beijing with a verbal flick of the wrist: "We have never valued ingenious articles, nor do we have the slightest need of your country's manufactures." And of the last Ming, who hanged himself for shame at the loss of his empire, of Guangxu and the Pearl Concubine, of the pathetic Puyi, the last emperor of all, whose toy court lingered on here until 1924.

I found artifacts from Puyi's childhood on display in one of the halls. There were scepters of carnelian and ivory, and jeweled crowns, and the robes dense with dragons that Chinese emperors had worn since the beginning of time. Alongside these confections were a popgun and tin dreadnoughts that any American boy might have bought in a corner toy store, and binoculars ornamented with rubies and gold, and a gramophone sloganed "Snapshots of Your Voice," and then photos of Puyi posed with the studied nonchalance of a 1920s playboy in tennis whites and in a tuxedo. The effect was disconcerting; it was as if archaeologists had unearthed a toy steam engine and spats in the palace of the last Roman emperors.

If there was a single spirit who presided over the palace, it was that of the Dowager Empress Cixi. She was an icon to turn-of-the-century Europeans, as fascinating and loathsome as Old China itself. "The most remarkable woman sovereign and the most unbridled despot the world has ever known," proclaimed Scidmore, who could always be relied upon for superlatives. She was less than that. But she did personify the last tawdry years of the empire; the xenophobia and corruption, the fatal solipsism.

There was something lurid about her, this last true ruler of Cathay. Old photographs show a fantastic creature poised like a bronze idol on her throne, flanked by wizened eunuchs who seem hardly more human than she. She was barely five feet tall, with delicate hands and four-inch nails which she wore in sheaths crusted with rubies and pearls. She breakfasted on lotus-root porridge with milk squeezed from a young mother's breast; for dinner she preferred sea slugs, shark's fin, and ducks' tongues, of which she ate thirty at a sitting. She slept on pillows filled with rose petals and swallowed crushed pearls in the belief that they would restore her beauty.

Her vanity fed the foreigners' exaggerations. "Do you know, I have often thought that I am the most clever woman that ever lived," she told the princess Der Ling. In fact, China grew ever-feebler during her long rule. The Russians gnawed at Manchuria, the Japanese at Korea, the French at Annam. The Germans demanded and got rights in Shandong, and the British in the Yangzi Valley. Burma was lost; Tibet and Turkestan began to slip from the imperial orbit. Cixi's cleverness was the brilliance of the seraglio, where politics reduced to conspiracy, and information-gathering to ears pressed against doors and walls; the only mode of government she knew was by threat and fiat.

She entered the Great Within as a concubine. Her route to power was the delivery of a son to the emperor. When the emperor died in 1861, she was just twenty-six; she outmaneuvered veterans of court intrigue twice her age to stage what amounted to a coup d'etat of the harem, producing a forged document that declared herself and the ineffectual concubine Niuhuru co-regents over the infant successor.

For the next forty-seven years she ruled China with unsparing determination, issuing commands from behind a yellow silk curtain, like an unseen god. "The court listens eagerly to the opinions of all and seeks truth about conditions. You officials should purify your hearts and tremblingly obey the repeated imperial commands to reveal your loyal counsels. But you must not irresponsibly offer your personal opinions." Those who did sometimes left their heads on the pavement of the public marketplace.

Perhaps not surprisingly, Cixi had a special affection for eunuchs. Since no unmutilated men except for the emperor were permitted to live in the Forbidden City, eunuchs performed every duty that was necessary to keep the palace functioning; they were cooks, janitors, guards, carpenters, masters of protocol, spies. Three thousand of them served the imperial household in the Empress Dowager's time, siphoning off without the empress's interference an estimated one-fifth of the immense wealth that entered the palace. The eunuchs loved her in return. During an illness, she remarked to the Chief Eunuch Li Lienying, "I know I am going to die, because I have no one so devoted to me that he will give me the only medicine that would cure me of my sickness." Understanding her meaning, the Chief Eunuch had a piece sliced from his thigh, cooked, and sent for her dinner; her recovery, it was said, was rapid and complete.

Outside the palace walls, the eunuchs were widely despised for both their mutilation and their arrogance toward commonfolk. Yet they were not completely unsympathetic. They were required to carry their severed testicles in little pouches at the waist and to produce them for imperial inspectors on demand. Eunuchs were so sensitive, it was said, that they could be hurt by the mere mention of a teapot without a spout or a dog without a tail.

The Empress Dowager's given name was Yehonala. It was hard, without irony, to use her honorific Cixi, which she preferred; it meant "Maternal and Benevolent." Her natural son, the Tongzhi emperor, died at the age of nineteen, apparently from syphilis contracted during incognito carousals in the fleshpots of the city. She then foxed her rivals a second time by adopting the son of a minor prince as her own, thereby ensuring herself another long and lucrative regency.

The new emperor was titled Guangxu: "of the Glorious Succession." He was small and sickly, and tubercular lungs made his voice "light and thin like the hum of a mosquito." He grew up with no one but eunuchs and women of the court for companions; Cixi perhaps wished him to become as effeminate and pliable as his predecessor. But Guangxu proved to be made of less predictable stuff. He had books on astronomy and engineering brought to him and obtained a miniature steam railway from Germany, to carry him from the palace to the pleasure garden at Beihai; when the engine blew up, eunuchs pulled him along the tracks with silken cords.

In 1898, when he was twenty-eight, the emperor made his bid for independence. Inspired by modernizers who had been influenced by Japan and the West, he declared freedom of the press and emigration, free trade with the outside world, the conversion of temples into modern schools, and legal reforms that would have made China a constitutional monarchy. But he was no match for Cixi. Within three months, the reform movement was dead.

One can picture him, the emperor wheezing apologies in that strange mournful voice, confronted by the Empress Dowager in his private apartments, from which there was no exit except through Cixi's own. An official described the empress in a temper: Her eyes "poured out straight rays; her cheekbones were sharp and the veins on her forehead projected. She showed her teeth as if she was suffering from lockjaw." She told Guangxu, "Do you know the law of the imperial household for one who raises his hand against his mother?" But she let him live, languishing for another ten years, a prisoner in the heart of the palace until his death.

NORTH OF the halls of government, the palace's grand terraces dropped away into a labyrinth of much smaller courtyards linked by walled passageways of such complex configuration that I never managed to sort it out completely. There were always courtyards I'd never noticed, hidden corridors that I'd missed. The Empress Dowager's apartments lay here. They were low and surprisingly cramped, and built of the same prosaic gray brick as everything else in Beijing. But they were stuffed with incredible objects. There were coral trees with jade leaves and pearls for plums, and golden elephants, and cloisonné cranes with the fungi of immortality clutched in their beaks, and pewter dragons and phoenixes, and appalling rococo clocks. The eye fairly gagged on the too-muchness of it.

Before his imprisonment, Guangxu lived in a small cluster of apartments nearby. You could see through the smudged glass the "go" board he had played on, and a golden clock, and ivory and jade bijoux, and the imperial bed. The empress sent concubines to him here wrapped like succulent caterpillars in rugs, on the backs of eunuchs. White silk straps hung from the imperial bed, to tie the concubines' legs so they wouldn't bruise the imperial buttocks. During the act of love, eunuchs stood outside the door, shouting, "Don't strain! Protect the imperial health!"

I liked the quietude here. When I worked in Beijing, I often cycled over from my office at the news agency with a lunch of apples and crusty, freshly baked rolls in my pockets, and settled in a corner to read in the sun. The agency's headquarters were not far away, on the site of the imperial elephant stables; work was organized in small self-contained units that in spirit resembled nothing so much as the walled courtyards of the old city, so that it was rare even to encounter anyone from a different section. The dozen journalists on my staff were mostly old hands who had served the agency since the days when no one troubled to distinguish between news and propaganda. They rarely lied, but they knew when to omit inconvenient truths, and they never thought of challenging the mysterious people who labored somewhere in the building's bowels, removing from stories anything that seemed unhelpful to the interests of the Communist Party and the People's Republic.

It was typical that weeks passed before anyone explained to me that Chen Ruining was the unit Party leader, as well as the chief editor. That meant that he also approved housing assignments, private travel, pregnancies, and divorces, and presided over the dossiers that detailed each staff member's class origins, family political history, and ideological reliability. Chen was fifty-two, part of the generation that was inheriting power as China's geriatric leadership gradually retired. He had earned a certain notoriety during the Cultural Revolution when, as a correspondent in Pakistan, he dared to sit in the Chinese ambassador's chair for several hours, when Mao called for a general revolt. Although he had advanced steadily in the agency, he wore a perpetually insecure air that revealed itself in a moist and nervous laugh and in exhausted eyes that flickered uneasily around him when he spoke.

Chen worried when I said I was buying a bicycle.

"You should stay in your room and rest," he said.

When I asked him what he did for recreation, Chen said, "I sleep."

I bought the bicycle anyway. During the long lunch break, when Chen and the rest of the staff curled up on their desks and slept, I would cycle off to the palace, or the Lama Temple, or the Fa Yuan Temple in the south; on weekends I might ride out to one of the temples in the Western Hills. Some of these had been splendidly restored, and before I knew better, they seemed to promise still greater riches yet to be discovered. Eventually I learned that there had been two hundred temples around Beijing before the revolution; the half-dozen that now remained were token showpieces, pseudo-places ultimately, beautiful in the way that objects beneath glass in a museum may be beautiful, and sterile. Even so, the old spaces still soothed with an elegance that the crabbed Chinese present so conspicuously lacked.

The atmosphere at the agency made me uncomfortable, but I tried to make a game of it. Once I went with a reporter to the new "Children's Palace," where there were displays for the young on astronomy and computers, and instruction was given in dance, painting, martial arts, and the like. It was well known that the place was a former residence of Mao's wife, Jiang Qing.

"Who do you suppose lived here?" I teased.

The reporter answered deliberately. She was a wary woman who had survived without trouble at the agency for many years.

"I think someone did."

"But who do you think it was?"

"Oh, I don't think I know."

"It must have been someone high in the Party, don't you think?"

"Maybe it was."

"Do you think it might have been someone in the Gang of Four?"

"It's possible."

"Could it have been Jiang Qing's house?"

The reporter raised her eyes to the sky and stared at it like a dog at the moon.

I told Chen Ruining what had happened. I expected a laugh. I was still new at the agency then.

"Our job is to give people abroad the correct idea of what is happening here," he said.

Warnings hid like that in non sequiturs.

Ouyang was seventy-two, but people at the agency said she had been a great beauty in her day. It was easy to see that her huge melancholy eyes must have intoxicated men in a less puritan Beijing. She was supposed to have retired, but she kept reappearing at the office like a force of nature with some story about a newly discovered tomb, or a mummy that had just been unearthed somewhere in Xinjiang.

I took Ouyang to lunch one day at the Sichuan restaurant near the office. What was ordinarily a ten-minute walk took thirty, but she moved with such olympian grace that she transformed it into an imperial progress through the shuffling noontime crowds. Mostly we talked about New York, where she had lived in the 1940s, and about Columbia University, and good food. And about Japanese; she had just begun to study it.

She said, "It might come in handy in the future."

But a few weeks later, when I proposed another lunch date, she was evasive.

"It may not be convenient," she finally said.

The phrase warned off.

After that, odd things began to happen. Ouyang avoided me altogether. Budding friendships hesitated and atrophied. Chen Ruining would suddenly appear next to me, leaning into my conversations, unembarrassed, noisily sucking back spittle. I would look up from a manuscript to discover him staring at my desk, straining to see what I was writing. A reporter told me that he had detailed her to sit near me in a theater, to find out whom I was with and what I might say.

Something had happened, but no one would tell me what. The reporters went on fossicking about their commas and colons. The stories hailing new achievements in oil extraction and coal production continued to flow in; everything, the masters of punctuation assured, was always improving.

"Don't worry," one of them said to me. "It's not important."

It was meant to be soothing, the way you would hush a child.

"Why am I not allowed to speak to anyone?" I asked Chen.

"But that is not true," Chen protested, with his moist grin and unsteady eye. "You can talk to me."

TROMPE L'OEIL paintings of scenes from the *Dream of the Red Chamber* were painted onto the walls behind the veranda that ran around the courtyard in the rear of Cixi's apartments, so that where the wooden galleries left off, painted ones continued into an exquisite garden where lissome girls sipped tea in graceful pavilions, glided over dainty bridges, and whispered by lotus-filled pools. It was easy to imagine the Empress Dowager breakfasting here on her fresh-squeezed mother's milk and porridge, sending her eunuchs scurrying through the courtyards to organize the hundred dishes that would appear each evening on her table, or to search out some famous craftsman to carve a bit of jade to delight the imperial eye.

I had looked forward to seeing the courtyard again, and those murals. But now it felt odd to be back. The last time I had been here was the day I realized that something had happened to Ouyang. Even across the space of six years, the memory was painful, and now, as I sat on Cixi's veranda and looked into those wonderful *trompe l'oeil* galleries, I wished I could walk away into them.

THE PEARL Concubine was the kind of woman Cixi feared; curious, intelligent, even independent within the constraints of court etiquette. Despite the ubiquitous eunuchs, she and Guangxu actually seem to have fallen in love. She could have saved herself by keeping silent when Cixi fled the palace with her imperial captive after the failure of the Boxer Rebellion, in 1900. But instead she begged Cixi on her knees not to disgrace the dynasty by running away. Perhaps Cixi saw danger in the girl's will, or simply decided to take advantage of the situation to punish Guangxu further. The Empress Dowager gave an order to her eunuchs; Guangxu, disguised like the fastidious Empress Dowager herself in peasant's rags, watched helplessly as the eunuchs took hold of the only person he had ever loved and threw her into a well, to her death.

I went looking for the well one day. I knew that it was somewhere in the northwest quarter of the palace; I paced the walled lanes for most of an hour, but the gates to it were locked or the courtyard sealed off, and I finally gave up. I had parked my bicycle inside the northern gate. On the way out, a voice bellowed at me to get off my bike. Six young men in olive-drab greatcoats piled out of the gatehouse.

"Get off! You must get off!"

They ordered me into the guardhouse, where their sergeant struck a pose, square jaw thrust forward.

"Why didn't you get off your bicycle?" he bellowed. "Where were you going? What were you doing here?"

"There was no sign telling me to get off," I said.

We all went outside again. There was a sign after all, but it was facing backwards, so that someone exiting the palace couldn't read it.

"You said there was no sign!" The sergeant smiled triumphantly. "There it is! You're guilty!"

His face went purple.

"You must know the rules!" he howled. "You must know the rules!"

THE IMPERIAL pleasure garden that was now known as Beihai Park lay across a busy avenue from the palace. The day was unseasonably warm, and the park was full of Pekingese taking in the sun. Even middle-aged cadres cavorted and mugged while friends photographed them framed against the *dagoba*, the huge, white, bell-shaped construction that dominated the lake. The park was a popular trysting place, and young couples probed the shrubbery like mine-sweepers, in search of privacy. I kept stumbling on them in the pavilions and rockeries, and among the trees below the *dagoba*, on the island that Marco Polo knew as the "Green Mound."

The man in the white loafers had that seedy, calculating look of petty predators the world over; I pegged him as a money changer from the start. He was probably in his twenties, and along with the loafers he wore a canvas rain hat and a battered nylon Mao suit that was lumpily buttoned, as if there were something hidden underneath. He ambled around me in vague but meaningfully shrinking circles. I tensed instinctively.

"What is your country?" he asked.

I told him. He sidled away and then circled back.

"U-n-i-t-e-d S-t-a-t-e-s," he declared, painstakingly spelling out each word letter by letter.

"Yes."

"I am C-h-i-n-e-s-e."

"Yes."

"What means 'U-S-A?' "

"The United States of America."

"Ah! U-n-i-t-e-d S-t-a-t-e-s?"

I slipped away into the crowd, but I could see him still eyeing me as I dodged up the stairs to the small walled hill called the Round City. On top, there were a few old pavilions that had been turned into souvenir shops, a white pine tree that two centuries ago was already so old that the emperor Qianlong ennobled it with the titles of a Chinese earl, and an enormous black jade bowl that legend held had fallen from Chang E's palace on the moon. The bowl was in fact all that remained of the palace from which Kubilai Khan ruled the city that Marco Polo knew as Cambaluc.

The "Green Mound" fascinated the Venetian. Whenever Kubilai heard of a particularly fine tree, he had it dug up, roots and all, transported by elephant to the capital, and planted on the hill; he covered the hill with rare green stones, then erected a completely green palace on the topmost point. "And I give you my word that mound and trees and palace form a vision of such beauty that it gladdens the hearts of all beholders," Polo swore.

Now the island was built up mostly with dilapidated Qing studios and a maze of galleries and stairs that climbed through miniature caverns and curiously shaped doors. Cixi liked to come here to paint, looking out toward the dainty pavilions that dotted the lake's northern shore, and the sweeping roof of the temple of the Great Western Heaven, where the hundred stages of reincarnation were sculpted in painted plaster, in lurid detail. One could picture the entourage of handmaids and eunuchs that trailed after her wherever she went, standing in bated silence while she drew one stroke after another, as if each mediocre splash of the brush were a solemn event, potent with manna.

Kubilai's green palace probably stood where the spacious terrace now lies around the foot of the *dagoba*. The Great Khan delighted in travelers' tales, and it must have been here, at the center of medieval Cathay, that Polo told of his epic journey from the Taklamakan and the Hindu Kush, Persia and the Holy Land, and from what must have seemed, with the greatest city in the world now spread out before him, the puny faraway port of Venice. He was dazzled by the capital's immense whitewashed walls, the chessboard regularity of its blocks, the mansions with their ample courtyards and gardens, the palace so splendid that "no man in the world could imagine any improvement in design or execution." He cited statistics like an incantation: the 1,000 cartloads of silk that entered the city each day, the hall so vast it could seat 6,000, the 10,000 maids who served each wife of the Khan, the 20,000 courtesans who served the city's brothels, the 100,000 white horses the Khan received as gifts at the New Year. The astonishing numbers, the dreamy vision of the city beyond Europe's imagining, fed the legend that became Cathay.

Polo did not invent the name "Cathay." Ironically enough, it was not even a Chinese word; it derived from the "Khitai," plundering tribes who swept down upon northern China in the tenth century. Long after they had passed into oblivion, their name continued to creep westward along the trade routes, blurring as it went and gathering magic, to finally become immortalized in the fantasy of a whole civilization of which the barbaric Khitai themselves had probably never even heard.

I stood at the parapet beneath the *dagoba* and scanned the city, trying and failing to pick out the line of the city's old walls and gates. They were all gone now, torn down to build backyard smelteries during the Great Leap Forward, and then air-raid shelters when Mao feared a Russian nuclear attack. Now high-rise developments were nibbling everywhere at the ancient symmetries. Bulldozers were sweeping away the old courtyard dwellings; often, cycling through the lanes, I would see them torn open, with their centuries-old beams and sculpted latticework, and moon gates in ruins where the machines had passed through.

George Kates came here often. On blustery days the terrace reminded him of a galleon's poop rocking high over the yellow ocean of palace roofs that spread away to the south. In the 1930s he could look down upon a city that was not so very different in its essentials from the one that Polo had seen six hundred years before. "Beijing was simply the most beautiful city in the world. The symmetry of its grand plan made all other great agglomerations untidy and uncouth by comparison, and its scale could transform a Versailles even, into mere decoration for a wedding cake. The beauty was so constant that I seemed to swim in it as in a new sea, past new shapes and forms almost every hour of my waking existence."

It was an extraordinary time in Beijing. The city was more open to foreigners than it ever was before, or has ever been since. Even an independent scholar of limited means, like Kates, could afford a traditional courtyard home along with a couple of servants "who would do credit to a good Newport establishment." He prized above all the tranquility that enabled him to pursue his penetration of the language, a quest that became, as time went on, the center of his life. Through it, he felt himself "climbing those beautiful Chinese mountains where, half-seen in the mist, lay an art and a culture so grand that on earth it had no equal."

He shunned the expatriates of the Legation Quarter, who called him "the clam." His quest for solitude wasn't misanthropy; he adored the Pekingese. He found them "friendly and loveable beyond any anticipation." He admired their gravity too, the instinct for high ceremonial and etiquette that had to reflect, he thought, the sheer grandeur of the setting in which they lived.

The "small-town country silence" of his neighborhood seduced a man who had found Hollywood and Oxford and New York too limiting. Years later, memories came to him again and again in musical metaphor. "Conversation was tranquil and voices melodious." Tinkers and vendors announced their approach with a clamor of ingenious trumpets, clappers, and tuning forks, like repeated themes in a symphony. "Kindling or cabbages, garlic and leeks, each had its own motif, each had its special praises lifted insistently for a moment above the continuing background of sound."

Something he said to me on that stark New England afternoon kept coming back: "It seems, when I look back, that everything that happened before I came to Peking happened to another me. What that me desired, it found there, and having found, desired only in those troublous times not to be separated from." It was difficult to imagine now that Beijing could ever have given such happiness.

The man in the white loafers had come up suddenly behind me.

"You are student," he declared.

"No."

"You are teacher."

"Writer."

"Yes, teacher."

"No, writer."

"Yes, student."

"Yes, student," I said.

"How long in China?"

"Several months."

"Oh, three days."

"No, several months."

"Yes, three days."

It went on like this. It was all I could do not to push him away bodily.

I said, "I don't want to change money."

"C-h-a-n-g-e m-o-n-e-y?"

"No!"

"I don't know."

"What?"

"I am a bus conductor."

"You're not trying to change money?"

"I am sorry," he said. "No money. Only paintings."

"What?"

He pulled a folder from inside his jacket, opened it, and shoved it at me.

"You want beautiful Chinese paintings as a souvenir," he said.

The words rolled off his tongue with unexpected speed. It must have been a memorized sentence.

"I want to sell my beautiful paintings," he said. Another memorized sentence. "Not expensive."

"No," I said, taking in a fleeting impression of plum blossoms and peonies and birds. "Leave me alone!"

I thought of George Kates's courtyard, unmarred by wires or pipes, aromatic with oleanders and chrysanthemums, and with fig trees that he had planted with his own hands. He knew what it was for him; he called it his "peach orchard beyond the world." It might lie out there still, somewhere in the smoggy gray honeycomb of the old city. I couldn't help visualizing it intact, a perfectly self-contained world, like one of those miniature landscapes that craftsmen used to carve from a lump of jade or ivory so small that it would fit in the palm of your hand.

The man in the white loafers said, "Wish you a very nice holiday."

Then he shuffled away without apparent disappointment, this time for good. I felt a gust of relief. Then I began to realize that the pictures I had glimpsed actually were beautiful. I saw him fighting his way, day after day, through the glutinous crowds on his bus, dreaming in the suffocating crush about peonies and snow-dusted plums, and weirdly shaped stones and darting orioles as he clutched for tickets in the stink and press of humanity. I ran after him, but the white loafers had disappeared in the crowd.

It was late now and getting cold, and I set off through the brush, back down the hill. Red pumps, sneakers, bobby socks, and blue cuffs poked out from every bush. Everywhere I stepped I was surrounded by whimpers and murmurs and sighs. The boys and girls clutched at each other under the shrubs, nuzzling in each other's arms like puppies. The entire hillside was alive and pulsating with repressed sexuality and lust. I felt that if I stumbled against anyone he would shriek or explode.

THE HOUSE lay behind a muddy gray wall, off a busy street in the northern part of the city. A maid let me through a red enameled door, and then across a courtyard, picking our way where someone had been breaking up coal. She led me to the central hall and told me to wait. There were a few bulbous armchairs, silk flowers in a vase, a plaster nymph with a clock, and on the wall, photos of the dead Japanese wife and of Zhou Enlai.

The man who entered was tiny and delicately made, like a toy. His bony, walnut-brown face was drawn tightly down at the sides of his mouth, and it gave nothing away. But he knew how to draw a laugh.

"Of course, this place is quite a bit smaller than the Forbidden City, but it's quite enough for me!"

The tiny man was Aisin-Gioro Pujie, brother of the Last Emperor of China, heir to the Manchu throne, former soldier in the Imperial Guard of Japan.

"I was just a few months old when Puyi was taken away to the palace," he said. "He ascended to Heaven, while I stayed down here on earth. After that I no longer had a brother anymore, I had an emperor."

Pujie grew up within the hermetic courtyards of his father's mansion. The servants called him "Second Master" and on holidays prostrated themselves before him, one after another, in ritual kowtow. "I took it for granted. That was the natural order of things then." He learned the Confucian classics from scholars of the Imperial Academy; "It was years before I realized that Confucius might not contain all that needed to be known in the world." Then he was sent to the palace as a study companion for Puyi.

"But I didn't know that the emperor was my own brother." The wooden face broke into an impish smile. "No one had ever told me, you see. We believed that the emperor lived in Heaven. It was forbidden for us to even speak of him. I imagined the emperor as an old man with a long beard. So the first time I was told to go to court to see the emperor, he turned out to be a little boy! I was astonished!"

The boys were eventually assigned an English tutor, a former diplomat named Reginald Johnston, who believed with blind devotion in the fallen dynasty. Pujie called himself "William," and the emperor took the name "Henry." They grew to hate the decaying palace and dreamed of going to school in England; they almost escaped, but Johnston dissuaded them. He shamed them with the ancient Chinese story of the King of Yue who slept on firewood and ate gall to remind himself of his humiliation, and bided his time, waiting for the restoration that Heaven had decreed.

So they stayed on, uselessly, in the rump court, with their tuxedos and tennis whites, and the gramophone that said "Snapshots of Your Voice." It was all make-believe; there was no party to go to, no Dusenberg waiting at the gate, just courtyard after empty courtyard, hall after dusty decaying hall, where the eunuchs waited, slavish, predatory, and alert.

Then in 1924 the warlord Feng Yuxiang drove the boys out of the palace and into the arms of the Japanese. Pujie went to military school in Japan and was married by order of the Japanese army to a nobleman's daughter. He was arrested with Puyi during the Japanese collapse in 1945, interned by the Russians, and then held for ten years more in a Chinese Communist labor camp. From the start, Puyi and Pujie were destined to serve as models of Maoist thought reform.

"We were traitors, collaborators," Pujie said. "We expected to be killed, but the Communists were very good to us. The warden fed us well and allowed us to play mah-jongg from time to time, and even to gamble a little, because he said that was what the exploiting class was used to doing. The Communists changed our thinking through persuasion, little by little, little by little. We had killed so many Communists when we were in power, my brother and I! But the Party gave us a good education in return, so that we at last learned to understand our past crimes."

Since his release in 1961, Pujie had made gratefulness a lifetime's work. He was rewarded with an appointment to the Standing Committee of the national legislature. A few months after I met him, he was one of the first high-ranking officials to publicly praise the army's massacre of the young people who demonstrated for democracy in Tiananmen Square.

I wondered whether he ever missed the China of his childhood.

"During the Cultural Revolution, ultraleftist views held sway," he replied stiffly. "They maintained that everything connected with the dynasty was evil. Now our thinking is completely free from such errors."

The ideological lingo was meant to fend me off. But I tried again. I wondered what he felt when he walked through the palace now.

"I have no feeling at all," he said blandly.

I knew I wouldn't get anything more. He wasn't expected to have feelings about such things. It wasn't part of his job.

Later I came across a story in a pictorial magazine about the former imperial clan. It strove for a breezy touch. Mao Zedong's "principle of humanitarianism," it said, had enabled the family "to turn over a new leaf." Now, "they live contented lives like ordinary Beijing residents." One sister lived with her husband in a room twenty-four yards square. "We go across the street to use the public toilet," she commented. Another sister peddled cigarettes while her brothers were in prison and "now sits at home with her old husband and either reads or talks to her goldfish as if they were human." Her only son died of malnutrition when he was eight. Several members of the clan had changed their surname to a Chinese one in an effort conceal their origins. "Oddly enough," the article said, "the Last Emperor's brothers and sisters would rather talk about the price of vegetables in the market than recall their life in the imperial court."

S EVERAL OF the imperial altars still existed. The most important one stood in a large enclosure in the southern part of the city. Visitors often mistook the cylindrical, azure-roofed Hall of Annual Prayers for the main shrine. The actual Altar of Heaven lay a mile to the south at the end of an elevated marble causeway. It was a simple triple-tiered platform, surrounded by a circular rose-colored wall and then by another square red wall: Heaven and Earth in a mystical embrace.

Here the emperor annually brought the world of man into fragile balance with the terrific powers of the universe in a ritual that had continued without fundamental alteration for five thousand years, until it guttered out in the aftermath of the Republican Revolution. Two hours before daylight, the Son of Heaven donned robes of plum-colored silk, a black satin cap, and blue satin boots, and entered the inner enclosure. The round blue gem that symbolized Heaven was borne in a sedan chair like a living thing from the Temple of the God of the Universe and placed on the round stone that was the center of the topmost terrace. Psalms were played on slabs of jade and deep-throated drums. The emperor ascended the altar and prostrated himself nine times, offering up as he did so bolts of silk, jade cups, a pig, a ram, and a bull. What relief those who witnessed it must have felt, believing that in those gestures of unimaginable antiquity the universe itself was made an ally and that the empire was safe for another year!

I found the Altar of the Sun in a modern park, in the middle of the embassy quarter; it was a square platform that lay within a circular red wall that was crested with green-glazed tiles. It was a bitterly cold day, but there was an elderly man wearing a down jacket and a painter's cap with "Murphy" written on it sitting on the steps of the old bell tower nearby. He was playing tunes on an *erhu* that he had propped between his knees.

He said his name was Ma Erfei. "It means 'good luck,'" he giggled. "In English it sounds like 'Murphy.'" He pointed to his hat.

Murphy's eyes were merry and his mouth was caved in where his teeth had gone; a few silvery hairs straggled over his lip in search of a moustache. He spoke English with an American accent that he said he had learned "once upon a time" in a missionary school. He opened his wallet and showed me a colored picture of Jesus.

With a sly smile, he opened his coat to reveal a windbreaker that said "Columbia Records."

Before World War II he had been "in import-export." He had had a shop outside the Front Gate.

"Do you know the Peking Hotel?"

"Of course," I said.

"I did deals there, big deals. Do you know the Wagon-Lits Hotel?"

It had been gone since the 1950s.

"I did big deals there!"

I wondered what had happened to his business after 1949.

"I had to change my job."

The euphemism gently elided a revolution. For the next thirty years, until his retirement in 1980, he had been a cashier in a government canteen.

"Watch the water," he told me, pointing to a fountain that played over an artificial rockery nearby. He played to the spray. The melody dipped and rose mournfully, with an almost heartbreaking fragility. Then he played a Cantonese dance and something Russian that I didn't recognize, and then "Jingle Bells."

"Now I study the water," he said.

I told him I wanted to find the Eastern Peak Temple, which I knew was somewhere nearby. It used to be the most popular temple in the city, sheltering almost every folk deity from the Spirit of Plagues and Boils to Old Mother Wang, who doled out the Chinese equivalent of chicken soup to souls on their way to the underworld. In an extension of the temple, the bureaucrats of the eighteen hells supervised demons who burned the condemned in oil and hooked out their eyes, and pulled out the tongues of people whose habits of speech did not please the gods.

"It's right up there, just to the north," Murphy said. Then he frowned. "But maybe it's not there anymore. Maybe they pulled it down. It's hard to say."

He squinted ambiguously, in the way of Chinese who have seen much that they prefer not to describe.

"There were monks. But they're all gone now."

"What happened to them?"

"They had to change their jobs."

He made a sweeping gesture. "Things changed." After a while he said, "Go, maybe there is something there."

The Eastern Peak Temple lay just where Murphy said it would be. But where the old wooden gate would have been, there were iron doors. They were chained shut; through the crack I could see an overgrown courtyard, dilapidated halls, and a few Russian-style jeeps. A plaque identified the work unit that now occupied the temple; I copied down the ideographs. Later I asked someone to translate them for me. The temple was now a training school for the Public Security Bureau, China's KGB. I wondered if the commissars had a sense of humor after all.

I walked back to the Altar of the Sun, but Murphy had gone home. There was only one other man in the enclosure. He wore a shabby Mao jacket and baggy trousers, and he was stalking strangely across the altar, twittering and barking to himself. Suddenly he threw himself on his knees and kowtowed to the south. At first I supposed he was practicing an arcane form of *qigong*. Then I realized that he was mad and acting out some neurotic drama on the ancient celestial stage. He rose with his hands uplifted to the heavens and then abruptly pressed his face again to the altar. Then he spread his arms, turned his face to the sky, and hooted with the long raw cry of some great mountain bird.

THERE WAS the sense in Beijing, that winter, of a city waking from the long Maoist sleep, rubbing its eyes, trying to get new bearings. Billboards looming over the gray lanes proclaimed dream images of a future Beijing of skyscrapers and freeways. There were commercials on television for giant radios and computers, and color TVs. Dissidents were talking about new political parties and a serious parliament. Hotels that were carbon copies of ones in Palo Alto or Atlanta were going up everywhere; everyone was building them, even the Foreign Ministry and the Security Police. There were traffic jams too; government agencies were buying fleets of Toyotas the way the emperors used to squander the treasury on rococo clocks. It seemed as if communism had become as hollow as the empty palace at the city's heart, peopled only by its own enfeebled retainers and by the ghosts of a more heroic time.

I knew an American who had come to China in 1948 and had stayed on to make revolution. He lived in an old courtyard home near one of the back lakes; the neighborhood was really a slum, but Party leaders lived there and it had cachet. He was not happy about the way things were going in China.

"Things are getting worse and worse," he said, with the rasping side-of-the-mouth inflections picked up a lifetime ago on the streets of Flatbush. "The corruption is something awful. It's everywhere. And the ads I see on TV, they're worse than the stuff I left behind forty years ago. You know, there's nothing wrong with a little democracy, but there's nothing wrong with some more socialism or collectivism either."

He remembered the 1950s as a halcyon time. "The milk of human kindness was flowing all over the place. You'd see fifty thousand people leveling a mountain or building a canal with little baskets on carrying poles, and singing all the while." The Cultural Revolution had started out all right. "The bureaucracy was inefficient. The system needed a shake-up. People sort of deified Mao, and so did I. There was a reason for it. He was an amazing guy. But then the hopheads got control of things, and everything went to hell."

The hopheads. The creaky slang made me think of some melodrama of the 1930s, of the thuggish young Cagney or Bogart, of Mao as the decent fella, Pat O'Brien say, trying to clean up the block.

The American had good taste. There were fine scroll paintings on the wall. But the room was dominated by a portrait of Zhou Enlai and by a photo of the youthful Mao. Except for the imperial portrait that hung at the entrance to Tiananmen, it was the only picture of him that I saw in all Beijing.

Outside, the whole neighborhood seemed to have taken to the frozen lake. There were workers pedaling three-wheeled carts, and pig-tailed girls tugging kids on stools with cords tied to the legs, and old women perched on little wooden thrones and propeling themselves with picks that they held in each hand. There were entrepreneurs selling fruit and sharpening knives, and people fishing through holes, and people frying lunch on portable stoves. The wadded clothes made everyone seem improbably fat, as if they had been drawn with a wide brush in broad earthy strokes. There was a Brueghelesque feel to it all, an impression of something medieval having come back to life and enjoying itself immensely.

A FRIEND IN New York had written to Wei with an introduction and asked him to lend me a hand if I needed help. Wei was broad-faced and large-boned, and wore his hair combed forward in a sort of Caesarean fashion; he worked a few days a week for a magazine for independent businessmen, but he regarded himself as a poet. Mostly he thought the old culture was a waste of time. When I asked what he thought of traditional painting, he contemptuously replied, "Birds and flowers!" He had never been to a classical opera in his life. "When there's one on TV I turn the sound off." His taste ran to T. S. Eliot, John Ashberry, and Baudelaire.

Wei had once been arrested for publishing an underground magazine. He was released after a few days, but the experience had frightened him. The aftermath depressed him even more. Friends who made self-criticisms had been rewarded with state salaries and invitations to join the official writers' union. He said, "So then they began to oppress the younger poets just the way they were oppressed before."

The party Wei invited me to was in an apartment in one of the new high-rise developments beyond the Altar of Heaven. From a distance the buildings looked like the billboard fantasies of twenty-first-century Beijing. But when I got closer I could see that gouts of concrete were falling off the buildings, and inside the halls were just bare concrete and already stained with graffiti.

The apartment aspired to the bohemian. There was a fishnet hanging from the ceiling and a plaster bust of Beethoven on an upright piano. Poets and writers were gobbling oysters from a tureen and swigging at a bottle of Gordon's gin. The strains of a classical lute issued from a cassette player. Later someone put on Michael Jackson, and then Mozart.

Wei introduced me to a girl who wanted to study structuralism at the University of Michigan, and then to a Taiwanese journalist who was trying to get people to make nasty remarks about the Communist

Party, and then to a young poet who was translating Gay Talese's *Thy Neighbor's Wife*.

"There's no money in poetry," the translator said.

People said Talese's book was pornography so he thought it would be easy to get a publisher. I wondered what arrangement he had made with Talese for royalties.

"What are royalties?"

Then Wei introduced me to a tipsy novelist who had spent a year as a writer-in-residence at a college in the Midwest. I asked him what he thought of American writing.

"Americans eat too much," he said. "It's bad for literature."

The novelist nodded toward a long-haired man wearing baggy corduroys and a beret.

He said, "There goes a serious Taoist."

The Taoist was infatuated with Rabindranath Tagore.

Tagore had traveled in China in the 1920s and made a terrific impression on the poets of the era. Like much else that had lain fallow during the Maoist years, he was now being rediscovered in this twilight of communism.

"Ultimately the West is wanting, too," the Taoist said. "We can learn economics and technology from you, but the higher teachings of the spirit will come from Asia."

Two women next to us were arguing about the idea that a constant interplay of action and reaction was the driving force of revolution.

"Marx was misunderstood," one said defensively.

"That's Mao, not Marx," said the other.

"That's Lao Tze, not Mao," said the Taoist.

Then I talked to a depressed woman who taught Chinese at a middle school.

"China is a complete failure," she said. "China used to be complete in its government, its social organization, its aesthetics, its religion, everything. But it all failed. Then China was defeated by the West. Then it tried Marxism. Then that failed too."

Lately she had experimented with Christianity.

"They have so much certainty!" she said enviously.

She wanted to teach her students the Greeks. But she said it wasn't worth the struggle, that you weren't allowed to say what they really meant.

"Chinese education is just propaganda!"

I looked around for the Taiwanese journalist. But he was eavesdropping on a different conversation.

"We have to explore ourselves!" the poet who was translating Gay Talese said vigorously. "We have to investigate our feelings!"

"If they won't let me teach Plato, maybe I'll try Sartre," said the teacher.

"We must know who we are!" said the poet.

Before I left, I asked Wei if he would help me find George Kates's house. He hesitated long enough for me to see that he didn't really want to, but he said yes.

On the way out, I saw the writer who had been to America. He was quite drunk now. I asked him what he had liked best in the United States, and he said Abraham Lincoln's home in Springfield, Illinois.

"It wasn't the old house, or anything like that," he said. "There was a bronze bust of Lincoln there. So many people had gone up and rubbed his nose that it was shiny. It was amazing. No Chinese would ever have even thought of rubbing Mao's nose."

ZHAO AND I had not been close at the agency. But he was earnest and likable, and I knew I could trust what he told me. I suggested dinner at the Beijing Hotel; he said he lived near the Summer Palace and that it would be better to meet there. I wondered if even now he was wary of being seen with me in the center of town. But I was happy that he agreed to meet me at all. Things had changed, at least a little.

I cycled out the familiar route, first to Xizhimen and then northwest past the walled compounds of the universities and the technical institutes, and the Friendship Hotel where I used to live, pedaling hard against a stiff, dusty wind. Zhao was waiting for me at the gate of the Summer Palace, swathed in the sort of puffy down coat that made him look, with his large bespectacled eyes, like a fat blue owl. It was typical of him that the first thing he said was, "You're two minutes late." Then he smiled in the noncommittal way that I remembered and handed me an entrance ticket. It had cost him only a few cents, but it was a friendly gesture.

Zhao had been a lawyer before the revolution, until the legal profession was abolished as "bourgeois." Because he had studied English, the government decided that he would become a journalist next. That was all I had learned about him in a year of daily contact. He told me now, a little giddily, that one of his sons had just had a baby. Both sons, he said, worked in factories. During the Maoist years it was wise to have workers in the family, but Zhao came from the old intellectual class, and I wondered if he regretted their lack of education now. I began to ask, and then thought better of it.

Instead, I said, "I never even knew you were married."

He replied, "You can sit next to someone for thirty years and never know if he is married."

We crossed a courtyard populated by bronze gargoyles and dragons and foamy stones, and then went through a web of alleys that brought us out upon the most handsomely proportioned landscape in North China. A large pagoda capped the steep hill to the north, and below it a madder-rose fizz of galleries and pavilions covered the lower slopes as far as the shore of the iced-in lake that spread out before us. A causeway with camelback bridges copied Su Dongpo's dike at Hangzhou. So perfectly did the purple hills to the west complement the scene that they might have been erected by coolies like the rest of the garden, at the Empress Dowager's imperious command.

"I am aware that the emperor's desire to restore the palace in the west springs from his laudable concern for my welfare, and for that reason I cannot bear to meet his well-meaning petition with a blunt refusal," she declared when construction began in 1888. "Moreover the costs of the construction have all been provided for out of the surplus funds accumulated as a result of rigid economies in the past."

This was hogwash, of course. Poor Guangxu had no say at all in the matter. There had certainly been no "rigid economies," and there were no "surplus funds." Cixi simply plundered the money that had been allocated to build a modern navy.

We followed the long arcade that skirted the lake's northern shore and ended at the marble barge that Cixi built in lieu of real warships. We stood for a while on the immobile prow, watching the skaters; there were scores of them on the lake, young men mostly. They skated gravely and silently, bent against the wind, each in a perfect circle that he had marked on the ice. It was a scene that I thought George Kates would have found stunningly beautiful.

I told Zhao what was on my mind. I wanted to know what had happened to Ouyang.

He kept looking at the skaters bent against the wind, going around and around in their lonely circles. I could see that he was deciding whether to answer me.

Finally he said, "She didn't ask Chen Ruining for permission to have lunch with you."

"She was seventy-two years old!"

"She wasn't correct," Zhao said blandly. "She was ordered to criticize herself. Very embarrassing."

He made a gesture of ripping his face off. It was an awful image.

Then he said, "Chen said you might have been asking her questions about something."

"About what, for heaven's sake?"

"I don't know."

The way he said it, I knew he was telling me not to press for an opinion, and that if I did he wouldn't give me one.

"But how did Chen find out about it?"

"You told Li. Li told Chen."

I had liked Li. He was a quick-witted and engaging man of sixty or so, and gregarious by office standards. He often asked me where I had been and who I had met, and in a way that always reassured.

Zhao said that Li had belonged to a Kuomintang youth group before the revolution. It had blighted his life. He performed extra duties to prove his loyalty.

"Everyone knew he was a spy, but no one was allowed to tell you."

"What happened to him?"

"They finally allowed him to join the Party. It was part of the liberalization. The Party is recruiting more intellectuals now."

I searched for irony in his tone but didn't find it. I didn't know what to feel. I wondered if Zhao would even have understood what it was that upset me. He was a man of the system too, and he took spies for granted.

Something still puzzled me.

"It must have started when I went to the Children's Palace and kept asking about Jiang Qing's house."

"No, it was the bicycle. It drove Chen Ruining crazy. He never knew where you were going."

This was where the old empire survived, I thought, in men's souls, invisibly, in the craving to control and obey, in the lust for secrecy, in the incessant scraping at one's fellow man. The gates and walls and moats of the old city still stood there too, in every encounter; secrecy, suspicion, petty cruelty were part of the fabric of the place, as inescapable as the yellowish-gray walls that had flanked every lane in the city since it was the Cambaluc of Kubilai Khan.

By now we had come back around the lakeshore to Guangxu's prison. It would have been a pleasant enough dwelling; it was called the Pavilion of Jade Billows, and it was sited to take in the best view of the lake. But Cixi had the windows bricked in so the unfortunate emperor could see nothing at all.

Occasionally he would be trundled out, like some antique talisman, to renew the dynasty's ever more fragile mandate at the Altar of Heaven. The commoners would be driven from the streets, the silken curtains hung, the musicians gotten up in their regalia, the show put on as if the Son of Heaven still ruled in Cathay. But it was all a sham now. House owners let foreign tourists peer through curtain slits as the imperial cortege passed. One found "the dragon countenance a pale and sickly one, the glance timid rather than terrifying," and the imperial robes as greasy and threadbare as a street pedlar's. If the Cathay of panoply and mystery, the exotic land that enchanted the imagination of travelers since Polo's day, can be said to have died at any particular point in time, it was perhaps at that prosaic moment somewhere along the sacred axis, with the forbidden face for sale to tourists, a shilling a look.

The custodians were locking up, and there was barely time enough to trot around the courtyard and peek through the windows at the emperor's apartment. All I could make out was a clock crusted with rubies and diamonds, a bed in a shadowy alcove, a writing table, some cloisonné curios, and a pair of life-size cranes, symbols of good fortune that the Empress Dowager must have intended to mock the emperor's fate.

Cixi and the emperor died just two days apart, in November of 1908. The Empress Dowager was suffering from severe dysentery and apparently knew that her own death was imminent. Guangxu began inexplicably to sicken at the same time. The palace doctors blamed a weak liver; whisperers said that Cixi had finally poisoned the emperor, although there was no clear-cut proof. At the last moment, Guangxu petulantly pushed aside the sacred Robes of Longevity that tradition required the Son of Heaven to wear on his deathbed. It was the last feeble gesture of independence left to him. Guangxu's death worked on Cixi like a tonic. She rose from her sickbed to gorge herself on clotted cream and crab apples. Within hours she was dead.

The place suddenly depressed me. The walled-in courtyard, the too-ornate curios, the thought of the eunuchs with their ears forever at the door, the wasted years of loneliness made me almost physically sick.

I said, "I wonder how he ever bore it."

"The Chinese know how to bear suffering better than anyone else in the world," Zhao said. "It is our greatest strength."

I could see that it was something in which he took pride. But what he saw as strength I thought was the greatest Chinese weakness of all, a resiliency that approached the tragic.

The atmosphere had taken on an extraordinary softness. A pagoda to the west stood etched in stark exclamation against the blue mountains. Then, so dramatically that it seemed strange that it was not accompanied by sound, a moon the color of old ivory broke free from the hills and lofted into the violet sky.

Even as the light dimmed, the skaters kept on in those perfect, lonely circles. I waited for one of them to break loose and rocket off across the ice. But none did. It wore me out watching them, and finally I turned away.

I said to Zhao that I hoped we could meet again before I left Beijing. He looked embarrassed.

"I don't think it would be convenient," he said.

I HAD AN address scrawled in George Kates's shaky hand: "35 Laku Hutong." Wei and I found the street in a maze of lanes a little distance north of the Forbidden City. Long ago, the area had been inhabited by Manchu aristocrats, and superstitious people said the atmosphere was still saturated with the lingering *qi* of the departed princes.

We had already been up and down the lane. Kates's courtyard, if it still existed, was just yards away from where we stood. But the numbers were all wrong, or had been changed. Where No. 35 should have been there was just a blank wall.

I stopped cyclists and passersby, anyone who looked old enough to have lived on the street fifty years ago. A jowled man in a boiler suit grudgingly paused.

"There are no Americans here," he said patronizingly. "This is China."

An elderly man stepped out of his door and when he saw that I'd caught his eye, dodged back in. But when Wei called politely he stepped out again. He was nervous and obviously wanted to break away. Then he warmed a little and said, "Speak to Old Zhang. He grew up in the lane."

Old Zhang's home was further up the street, in a brick barracks that had been wedged into what had once been a princely courtyard. The middle-aged woman who answered our knock didn't bother to conceal her surprise at the sight of a foreigner. I told her how fondly Kates remembered the neighborhood and that he wanted to know before he died how things stood there. It was the kind of appeal that Chinese understood.

The woman went away, and after a while an ancient, lantern-jawed man appeared. He bent forward and listened, nodding vaguely. Then he smiled vacantly into the wind.

"Meiyou," the woman said. "Nothing there."

We wandered back down the lane, pressed against the coal-stained wall to escape the wind. I could see that Wei wanted to go home. We had been the length of the lane three or four times now, and he knew we had been noticed.

I wondered to myself what anyone in my own neighborhood in New York would remember about me fifty years hence. If a nosy Chinese came asking questions, what would the laundryman say, or the grocer, or the Yemeni who sold me my morning paper? I felt defeated and depressed.

An elderly man was selling skewered fruit from a little bamboo cart at the corner, crying out his wares in an operatic falsetto that resonated the length of the lane.

"Sugared fruit on a stick! Just stuck the sugar on!"

Pale grapes and crimson hawthorne fruit and tiny glazed oranges lay inside a glass box in neat glistening rows. The hawthorne fruit was cold and tart, and I stood eating it slowly in the wind so that I could keep listening to the old man's wonderful cry. He had a grizzled, jolly face and a mouthful of holes where most of his teeth had been, and he told me that he had recently returned to selling fruit after forty years' hiatus.

"I changed my job after the revolution," he said.

I had an impulse.

"Were you ever here in the 1930s?"

"This was always my corner!"

"Do you remember any foreigners who lived here in those days?"

"Just the American."

"The American!"

"The American. Before I sold fruit I pulled a rickshaw. I pulled him often."

"Can you remember where he lived?"

"Right there," he said smilingly, pointing down the lane to a door that we had passed half a dozen times. "Over that wall."

"What was he like?" I asked.

"I couldn't tell you. I pulled and he rode. That was the way it was."

Wei and I stepped through a door in a gray-brick wall into a junkyard litter of rubber hose, empty bottles, rusty tins, used planking, and coal that had been heaped up in anticipation of future need. Cabbage had been spread out to dry on the cracked flagstones, and above them clotheslines sagged with the weight of lime-green long johns. Gradually I began to to be able to make out the lines of the old halls beneath the crust of jerry-built sheds, and then the fig trees submerged beneath the laundry and lumber.

The courtyard seemed deserted. Wei started when we peered through a window and saw a man in a boiler suit hunched over a wok. He saw us at the same instant and darted for the door. I felt Wei stiffen. But instead of driving us away, the man took hold of us by the arms and pulled us bodily inside, and told us that we'd come just in time for lunch. The oily aroma of fried cabbage radiated through the room.

Xu was short and sturdy, somewhere in his late fifties, I guessed; his iron-gray hair stood up stiffly, in military fashion, giving him a rather severe look. But he had an unexpected mildness of manner that put me instantly at ease. Wei liked him right away. "Old Beijing," he said. It was a compliment. He meant someone who was still capable of politeness, who had a certain kind of gravity, and graceful humor.

The hut was insulated with brown wrapping paper pasted to the walls and heated by a pot-bellied stove. There was a Naugahyde couch, a pinewood desk, an alarm clock on the Formica table, a television, a Chinese-made stereo. I could see that Xu was proud of it.

Xu's son and daughter-in-law lived on the other side of a partition. His aged mother lay curled on a bed in the inner room; her eyes peered eerily from the shadows, and later, when she pulled up the quilt over her head, I could see that she had a pair of ruined bound feet.

Xu was a Maoist success story. He said he had grown up a peasant in a village where money was rarely seen; now he was an assembly-line worker in a plant that made Chinese jeeps. It was the kind of job that had carried immense prestige when workers were still referred to ritually as the "vanguard of the revolution."

We got off on the wrong foot. Meaning to be polite, I asked Xu to tell me what his life had been like before the revolution.

"I won't talk about the past," he said.

I misunderstood his tone and asked why not.

"I won't tell you anything about it," he said abruptly.

There had been famine in the villages in those years. Children were sold for food. You never knew what people remembered.

I asked Xu about George Kates, but he looked blank. He had moved into the courtyard in 1960, but he had never heard of an American there.

Then I read him Kates's description of the "old palace eunuch, bobbing and rotund," and his "harridan of a wife, whose bad temper and scolding tongue" had scandalized the neighborhood.

"That's them!" Xu exclaimed. "That's them exactly!"

The eunuch was "a very kind person," but always remote, never intimate, Xu said excitedly, plainly thrilled that his memory had been enshrined in a foreigner's book. The eunuch's wife was vivid in his mind.

"She looked down on the rest of us because she had been the Dowager Empress's handmaid. She was angry a lot, but I suppose you could understand why."

Xu laughed as I supposed Kates's servants had half a century ago at the poor woman's frustration.

"So angry! She screamed at the children when they picked the figs. But she wasn't really bad. She gave them the fruit later anyway."

Kates's figs, I thought, from the tree that he had planted and coddled. Kates left the courtyard in 1940; the eunuch must have taken the house over for himself sometime after that.

I tried to imagine them, the sexless old man, the crabbed wife, bastioned in their imperial reserve, living anachronisms, struggling to stay afloat in the tidal wave of revolution. To Kates, the courtyard was the Peach Blossom Spring, a last and perfect refuge from the lesser world that lay beyond China. But to the eunuch and his wife it must have seemed the last patch of sacred imperial ground, the Great Within shriveled to the dimensions of a single yard.

Xu said that in 1960 the eunuch and his wife were told to make room for "productive workers" who had been given permission by the government to erect their own huts in the courtyard. A few years later, they were informed that they only needed one room for themselves, and more strangers were crowded into the central hall. Fourteen people now lived in the courtyard.

A worker's family occupied the main hall. Xu went across the courtyard and told them that someone had come from America to see their home. A mother and her two daughters silently made way for me as I pushed through a wooden door into Kates's inner sanctum. The wooden walls had been buried beneath bricks and plaster to resemble the concrete-block apartments that Chinese thought of as modern. The room was crammed with couches and beds; plastic flowers stood in a drinking glass, and on a shelf there was a thermometer affixed to a silver plastic boat. I tried to picture Kates here in his skullcap and robe, in his precious solitude, poised over some arcane text, happily parsing out ideographs.

Here Kates had found Cathay; an inner Cathay of which the chinoiserie-come-to-life of aging pavilions, lotus-filled lakes, and hieratic servants were but the facade. For the rest of his life there would be a secret Chinese in the aging body of a small patrician Jew, scribbling in a Salzburg hotel room about a Scottish queen who had lost her country, alone with his seals ("Kates meditates upon the Way") and dainty ivories, gradually forgetting everything except a China that was himself.

The woman stared at me and waited for me to leave. But Xu had gotten caught up in my enthusiasm and, ignoring her unease, he led me eagerly around the room.

"There were wooden screens over here, beautiful things," he said. "There were ancient cabinets, and over there old-fashioned shelves that divided the room, and over there a big table with curved ends, like an altar. During the Cultural Revolution we condemned things like that as 'old culture,' and people had to get rid of them. One day we pulled them out and threw them into the street outside, and crews came and took them away. We called it 'making revolution.'"

I remembered Chuck, the gregarious former Red Guard I had met in Wuhan. His job was cataloguing antiques confiscated from old

Manchu homes. I wondered if the eunuch's furniture had passed through his hands.

"Did the eunuch die from old age or politics?" I asked Xu.

Wei said, "We're lucky the police haven't come yet. Every court-yard has its eyes."

He was very nervous. I knew he was hoping I wanted to go.

Xu said the eunuch's wife died of malnutrition during the "three years of difficulty." That was the euphemism the Maoists taught people to use when tens of millions died of starvation after the failure of the Great Leap Forward.

"Then when the Cultural Revolution began, the daughter-in-law came," Xu said. "She was a nasty type."

"Daughter-in-law!" I exclaimed.

Xu said, "The son's wife, naturally."

"Son!"

Xu explained that before the revolution, the eunuch had adopted a peasant boy who continued to live with his natural parents in a village outside Beijing. The boy's sole duty was to await the eunuch's death and thereafter to make the offerings at his grave that befitted the dignity of a eunuch who had once served the Son of Heaven. Such things were important in the days when the old gods still ruled.

"During the Cultural Revolution, workers and peasants were encouraged to abuse people who belonged to the old culture, in order to express their revolutionary spirit," Xu said. "We had never seen the daughter-in-law before. She just moved in one day and said she was going to take care of the old man. But she was really after his money. She squeezed all his savings out of him, and then when there was nothing left, she abandoned him and went back to the village. She said she was 'making revolution.' The Red Guards took what was left. They found two jade belts that the eunuch had hidden somewhere. I saw them. So beautiful! They must have been the last things he had from the palace."

"How did the eunuch feel?" I asked.

"No one asked," Xu said. "It wouldn't have been polite. Then one day the Red Guards came for him. They said they were sending him to the countryside to be 'reformed.' He never came back, of course."

The ironic thing was, the eunuch had probably been born a peasant himself. Many of the court eunuchs were poor men who traded their testicles for entree to the palace. But the empire had capsized and left him beached in a world that had no use at all for men of his kind.

When we emerged again into the courtyard we found a dozen or more people watching us silently from the shanties. The courtyard hadn't been empty after all. A lean woman in a goose-down vest stepped forward with an expression of chilly expectancy. I said hello but she didn't respond. Wei understood at a glance.

"She's from the block committee."

"Foreigners are not permitted," she declared. "You must have permission. You must be officially accompanied."

I couldn't read Xu's face. But Wei was scared.

The committeewoman glared at Wei and demanded, "What is your work unit?"

"Don't answer," I said. "Let's go."

"Tell me your unit," she demanded.

He didn't and she drove us to the door in the outer wall, like thieves caught in the act. Xu looked at her stonily and declared that we should be seen to the gate properly, and then went on through it with us and down the lane, and the next lane too, until we reached the avenue, so that people could see plainly that he was with us.

"I have enjoyed your visit," he said. "Please come again. I hope you are enjoying your trip to China."

They were formulas of politeness and didn't require a response, but I knew that it would have been easier for him to have stayed in the derelict courtyard and said nothing at all. He spoke with grace and dignity and gentleness, and when he left us at the corner and sturdily turned back toward the courtyard, I almost wept.

We got on our bicycles and rode back toward the Avenue of Eternal Peace, pedaling hard against the dusty wind. There was a ghostly quality to the streets, which were only faintly lit by the grainy beams of streetlamps. Cars prowled without headlights to save power, maneuvering slowly through the herds of silent, bundled cyclists. We moved silently along with them, numb from the cold.

T HE CHINESE New Year began at midnight. When the clock struck twelve, the entire city began to roar. In the lanes, boys and their fathers, young toughs and lumpy old women, set off yards-long strings of firecrackers that hung from branches and drainpipes, and from the ends of long sticks. Roman candles whizzed off in wild cannonades in every direction, spattering showers of sparks against walls and roofs. Like signal flares before a barrage, pink and green balls of fire arched high over the gray lanes and the courtyards. Gunpowder floated in clouds down the boulevards, turning them lurid in the light of the streetlamps. Somewhere in the distance there was a scream where a fireball had struck someone, and then sobbing.

I cycled up to the Avenue of Eternal Peace and then west through Tiananmen Square. The square was empty except for a few clumps of policemen stamping against the cold. Mao's limpid Buddha-face peered down from the Gate of Heavenly Peace with deceptive softness through the gunpowder fog. A few blocks away, red flares rose over the walls of Zhongnanhai. I wondered if, had I been able to penetrate the imperial sanctum, I would have seen China's leaders disporting like wizened children, firing their toy rockets off into the night. But the fortress doors were closed and the guards with their submachine guns were as motionless as pewter grenadiers in the acrid haze.

I found an all-night variety show on television when I got back to my room. First, young men in Han-dynasty robes flipped and spun in a routine entitled "Break Dancing in the Dragon Palace." Next, the station's English-language news readers gathered like American hayseeds on a farm wagon and sang "Old McDonald Had a Farm." "With a moo-moo here, and a moo-moo there," they sang, grinning vast Jimmy Carter smiles ear-to-ear, "eeay, eeay, oh!" A ballet troupe from the People's Liberation Army came next. They danced classical ballet to a pulsing disco beat as strobe lights played over their uniforms. In their hands they brandished clubs and riot shields as they leaped through the air with breathtaking grace.

THE NEXT morning, I went to Chang's house to say good-bye. Friends had been by with New Year's gifts, and jars of quail's eggs and pickled hawthorne fruit stood in delectable regiments on every shelf. I asked what he was doing to celebrate the holiday.

"Not a darned thing!" he declared happily.

But he was worried. Since I last saw him there had been rumors that the bulldozers were coming, that the neighborhood was finally going to be cleared.

He said, "We never know if we'll wake up one day and find them pushing us out of our home."

We talked for a while about his life. He had survived, like the irrepressible Tao, by offering no resistance, by changing shape to fit each new power in his unfortunate city. An American missionary had saved him from the streets and made it possible for him to learn English, and then to find a job translating orders for a California firm that exported textiles. When the Americans fled just before World War II, he learned Japanese and became a reporter for a Japanese-run newspaper. Then when the Communists came, he taught himself Russian; he had spent decades translating documents for the inner circle of an important agency.

"I never belonged to the Party, but I worked so hard for them that for years they automatically took Party fees out of my salary. I don't think I would have gained by setting them straight."

But somewhere in the inner courtyards of the self, I thought, there was a man who had survived untainted by any of this, as innocent as that child running frantically through that garden of long ago, watching the poetry blow away in the wind. There was a lot I would have liked to talk about, but there was no time. I had a plane to catch; I was expected in Hong Kong, and then in a few days in Paris and New York. But I kept lingering. I liked it here in the silent courtyard, with the old palace walls at the end of the lane, like a coastline or the end of the world.

I told Chang about finding George Kates's house.

He heard me out and then said, "You know, I knew Kates."

He enjoyed my surprise.

Then he said, "When the Japanese came, Kates ran an American flag up over his house. It was the biggest flag I ever saw. He lived here all those years like a Chinese. But when things got tough he ran up the Stars and Stripes. I had no flag to run up."

I sensed that there had been a more personal slight of some kind, long remembered, never quite forgiven. But he wouldn't say anything more.

I must have been hearing the sound for some time without realizing it. At first it was just a soft hum, like the sound of wind on a high tension cable, and I didn't pay it much attention. Then a little later I heard it again, much closer, almost overhead. It faded and swelled, and then it seemed to be everywhere all at once. I turned around and looked through the window, and I saw the gray flecks against the smoggy sky.

Twenty or more fluting pigeons were wheeling and diving in wide arcs overhead. After a while they disappeared over the gray walls, but I could follow the haunting vibrato as they drifted and dove over distant courtyards. Then with a shift in the wind they were back, hurtling over us, and then away again over the stupendous yellow roofs of the Forbidden City.

I tried to keep Chang from getting up, but he insisted on seeing me to the outer gate. It was the way people of his generation did things.

I was halfway out the gate when he chirped, "You know, there are nights when I lie awake in bed thinking about my life. And I think, 'Damn it, I'm a lucky bird!' I'm lucky to have been born Chinese, and to have seen so much and lived so long!"

Further down the lane I heard the eerie hum again. I stood for a long time and waited for the pigeons to come back. But they never did. It was just the wind on a wire, or nothing at all.

EPILOGUE

THE NURSING home was as I remembered it: the nurses in the mint-green uniforms, the soap operas whispering in the tidy identical rooms, the frail figures hovering hopefully around the nurses' station. I remembered the woman who had surprised me with a kiss the year before, but there was no sign of her this time.

George Kates was lying in bed with his fingertips over the edge of the coverlet, like a child. A nurse told me that he had undergone an operation, that he had lost weight. I could see the anticipation on his face as I entered.

"Have you brought lunch?" he asked.

He didn't recognize me. But my letters were there; I could see them tacked onto his bulletin board along with postcards of Newport homes and the Summer Palace at Beijing, of something by Renoir, and Oxford, and Billy Graham in front of the Altar of Heaven. His little collection of boxes and seals, *les petites bijoux,* was spread out on the Formica table that was attached to the bed.

I said, "I've come from China."

He looked at me with an expression that I couldn't read. It was some time before he spoke.

"Has China changed?"

"It has," I said.

"Does it give the same pleasure?"

"Perhaps not," I said.

297

He was silent for several minutes.

"What a loss."

I found a nurse and arranged for his lunch to be brought. There was creamed spinach and a wad of fish salad on a bun. The nurse scraped the salad off and fed it to him with a spoon.

"I've brought you something from China," I said.

It was a box of tea from Qingchengshan. When I opened it, the leaves radiated that faint, wonderful aroma, like rhododendron. It brought back the viscous mist and the monks on the veranda, the temple bells ringing into the damp forest.

I told the nurse that I'd brew the tea myself. I supposed that when he lived in China Kates drank good tea with rainwater, as connoisseurs did. I had meant to bring a bottle of spring water, but I'd forgotten it. Then there was no kettle in the kitchen, and I had to boil water in the microwave. I carried it back with a plate over the top so it would at least brew properly.

"What's this?" he asked.

"Tea."

He finally took the cup.

"Yes, tea," he said after a while.

There was milk on his lunch tray. He poured some of it into the tea, spoiling it.

"I found your house," I said.

He looked blank.

"Your house in Beijing."

"There was a courtyard," he said after a while. "It was mine. It was very intimate."

He picked up a lacquerware box that was shaped like a cloud. Opening it, he removed a pair of cuff links of finely wrought gold filigree; a tiny luminous blue cylinder was fitted neatly into each one. Last year, he told me that he had had them made from an azure tile that had fallen from the roof of the Temple of Heaven.

"Don't they look nice?"

"What do you do with them now?" I asked.

"Dream," he said.

He opened the box again and looked into it.

"It is waiting to have something put into it," he said.

He was silent for a minute or two more, still staring at the box.

"There was a flower pot on each side of the door," he said. "There were chrysanthemums in them."

I kept groping for a concrete memory, trying to anchor him. I asked him to tell me about the eunuch, but he looked at me blankly.

Then I said, "I found your rickshaw puller."

"I took the same rickshaw most days."

"What did you talk to him about?"

"I talked about what interested me."

It was difficult. The silences lengthened. He rarely met my eyes. Finally his eyes closed. For five or ten minutes I simply watched his face, limpid and opaque, Chinese, full of secrets.

I started. I couldn't see any breath. I called to him, but he didn't respond. I was frightened that he had died right in front of me.

But then his eyes opened slightly and he turned toward me.

"Do you know me?" he asked.

I said, "I'm not sure."

"What do you want?"

"I came to talk to you about China."

He looked at me for a long time.

Then he said, "I used to live in China."

Suggestions for Further Reading

Aisin-Gioro Pu Yi. *From Emperor To Citizen*. 2 vols. Beijing: Foreign Languages Press, 1983.

All About Shanghai. Shanghai: University Press, 1934.

The Analects of Confucius. Translated by Arthur Waley. New York: Vintage.

Arlington, L. C. and William Lewisohn. *In Search Of Old Beijing*. Reprint. Hong Kong: Oxford University Press, 1987.

Barnhart, Richard M. *Along The Border Of Heaven: Sung & Yuan Paintings From The C. C. Wang Family Collection*. New York: Metropolitan Museum of Art, 1983.

Barnhart, Richard M. *Peach Blossom Spring: Gardens & Flowers In Chinese Painting*. New York: Metropolitan Museum of Art, 1983.

Bird, Isabella. *The Yangtze Valley & Beyond*. Reprint. Boston: Beacon, 1987.

Bland, J. O. P. and Edmund Backhouse. *China Under The Empress Dowager*. Peking: Henri Vetch, 1939.

Blofeld, John. *City Of Lingering Splendor: A Frank Account of Peking's Exotic Pleasures*. Boston: Shambala, 1989.

Blofeld, John. *Taoism: The Road To Immortality*. Boston: Shambala, 1978.

Bredon, Juliet. *Peking*. Shanghai: Kelly & Walsh Ltd., 1920.

Bussagli, Mario. *Central Asian Painting*. New York: Rizzoli, 1979.

Cao Xueqin. *The Story Of The Stone*. 5 vols. Translated by David Hawkes and John Minford, London: Penguin, 1973–1986.

301

Chen Lifu. *The Confucian Way*. London: KPI, 1987.

Cooper, Arthur, ed. *Li Po and Tu Fu*. London: Penguin, 1973.

The Courtesan's Jewel Box: Chinese Stories of the Xth–XVIIth Centuries. Translated by Yang Xianyi and Gladys Yang. Beijing: Foreign Languages Press, 1981.

Creel, Herrlee G. *Chinese Thought from Confucius to Mao Tse-tung*. Chicago: Chicago University Press, 1953.

Crow, Carl. *Foreign Devils In The Flowery Kingdom*. New York: Harper & Bros., 1940.

Deng Youmei. *Snuff Bottles & Other Stories*. Beijing: Panda Books, 1986.

Franck, Irene M. and David M. Brownstone, *The Silk Road: A History*. New York: Facts on File, 1986.

Gernet, Jacques. *Daily Life In China On The Eve Of The Mongol Invasion 1250–1276*. Stanford: Stanford University Press, 1970.

Hackin, J., ed. *Asiatic Mythology*. New York: Thomas Y. Crowell Co.

Han Fei Tzu. *Basic Writings*. Translated by Burton Watson. New York: Columbia University Press, 1964.

Hirth F. *China And The Roman Orient*. Reprint. Chicago: Ares, 1975.

Hookham, Hilda. *A Short History of China*. New York: Mentor, 1972.

Hopkirk, Peter. *Foreign Devils On The Silk Road*. London: Oxford University Press, 1980.

Hucker, Charles O. *China's Imperial Past*. London: Gerald Duckworth & Co. Ltd., 1975.

Jin Shoushan. *Beijing Legends*. Beijing: Panda Books, 1982.

Johnson, Reginald F. *Twilight In The Forbidden City*. Reprint. Hong Kong: Oxford University Press, 1988.

Kates, George N. *The Years That Were Fat*. Cambridge, Mass.: MIT Press, 1976.

Keswick, Maggie. *The Chinese Garden*. London: Academy Editions, 1986.

Kong Demao. *In The Mansions Of Confucius's Descendants*. Beijing: New World Press, 1984.

Lady Macartney. *An English Lady In Chinese Turkestan*. Reprint. Hong Kong: Oxford University Press, 1985.

Lattimore, Owen. *Inner Asian Frontiers Of China*. Reprint. Hong Kong: Oxford University Press, 1988.

Li Chu-Tsing and James C. Y. Watt, eds. *The Chinese Scholar's Studio: Artistic Life In The Late Ming Period*. New York: The Asia Society Galleries, 1987.

Lowe, H. Y. *The Adventures of Wu: The Life Cycle Of A Peking Man*. Reprint. Princeton: Princeton University Press, 1983.

Morrison, George E. *An Australian In China*. Reprint. Hong Kong: Oxford University Press, 1985.

Morrison, Hedda. *A Photographer in Old Peking*. Hong Kong: Oxford University Press, 1985.

Morrison, Hedda. *Travels Of A Photographer In China 1933–1946*. Hong Kong: Oxford University Press, 1987.

Mulliken, Mary Augusta and Anna M. Hotchkiss. *The Nine Sacred Mountains Of China*. Hong Kong: Vetch & Lee Ltd., 1973.

Nagel's Encyclopedic Guide To China. Geneva: Nagel Publications, 1975.

Pan Ling. *Old Shanghai: Gangsters in Paradise*. Hong Kong: Heinemann Asia, 1984.

Payne, Robert, ed. *The White Pony: An Anthology of Chinese Poetry*. New York: Mentor, 1953.

Powell, William. *Mt. Jiuhua: The Nine-Florate Realm of Dicang Pusa*. Tokyo: International Christian University, 1987.

Princess Der Ling. *Two Years In The Forbidden City*. New York: Moffat Yard & Co., 1912.

Rawson, Philip and Laszlo Legeza. *Tao: The Chinese Philosophy of Time and Change*. London: Thames & Hudson, 1979.

Scidmore, E. R. *China: The Long-Lived Empire*. New York: The Century Company, 1900.

Sears Pictorial Description of China and India. New York: Robert Sears, 1851.

Sima Qian. *Records Of The Historian*. Translated by Yang Xianyi and Gladys Yang. Beijing: Foreign Languages Press, 1979.

Sir Aurel Stein. *Ruins Of Desert Cathay*. 2 vols. Reprint. New York: Dover, 1987.

Siren, Osvald. *The Chinese On The Art Of Painting*. New York: Schocken, 1963.

Smith, Arthur. *Village Life In China*. New York: Fleming H. Revell Co., 1899.

Spence, Jonathan D. *Emperor of China*. New York: Random House, 1974.

Spence, Jonathan D. *The Death of Woman Wang*. New York: Penguin, 1978.

Stover, Leon E. *The Cultural Ecology Of Chinese Civilization*. New York: Mentor, 1974.

Strand, David. *Rickshaw Beijing: City People and Politics in the 1920s*. Berkeley: University of California Press, 1989.

Sze Mai-mai. *The Way of Chinese Painting*. New York: Vintage, 1959.

Tao Te Ching. Translated by D. C. Lau. New York: Penguin, 1978.

The Travels of Marco Polo. New York: Dorset Press, 1987.

Van Over, Raymond, ed. *Taoist Tales*. New York: Meridian, 1973.

Vare, Daniele. *The Last Empress*. Garden City: Doubleday, Doran & Co., 1938.

Von Le Coq, Albert. *Buried Treasures of Chinese Turkestan*. Reprint. Hong Kong: Oxford University Press, 1985.

Wang Qinxiang. *China's Last Emperor as an Ordinary Person*. Beijing: China Reconstructs, 1986.

Warner, Marina. *The Dragon Empress: The Life and Times of Tz'uhsi, 1835–1908, Empress Dowager of China*. London: Hamish Hamilton, 1984.

Watson, William. *Style in the Arts of China*. New York: Penguin, 1974.

Williams, C. A. S. *Outlines of Chinese Symbolism and Art Motives*. Reprint. Dover, 1976.

Wu, Aitchen K. *Turkistan Tumult*. Reprint. Hong Kong: Oxford University Press, 1984.

A Note About the Author

Fergus M. Bordewich was born in New York City, and spent some of his childhood on American Indian reservations in various parts of the United States. He has worked in the Alaskan oilfields, sailed as a deckhand on a Norwegian freighter, and driven a taxicab in New York City. Mr. Bordewich holds degrees from the City College of New York and Columbia University. As a professional journalist, he has traveled widely in Asia, the Middle East, Europe, and Central America, and published articles in many periodicals including *The Atlantic, Condé Nast Traveler, GEO, Harper's, New York* magazine, the *New York Times Magazine*, and *Reader's Digest*. In 1982 Mr. Bordewich was invited to the People's Republic of China to train the staff of the English-language Features Section of Xinhua, the official Chinese government news agency, in Western journalistic techniques. His experiences during that year led him to undertake the journey through China that resulted in this book. Mr. Bordewich lives in Brooklyn, New York, with his wife and daughter.